Mourning and Mobilization
in the Americas

Mourning and Mobilization in the Americas

The Affective Politics of Women Killings

LYDIA HUERTA MORENO

EU GPSR Authorised Representative:
Logos Europe, 9 rue Nicolas Poussin, 17000, La Rochelle, France
contact@logoseurope.eu

For information, contact State University of New York Press, Albany, NY
www.sunypress.edu

Library of Congress Cataloging-in-Publication Data

Name: Huerta Moreno, Lydia, author.
Title: Mourning and mobilization in the Americas : the affective politics of women
    killings / Lydia Huerta Moreno, author.
Description: Albany : State University of New York Press, [2026]. | Series:
    SUNY series, Praxis: Theory in Action | Includes bibliographical references and
    index.
Identifiers: ISBN 9798855805239 (hardcover : alk. paper) | ISBN 9798855806090
    (epub) | ISBN 9798855805253 (PDF) | ISBN 9798855805246 (pbk. : alk. paper)
Further information is available at the Library of Congress.

*For all those who have been victims of transfeminicide, feminicide,
Missing and Murdered Indigenous Women and Girls
and Two-Spirit People, Missing and
Murdered Indigenous People, and their families.*

*For the survivors, families, activists, relatives, friends, scholars,
and educators who do the work to keep the memories of those
who have been murdered, bringing attention to this gender-based issue.*

Contents

A Note to the Reader

The pages that follow contain descriptions of violence toward trans and nontrans women's bodies. Throughout the book I've committed to recounting an event if needed or declined to do so, encouraging you to look for those details elsewhere. While perhaps this commitment is flawed, I recognize that the material may be emotionally challenging and upsetting, and difficult to process. I encourage you to read with care. Approach these pages at your own pace, taking breaks when needed and allowing yourself space to process and reflect.

If at any point you feel overwhelmed, please consider setting the book aside temporarily or discussing its contents with someone you trust. Your well-being matters.

Acknowledgments

I am deeply grateful to the many people who have supported the creation of this manuscript, as writing and ideas never emerge in isolation. First and foremost, I thank my ancestors, elders, and relatives for their enduring guidance. I am privileged to have an immediate family that has loved me unconditionally, believed in me, and supported me both emotionally and financially—mil gracias de todo corazón—mamá, Kurt, Ale, Yvan, Jessi, Pablo, and Rodrigo. I am thankful to my extended families in Mexico and the United States, especially those who have provided support to me during the process of writing this book—Agustin, Bernardo, Patricia, Lourdes, Rosa, Gaby, Sofy, Luly, Pily, Dani, Juan Carlos, Felipe, Rafaela, Tati, Mimi, Marco, Lynn, Gina, Leah, Ryan, Kathleen, Elizabeth, and Glenn. To friends who live across the continent, you know who you are; thank you for always believing in my ability to write this book and engaging me in thoughtful and thorough conversations on the topic. Special thanks to Malena, Diana, Lali, Irisel, Laurita, Arno, Roger, Alicia, and Daniel—your support and care packages have been vital. This manuscript was mindfully written in loving memory of my father, Jorge Huerta Wilde; my grandmothers, Frida Wilde Lorenzana and Lidia Campoy Mendoza; my friend Peter Garcia and Cofi, Iker, and Ze. Their presence in my life and their loss shaped much of this work.

Since 2007 I have had the privilege of working alongside extraordinary community activists and scholars who made this manuscript possible. I am especially grateful to Beatriz and Adela Lozoya Gutierrez, Yoch Otte, and el Colectivo Reziste, Kathy Benavidez, Chisa Oros, Debra and Nuba Harry, Lyla June Johnston, and Beverly and Autumn Harry for their trust, activist work, and enriching conversations. I also thank Carla Necke Conradi, Gregory da Silva Balthazar, Rodrigo Lopes, Gil, Cecília Soares, Linda Brasil, and the human rights students, lawyers and educators from both Universidade Estadual do Oeste do Paraná (UNIOESTE) and Universidade Tiradentes (UNIT). Their critiques and perspectives were instrumental in shaping this project's final version.

At the University of Nevada, Reno, I found a community of rigorous, kind, and compassionate colleagues. I am particularly thankful to Jen Hill, Melanie Duckworth, Deborah Bohem, Emily Hobson, Katherine Fusco, Meredith Oda, Debra Harry, Prisca Gayles, Guadalupe Escobar, Vadricka Ettiene, Ignacio Montoya, Nasia Anam, Allison Evans, Michael Aguirre, Deborah Achtenberg, Daniel Enrique Perez, Jen Lanterman, Clayton Peoples, and Tanya Nawrocki. I also want to thank the Core Humanities Program (Dan Morse and Chris Stancil) and the Ozmen Institute for Global Studies for their research grants. More broadly, I am indebted to the scholars whose work continues to inspire me—especially Karma Chavez, Aisha Durham, Rosa Linda Fragoso, Wanda Pillow, Guillermina Nuñez-Mchiri, Loretta LeMaster, and Emma Bailey. Their encouragement at conferences and invaluable conversations validated this project's merit. I am also deeply grateful to Rebecca Colesworthy at SUNY Press, whose enthusiasm and belief in the work were evident from our first Zoom call, as well as to the entire editorial team whose efforts made this book possible. I extend my heartfelt thanks to my spring 2024 students in the GRI 710 and SRJS 720 graduate seminars for their patience with me and their engagement with this project. Special thanks to Hector Dominguez Rubalcaba, Hannah Wojciechowski, Jill Robbins, Jossianna Arroyo, Sarah Blithe, Margarita Wulftange, and Adela Pineda whose mentorship and friendship over the past decade have been foundational to this work.

My immediate support network during the writing process deserves special recognition for their willingness and contributions to this process: Sayak Valencia for providing the concept I needed to write this book, for her generosity in helping me think through ideas, and for writing the foreword to this text. My local friends, Billie, Mel, Vanessa, Rose, Felicia, and Emily, let me stay and write in their homes, feeding me and providing distractions. To Ceci for your meticulous editing and steadfast camaraderie throughout this journey. To Gigi, your feedback regarding accessibility and framing and your emotional support made this work stronger. Prisca, thank you for being a grounding force during the obstacles I faced in this journey and for being the best "no" advocate. Semra and Zach, on a humid Houston night of intellectual banter, revamped the title of this book. To Diego/Lupe, whose artistry is behind the image on the cover of this book and who is always a guiding light in my life. And, Ruthie, beyond your thoughtful editorial contributions, you nourished both my body and spirit, filling our home with music and laughter when I needed it most. Your gift for transforming my moments of doubt and exhaustion into occasions of joy and possibility has been invaluable. This manuscript bears the invisible imprint of your patience and support.

Finally, in the words of Rosa-Linda Fregoso (2023), "Writing about feminicide is painful, yet this agony pales in comparison to being its victim" (57), and being able to write to remember and write through the pain also involved a team of people who believe in the importance of non-Western healing modalities. My heartfelt thanks go to Kathy, Ale, Flor, and Dee for their healing gifts and connection to other realms. I also thank April, Gretchen, Johnathan, Prattna, Aleks, Stacey, and Christina for helping me keep my body and mind mobile while writing this book.

Overview

Introduction: When the Dead Speak
Organizing Question: How do the dead speak through the living?
Keywords: transnational, Americas, affect, social movements, feminicide

Chapter 1. Impotence and Frustration: Breaking the Silence in Ciudad Juárez
Organizing question: How did the postmortem politics of activists, scholars, and relatives become known around the globe?
Keywords: Ciudad Juárez, S Taller, transurority, visual art

Chapter 2. Fear and Rage: Legislating Feminicide Across the Americas
Organizing question: How did counteracting gender-based violence against nontrans women become an interconnected call for the legal codification of feminicide/femicide?
Keywords: legal advocacy, social media, Ni Una Más, Ni Una Menos

Chapter 3. Determination and Tension: The Continuous Struggle for Recognition
Organizing question: How did legislating gender violence affect Brazilian hegemonic culture?
Keywords: international law, social media, national politics, luto é luta

Chapter 4. Indignation and Persistence: Lessons from Indigenous Activism in Canada and the United States
Organizing question: What can we learn from Indigenous activism on MMIWG2?
Keywords: colonialism, content creation, mourning, land

Conclusion: The Perseverance of Transmuting Grief
Organizing question: How can we take steps to eradicate gender-based violence?
Keywords: pedagogy, efficacy of sound, coalition, interconnectedness

Foreword

Sayak Valencia

En el contexto actual caracterizado por el asesinato sistemático de mujeres cis y trans, personas migrantes, lideres ambientales, personas racializadas, entre muchas otras, la violencia se convierte en un centro persistente para la organización y propagación de la modernidad-colonialidad occidental. Así, la muerte violenta como herramienta aleccionadora tiene como subtexto doblegarnos afectivamente, creando una especie de tecnología civilizatoria que persiste en nuestros días y conecta el contexto actual con la intermitencia colonial, a través de las tecnologías del asesinato como una forma de aescarmiento, pero también como un dispositivo dinamizador de las economías de la muerte.

Por ello, encuentro que es necesario profundizar en las reflexiones sobre la muerte-asesinato como un motor de plusvalía de la necropolítica[1] y de expolio continuado en nuestros territorios y cuerpos que también activa y robustese economías sexuales, cuya plusvalía se genera a través de la supresión de ciertos cuerpos producidos como desechables o indeseables, negandoles radicalmente su "derecho a aparecer"[2], es decir, de hacer política pero también volviendo cada vez más deshables a un gran número de poblaciones, por ejemplo a las personas migrantes que se convierten en "botines" de guerra ante gobiernos autoritarios y conervadores como el de Donald Trump.

---

1. Achille Mbembe, *Necropolítica* (Barcelona: Melusina, 2011).

2. Judith Butler, *Cuerpos aliados y lucha política: Hacia una teoría performativa de la asamblea* (Barcelona: Paidós, 2017), 31.

Así, la violencia y la muerte como elementos comunes de la colonialidad del género[3] cuya consecuencia extrema es justamente la eliminación de poblaciones potencialmente indóciles, poblaciones cuyas intersecciones desmontan el dimorfismo sexual y desnaturalizan las opresiones de raza, género, sexualidad, estatus migratorio indocumentado, etc; como afirmó María Lugones: "la raza no es más mítica ni más ficticia que el género, ambas son ficciones poderosas."[4]

Y es en este contexto en el cual aparece este libro de Lydia Huerta quien nos muestra que es urgente realizar investigaciones que rastreén alianzas entre los movimientos (trans)feministas, los movimientos anti-racistas, movimientos ecologistas, a través de las Américas (la latina, la lusósfona y la anglo), pues estamos en la era donde los actos políticos parecen tener sentido solo de manera post-mortem.

Donde el reclamo feminista central es por no ser asesinadas; como lo muestran los movimientos transnacionales que se representan en redes sociales virtuales con los hashtags #NiUnaMenos, #VivasNosQueremos y donde las herramientas y discursos de nuestras luchas son expropiados por la cara amable de las democracias fascísticas a través de la mercantilización cosmética o la instrumentalización jurídica de nuestras demandas políticas por la justicia social hacia las mujeres cis y trans.

En este espacio social de convergencia entre mercados y protestas, la necropolítica se expande como exterior constitutivo que nos asedia y nos quiere inertes y segregadxs. Y frente a esta segregación e inmovilización surgen las políticas post-mortem que podemos definir como formas de representar dignamente a lxs muertxs y/o asesinadxs y de acuerpar los afectos que tenemos por aquellos que han sido exterminados por la violencia letal del Capitalismo Gore[5] y sus cientos de tentáculos.

Las políticas Post-Mortem son entonces, una serie de prácticas afectivas y políticas para dignificar a las víctimas y decir: nuestres asesinades no quisieron morir esa muerte, brindándoles agencia incluso después de la muerte, agencia que es acuerpada por los sobrevivientes de comunidades integradas tanto por familiares de mujeres cis y trans asesinas pero también de migrantes desaparecidos en transito, entre otros.

En este sentido, este libro propone realizar una investigación donde se profundiza en las características de estas comunidades de afecto y en sus

---

3. María Lugones, "Colonialidad y género," *Tabula Rasa*, July–December 2008, 75–101.

4. Lugones, "Colonialidad," 94.

5. Sayak Valencia, *Capilatismo Gore* (Barcelona: Melusina, 2010).

gramáticas no institucionales para colectivizar el duelo y re-elaborar el tejido social de forma situada y micropolítica. Para ello, la Dra Huerta realizó un mapeo de distintos despliegues comunitarios de las políticas post-mortem en las Américas, especialmente en México, Brasil, USA y Canadá, mostrando las gramáticas comunes de las resistencias (trans)feministas, anti-racistas y decoloniales que han venido creando estrategias no institucionales para la petición de justicia y la reparación. Estas indagaciones se presentan a lo largo de los capítulos que conforman este libro.

De esta manera, Lydia indaga también en la convergencia entre la búsqueda de justicia social, el artivismo, las Ciencias Sociales, las Humanidades y los estudios en Comunicación como enfoques transdisciplinarios que brindan herramientas de interpreta-acción para reflexionar sobre las políticas post-mortem como un lenguaje que contribuye a la elaboración de una memoria corpo-política y transgeneracional de las resistencias en el continente americano.

Lydia reflexiona además sobre las políticas del duelo público y colectivo desplegadas como espacialidades afectivas tanto en el mundo virtual como el real que frente al avasallamiento de la violencia letal y la indiferencia social, pueden proveer a las comunidades afectadas de otras imaginaciones políticas y otras herramientas para dignificar a las víctimas y contruir simbolica y colectivamente lugares de repara-acción.

Por lo anterior, me emociona profundamente redactar este prólogo para el libro "Mourning and Mobilization in the Americas" de mi querida colega y amiga Lydia Huerta. Me emociona porque finalmente veo materializado en un libro las innumerables conversaciones que hemos sostenido sobre temas tan dolorosos como el feminicidio y el trans feminicidio y su relación con el autoritarismo y el régimen colonial.

Y me parece especialmente relevante que este libro aparezca en estos momentos donde nos encontramos en una coyuntura tan compleja y cruel en contra de las mujeres cis y trans, de los estudios de género, del revisionismo en temas de igualdad y acceso a la justicia en todo el continente, pero especialmente en aquellos países donde el autoritarismo de ultra-derecha se vanagloria de estos recortes y censuras en los derechos de estas poblaciones como en los Estados Unidos o Argentina.

O en contextos donde la agenda izquierdista o centro izquierdista también están desatendiendo los problemas relacionados con la violencia patriarcal y donde las comunidades más vulnerables están cargando con la mayor parte de las consecuencias ante este ascenso de neoconservadurismo colonial y la insistencia a instaurar políticas regresivas en torno a los derechos de las personas, ya sean sexuales, reproductivos o de tránsito migratorio.

Quiero destacar otra de las grandes virtudes de este trabajo: su afectividad, porque además de la sensibilidad y el conocimiento profundo de los temas que aborda la escritura de Lydia tiene la capacidad de dignificar a la víctimas sin revictimizarlas.

Nos encontramos entonces con un libro bisagra que es necesario en un momento de intensa polarización y de rupturas políticas y afectivas dentro de los movimiento sociales y especialmente dentro del feminismo donde las posturas anti-trans están coadyuvando al acrecentamiento del odio y la expansión del discurso conservador y anti-derechos en contra de las mujeres trans, población N/B y queer.

Destaco entonces el gran esfuerzo realizado por la Dra. Huerta al tratar de crear puentes tanto generacionales como territoriales y lingüísticos a través de las Américas como un llamado a la unión por medio de estas páginas.

Repito que este libro es una bisagra necesaria para reactivar el diálogo feminista y transfeminista en todo el continente, ya que Lydia conoce a profundidad el contexto de violencia exacerbada tanto en México como en Brasil y en Estados Unidos y Canadá y se mueve fluidamente entre los tres principales idiomas del continente: Español, Portugués e Inglés.

Este hecho, hace que la autora no sólo tenga conocimiento del contexto y la lengua sino conocimiento y experiencia de campo que le permiten hacer propuestas firmes sobre la interdisciplinariedad y la aplicación de metodología mixtas para analizar certeramente un fenómeno, complejo y dolorosamente creciente, como el feminicidio y el trans feminicidio.

En este sentido, quien lea este libro encontrará una hoja de ruta por distintas temporalidades y genealogías del feminicidio que es un fenómeno ampliamente estudiado tanto en Latinoamérica como en Brasil, Lydia tiene la virtud no repetir discursos fáciles, ni escudarse en las cifras sin discutirlas, tampoco reproduce patrones de lectura a partir del conocimiento de décadas que se ha creado por parte de lxss activistas, lxs académicos y las instituciones de procuración de justicia y defensa de los derechos humanos de las mujeres cis y trans; sino que respetando esa genealogía propone centrarnos en el análisis de las formas de dignificar a las victimas a través de la producción de un duelo público por medio de distintas estrategias tanto activistas tanto en el plano de lo social como de lo virtual.

Así, la Dra. Huerta nos explica la necesidad de reflexionar sobre la potencia afectiva encarnada por distintos feminismos, transfeminismo y activismos de base como un motor crítico y de acción política que puede inspirarnos para hacer frente a la desatención estatal, la negligencia institucional, la revictimización a través de los medios de comunicación tradicionales y digitales, cuestión que es fundamental en un contexto como el actual plagado de turbulencias y innegable polarización.

Foreword (English)

In the current context characterized by the systemic murder of cis and trans women, migrants, environmental leaders, racialized people, among many others, violence becomes a persistent center for the organization and propagation of Western modernity–coloniality. Thus, violent deaths as an edifying tool have as a subtext to bend us affectively, creating a kind of civilizing technology that persists in our days and connects the current context with colonial intermittency through the technologies of murder as a form of admonishment, but also as a dynamizing device of the economies of death.

Therefore, I find it necessary to deepen reflections on death-murder as an engine of surplus value of necropolitics[6] and of continuous plundering in our territories and bodies that also activates and strengthens sexual economies, whose surplus value is generated through the suppression of certain bodies produced as disposable or undesirable, radically denying them their "right to appear";[7] that is, to make politics but also render increasingly a large number of populations as disposable—for example, migrant people who become "spoils" of war for authoritarian and conservative governments such as Donald Trump's.

The coloniality of gender[8] commonly features violence and death. The most extreme outcome is the elimination of populations that might resist control—specifically, populations whose intersecting identities challenge sexual dimorphism and expose the constructed nature of racial, gender, and sexual oppressions, as well as the marginalization of undocumented migrants; as María Lugones stated: "Race is no more mythical nor more fictitious than gender, both are powerful fictions."[9]

This book by Lydia Huerta Moreno emerges in this context and in this crucial moment, demonstrating the urgent need for research that

---

6. Mbembe, *Necropolítica.*

7. Judith Butler, *Allied Bodies and Political Struggle: Towards a Performative Theory of Assembly* (Barcelona: Paidós, 2017), 31.

8. Lugones, "Colonialidad."

9. Lugones, "Colonialidad."

identifies connections between (trans)feminist, antiracist, and environmental movements across the Americas (Latin, Portuguese-speaking, and English-speaking regions). This urgency is heightened by our current era, where political actions often only seem to gain significance postmortem, after deaths have already occurred.

In this era, the central feminist claim is for not being murdered. This is shown by the transnational movements that are represented in virtual social networks with the hashtags #NiUnaMenos and #VivasNosQueremos, and where the friendly face of fascist democracies expropriates the tools and discourses of our struggles through cosmetic commodification or legal instrumentalization of our political demands for social justice toward cis and trans women.

In this social space of convergence between markets and protests, necropolitics expands as a constitutive exterior that besieges us and wants us inert and segregated. And in the face of this segregation and immobilization, postmortem politics emerge, which we can define as ways of representing with dignity those who have died, been murdered, or both, and of mending the affections we have for those who have been exterminated by the lethal violence of gore capitalism[10] and its hundreds of tentacles.

Postmortem policies are then a series of affective and political practices to dignify the victims and say: Our murdered did not want to die that death, giving them agency even after death, agency that is supported by the survivors of communities composed of relatives of murdered cis and trans women but also of missing migrants in transit, among others.

In this sense, this book proposes to conduct research that delves into the characteristics of these communities of affect and their noninstitutional grammars to collectivize grief and reelaborate the social fabric in a situated and micropolitical way.

To this end, Dr. Huerta Moreno mapped different community deployments of postmortem politics in the Americas, especially in Mexico, Brazil, the United States, and Canada, showing the common grammars of (trans)feminist, antiracist, and decolonial resistances that have been creating noninstitutional strategies for seeking justice and reparations. These inquiries are presented throughout the chapters of this book.

In this way, Lydia also investigates the convergence between the search for social justice, artivism, social sciences, humanities, and communication studies as transdisciplinary approaches that provide tools of interpretation–

---

10. Valencia, *Capilatismo Gore.*

action to reflect on postmortem politics as a language that contributes to the elaboration of a corpo-political and transgenerational memory of the resistances in the American continent.

Lydia also reflects on the politics of public and collective mourning deployed as affective spatialities in both the virtual and the real world that, in the face of lethal violence and social indifference, can provide the affected communities with other political imaginations and other tools to dignify the victims as well as to symbolically and collectively construct places of reparation–action.

For the above reasons, I am deeply moved to write this foreword for this book by my dear colleague and friend. I am enthused because I finally see materialized in a book the countless conversations we have had on such painful issues as feminicide and transfeminicide and their relationship with authoritarianism and colonial rule.

And I find it especially relevant that this book appears at this time when we find ourselves in such a complex and cruel situation regarding cis and trans women, gender studies, and revisionism on issues of equality and access to justice throughout the continent, but especially in those countries such as the United States or Argentina where ultraright authoritarianism boasts of these curtailments and censorship of the rights of these populations.

The book is likewise relevant to contexts where the left or center-left agenda is neglecting the problems related to patriarchal violence and where the most vulnerable communities are bearing the brunt of the consequences of this rise of colonial neoconservatism and the insistence on regressive policies regarding people's rights, whether sexual, reproductive, or migratory.

Another of the great virtues of this work is its affectivity. In addition to the sensitivity and deep knowledge of the issues that Lydia's writing displays, she has the ability to dignify the victims without revictimizing them.

We find ourselves then with a book that is pivotal at a time of intense polarization and political and affective ruptures within social movements and especially within feminism, where antitrans positions are contributing to the increase of hatred and the expansion of conservative and antirights discourse against trans women, nonbinary, and queer populations. Lydia has striven to create generational, territorial, and linguistic bridges across the Americas as a call to unity in these pages.

This book is indeed pivotal to reactivating the feminist and transfeminist dialogue throughout the continent. Lydia knows in depth the context of exacerbated violence in Mexico, Brazil, the United States, and Canada and is fluent in the continent's three main languages: Spanish,

Portuguese, and English. This fact means that the author not only has familiarity with the context and the language but also knowledge and field experience that allow her to make cogent proposals on interdisciplinarity and mixed methodology as means of accurately analyzing a complex and painfully growing phenomenon such as feminicide and transfeminicide.

Hence whoever reads this book will find a road map through different temporalities and genealogies of feminicide, which is a phenomenon widely studied both in Latin America and Brazil. Lydia has the virtue of not repeating easy discourses, nor shielding herself in the data without discussing them, nor reproducing patterns of interpretation and extraction from the knowledge of decades that has been created by activists, academics, and institutions of justice and defense of the human rights of cis and trans women. Instead, while respecting this genealogy, she proposes that we focus on ways of dignifying the victims by producing public mourning with different activist strategies both in the social and virtual spheres.

Thus, Dr. Huerta Moreno highlights the affective power embodied by different feminisms, transfeminism, and grassroots activism that can inspire us to address state neglect, institutional neglect, and revictimization through traditional and digital media—an essential endeavor in a context such as the current one marked by turbulence and undeniable polarization.

Preface

In December 2021, with travel restrictions lifted after the COVID-19 pandemic, I went to Ciudad Juárez, Mexico, to visit long-term gender-violence and women-rights activists Beatriz and Adela Lozoya and the graffiti artist Yorch Otte. I had met them while conducting initial research on feminicide in 2008 and established a friendship then. On my routine visit a year earlier on December 14, 2021, I also visited Yorch at his new bakery, Panadería Rezizte, located on one of Ciudad Juárez's busy main streets that lead downtown. As the Uber dropped me off, I noticed a painted mural across the street that depicted a girl's head on top of a platform of sunflowers, and a turquoise-like aural glow around it. The girl had bangs and a bob and her face was painted in graduating tones of blue and red, highlighting a turquoise-white emptiness that filled her eye sockets. There was a tear in her right eye. In the background against tones of blue and maroon purple, there were many eyes with brown pupils and a phrase in the top left corner that read "Te observan,"[1] with a signature on the bottom right corner in bubble-style writing: "Isabel Cabanillas." I was captivated by this mural, the emptiness of her eyes, the phrase, and the colors—it was all so haunting.

I entered the bakery in a trance-like state and gave Yorch a hug, but was a little distant. Yorch asked me if I was OK. I told him I was a little disturbed by the mural outside the bakery, but that overall I was excited to see him and catch up. I also asked about the mural. Yorch told me that Isabel (whom I had briefly met at one of Yorch's events with Beatriz) had just finished painting it before being murdered two days later on January

---

1. t. You are watched. All translations in this book are my own. From this point forward the English translation will appear in the footnotes.

Figure P.1. My own picture of the mural by Isabel Cabanillas on December 14, 2021. *Source:* Photo by the author.

18, 2020.[2] Yorch pointed to her bicycle that he had hung on the wall as a sort of homage to her and to another mural he and his collective Rezizte had painted in her honor on a corner opposite Isabel's mural. I noticed the mural.

It was a side portrait of Isabel's face: She was smiling, she had purple hair and was surrounded by different types of flowers. Above her face, toward the top of the mural, there was another phrase painted in different tones of purple, white, turquoise, and pink: "Recuerdo el cepillo de mi bisabuela, con el cabello de ella enredado en él, ella ya no estaba, pero cabellito sí, así cuando yo muera probablemente ese cabello azul paseará junto con el aire y será como si yo siguiera aquí."[3] I sounded out the phrase aloud, feeling the weight of each word. There was something poetic in the echo of sounding each of the words, as if the continuation of sounding them was a continuation of her existence. I asked Yorch about the phrase. He said that it was something Isabel once shared with him that had become popular among activists and artists after her death. I stood quietly by the

2. See Aristegui Noticias 2020.

3. t. I remember my great-grandmother's little brush, with her hair entangled all over it. She was not here anymore, but her little hair was. Just like her, probably when I die, that blue hair will walk along with the wind and it will be as if I was still here.

Figure P.2. My own picture of the mural in honor of Isabel by Colectivo Reziste on December 14, 2021. *Source:* Photo by the author.

bakery's window. I could feel the crisp winter chill of Ciudad Juárez's air, and as I glanced at the mural, I felt suspended in time. I could not remember exactly when I met Isabel. I know it was on one of my last visits to Ciudad Juárez before 2020, probably 2018 or 2019; as I write this I still cannot

Figure P.3. Yorch, Beatriz Lozoya Gutierrez, and I in front of Yorch's *Ser Fronterizo* (Border Being) sculpture on January 9, 2019. *Source:* Photo by the author.

access the exact year, as time pre-COVID-19 is blurry to me. I remember that she was an artist, a member of the women's collective Hijas de su Maquilera Madre,[4] an occasional collaborator of the Rezizte collective, and a prominent activist against violence toward women in Ciudad Juárez. I remember that she had come out to one of Yorch's events in support of his monument, Ser Fronterizo (Border Being). Honestly, I cannot even remember what we talked about; just that it was a pleasant interaction, her gaze was both kind and powerful at the same time, and that we laughed.

Yorch touched my shoulder, and I came back to that moment in the bakery. I turned toward him and asked what had happened to her, how it came to be that she was murdered. He shrugged his shoulders and said, "Ya sabes, lo de siempre."[5] His response sent chills throughout my body. It was not the first time I had heard of the news of a woman I had briefly known or met being murdered, but it was the first time I was aware of my body's reaction to the news and the resignation in Yorch's response. Throughout the entire two hours I spent in the bakery talking to him, I could not stop thinking about Isabel, about her mural, about her murder.

Since 2006 I have become very familiar with the feminicides in Ciudad Juárez—and all the literature, scholarship, and activism attempting to theorize, visualize, and bring awareness to the killings of women. This social problem was the topic of my doctoral dissertation—and part of the scholarship I chose to desert shortly after successfully defending it. I discontinued it because I could not do research and write on violence against women while also experiencing various forms of violence professionally and personally. During those years, I peripherally kept up with the scholarship to engage with the topic of feminicide and other forms of violence against women. I was mostly involved through occasional activism and service. However, being in Yorch's bakery, with Isabel's mural peeking in through the door and the other mural in plain view through the window, made me ashamed of abandoning my scholarship on feminicide. I stood there in that bakery, haunted by Isabel's mural, aware and surprised by my body's reaction. Shameful thoughts began to enter my mind; I did not want to allow the sadness, impotence, and hopelessness to manifest as tears. I managed to wrap up the conversation with Yorch and left.

The next couple of months I had dreams where I saw Isabel. I felt chills whenever I taught about Ciudad Juárez in my classes, and I could

---

4. t. Daughters of Your Maquila Mother.
5. t. You know, what always does.

not put that mural out of my head. By October 2022, I felt that there was something pressing about the mural and Isabel's constant appearances in my dreams. Maybe I needed to return to my scholarship on feminicides—to rethink all of the work I had written about ten years earlier.

This book began as a collection of notes I would write on nights when I would abruptly wake up with the mural in mind or having just seen Isabel in my dreams. It has unknowingly been a work in progress over the last fifteen years. In *Mourning and Mobilization in the Americas: The Affective Politics of Women Killings,* I argue that grief and mourning mobilized by activists' responses to the killing of women in Ciudad Juárez opened an affective hemispheric dialectic with other responses by activists in the Americas. At the heart of this book is a reading of grief as an embodied affect that connects our bodies to our communities, not as a rational choice but rather as a felt compulsion with political power.

Introduction

When the Dead Speak

> The dead do not like to be forgotten, especially those whose lives had come to a violent end.
>
> —M. Jaqui Alexander[1]

This book cautions against discipline-specific studies and emotional rationality, showing the limitations of legal frameworks as solutions to feminicide. It offers what feminist theorist Rosa-Linda Fregoso calls "the force of witness" by reaching beyond the individual affective responses of bearing witness to feminicides and local-governmental solutions, to instead address social problems by moving toward a "dynamic, spirited connection between seen and unseen worlds" (Fregoso 2023, 2). Through a mixed-methods approach, this book urges us to examine the interconnectedness between affects and politics; it also asks us to consider the relational dynamics of a collectivity that is interconnected and interdependent across the Americas that demands the right to life in the face of how governments use this system to determine who lives and who dies, particularly among marginalized populations within an economic system that profits from extreme violence and death.

When the Dead Speak Through the Living

In graduate school, I gravitated toward the study of social movements that had been sparked by the death or disappearance of people. I took Hannah Wojciehowski's course "1968: A Year in Theory" and learned how the social

---

1. In *Pedagogies of Crossing* (2006), 317.

movements against authoritarian and often fascist regimes across the globe were mobilized by grieving families, students, mothers, and friends of the dead. While there is a plethora of academic studies centered on political, economic, and sociological understandings of the social movements of the 1960s and afterward, I could not find literature on how people's grief played a part in these paradigm-changing movements. What I did find, however, were testimonial works that captured the witnessing. One such text was Elena Poniatowska's *La Noche de Tlatelolco* (1998)[2] in which she captures testimonies from those who witnessed the massacre of students on October 2, 1968, in Mexico City a week before the '68 Olympics. Many of the works I read about massacres used testimonial narratives as their framework to theorize the violence that had occurred or to excavate the political implications of enacting such violence, or both.

After completing my doctoral coursework, I attended a talk featuring Deborah Paredez who had just published *Selenidad: Selena, Latinos, and the Performance of Memory.* I went to the talk because, besides being a great admirer of Selena Quintanilla, I was curious about how her identity was being thought about intellectually. As a first-generation Latine doctoral student, I struggled to find meaning in why I was pursuing a PhD and Paredez's talk challenged me to think about how academic literary and cultural research could be meaningful while also being dynamic and contemporary. I remember leaving the talk inspired and bought the book the same week. I immersed myself in the pages of *Selenidad*, in which Paredez argues that Selena's death and the mourning afterward brought Latinos together and changed what it meant to be Latina/o in the cultural, political, and economic landscape of the 1990s (Paredez 2009). Reading *Selenidad* changed the way I thought about my doctoral studies (at the time centered on representations of violence in twentieth-century Mexican literature), and it influenced me to change not only the topic of my dissertation but also to connect it to the cultural moment I was living in. Paredez's *Selenidad* gave me the courage to look toward Ciudad Juárez and pay attention to how the killings of women in this border city were being understood culturally, politically, and economically by people in Mexico and the United States.

I found the last paradigm-shifting text for how I thought about and understood gender-based killing of trans and nontrans women in 2015; it was Deborah B. Gould's *Moving Politics* (2009). I came across it while

---

2. The book was translated as *Massacre in Mexico* (1991).

doing some research about World AIDS Day for an event I was organizing as the codirector of the Center for Gender Equity and Social Justice (the Center), which I had cofounded with my colleague Emma Bailey at Western New Mexico University. In *Moving Politics*, Gould explores the relationship between activism and political feelings, and how emotions were harnessed as a political resource within the AIDS activism movement. Gould claims that "feeling and emotion are fundamental to political life, not in the sense that they overtake reason and interfere with deliberative processes, as they are sometimes disparagingly construed to do, but in the sense that there is an affective dimension to the process of social change" (3). After reading *Moving Politics*, I reflected a lot about how emotions had been harnessed by activists in Ciudad Juárez between 1993 to 2012 and how I did not center their voices in my dissertation—nor their feelings. I had a moment where I opened my dissertation file, skimmed it, and thought about how a lot of it could be reconceptualized to focus on the affective dimension of activism in relation to the killings of women in Ciudad Juárez.

However, by this point the first Trump administration had already begun, and I began work that felt more urgent at the time: protesting the treatment of transmigrants held at the Cibola Detention Center, while teaching at Western New Mexico University and running the Center. However, on sleepless nights I would think about these three texts. I began to understand them as interconnected and how they inextricably linked affect and social mobilization together for me. Specifically, I saw in all three how testimonies, performances, and public mourning influenced social mobilizations. I realized that in these testimonial narratives, performances, or both, the living would speak of those who were murdered; they would speak of their life. It was as though the testimonies of the living gave life to the dead, and I began to see a connection to my past research. When I officially began my research on the murders of women in Ciudad Juárez back in 2009, I noticed a similar pattern of the living (mothers, sisters, friends) giving a voice to the dead (murdered women and girls) through press interviews, funerals, rallies, during marches, and in poster art. While I noticed this pattern at the time, I did not name it. My doctoral work primarily focused on empathy and how it was created and achieved through these testimonies as calls for action to engage other citizens in the fight to stop the killings of women. My witnessing of Isabel Cabanillas's mural and Rezizte's response, however, also reignited this unarticulated, previous awareness of bringing the dead to life through testimonies and public mourning.

The haunting of Isabel's mural and Rezizte's honoring mural under-scored a dialectic between the dead and the living that confirmed what I had been observing in other social mobilizations. Through #Blacklivesmatter, #Niunamás, #Niunamenos, #MMIW, #NODAPL, #translivesmatter, #Say-hername, #MeToo, #familiesbelongtogether, #EuNaoMereçoSerEstrupada, and more recent stories from those who did not survive the COVID-19 pandemic, I observed that the dead became more alive than when they lived through the stories the living tell of them as the living gather support and mobilize for their respective causes. I shared this thought with several scholars and friends who responded encouragingly that I should write about it and theorize it, yet I could not find an anchor in Western scholarship. Thus, I turned to the Indigenous ways of knowing that have been present throughout my life through oral teachings, personal experiences, and gradual exposure to Indigenous scholarship.

I grew up celebrating Día de los Muertos (Day of the Dead). I had my first lesson on how the dead speak through the living at around age seven when my grandmother, my parents, my siblings, and I went to the cemetery in my hometown of Guadalajara, Mexico. I remember asking the adults why we were going to the cemetery and my grandmother explained that it was important to honor those whose bodies were no longer with us by going to visit them. She told my siblings and me that the dead never really leave us, that they are always with us and that they like it when we visit them, invoking them in our prayers and talking to them. She explained how in her family, her grandmother Teresa Ebberman had a close connection to the dead and sometimes would talk to them, and that her sister Rosa had inherited that gift. Then my mother added that in Mexico, this belief was also passed down by our Indigenous brothers and sisters and that the Spanish liked and adopted it as a celebration once a year on the first and second days of November. That was why we were going to the cemetery a day early to honor my aunt, Pilar, my father's sister, who had died from an overdose of anesthesia during surgery—a medical error. I remember being confused by this belief because the Catholic teachings in catechism school and some in the family said that when we died, we either went to heaven or hell. It seemed strange that my grandmother and the adults in my life would also have this perspective that at the time seemed antagonistic to the Catholic teachings.

My brother claims that I asked my dad and mom what happened to the dead if they did not go to heaven or hell and that their response went something like this: "Once people die, they transition. Their bodies leave and become part of the earth, but their spirits, their souls are made of energy, and they journey to the ancestral realm. Sometimes they come to visit us, check in on how we are doing through our dreams, by showing us visions or sending animals. Sometimes they bring messages or support through scents or actions people do that remind us of them. The dead are around us; they visit us the same way we visit them; they come and can sometimes speak through us." After this explanation, my little brother then told me that it really was very simple: "We visit the people who die and they visit us because we are connected."

My parents' and grandmother's explanations of our relationship with the deceased in part were influenced by the Indigenous teachings passed on to them. While we did not grow up in an Indigenous community, we had relatives who shared their knowledge. For example, my mom taught my siblings and me lessons that her Yaqui caregivers passed on to her.[3] She mainly taught us about the duality of life and death, where death is not an end, but rather a transition to another state of existence and part of our spiritual journeys. When we were older my mom shared with us a story about her best friend Clarissa Felix, who had died at twenty years old when a US Air Force jet crashed into her car and engulfed it in flames near the University of Arizona campus. When my mom shares this story, she always says she felt Clarissa's presence when she died, weeks after would see her in dreams, and continues to feel her presence at different moments.

My father and some of his siblings shared a lifelong search to connect to their Wixárika ancestors and learn their belief systems. My father's older brother, Manuel, and younger sister, Patricia, went in search of spiritual guidance and connection to our Wixárika ancestors in the 1970s and since then became the family's lifeline to Wixárika ways of knowing, rituals, and ceremonies. Manuel would tell us that when he died, he would come and tickle our feet so that we knew that we were not alone. The week he

---

3. My mother and her siblings also did not grow up in an Indigenous community. Her family history is further complicated by the story that her great-grandmother was Yaqui and had a child out of wedlock with a German by the name of Joseph Hoffer. Then, when she was abandoned with her baby, a rich Spanish family by the name of Mendoza took her in. They adopted her daughter and gave her their surname, letting my mom's great-grandmother stay close as the nanny. I share this story to further complicate the violence and legacies of colonialism within our own families and the ways in which whitewashing family histories occurs. My mother grew up being cared for by nannies, cooks, and service staff who were Yaqui; that is mainly how she and some of her siblings came to learn about Yaqui ways of knowing.

transitioned from being earthside, he came to me in a dream and we talked for what seemed hours. Patricia modeled showing respect for the land and for the beings on it and introduced us to different forms of rituals and ceremonies. One of the beliefs Patricia taught me was that Wixárika spirituality is heavily characterized by ancestral communication because life and death are cyclical, not linear. When a person dies it is believed that their spirit embarks on a journey to the ancestral realm and once they reach that realm, they visit the living through dreams. She also explained that Wixárika shamans have a way with knowledge that allows them to communicate with the spirit world. In a way, my mom's relationships with Yaqui elders and my aunt's relationships with Wixárika elders also made it possible for me to nourish friendships and meet elders that have helped me connect with my ancestors, both Indigenous and European. Through my family members, and my friendships with Indigenous elders, peers, and colleagues who have trusted me enough to teach me Indigenous ways of knowing, I have come to understand what it means to have a relationship with our ancestors and those who have passed and how they influence us—the living.

One of my most cherished teachers and friends, Peter Garcia (Hopi), a roadman and graffiti and mixed-media artist, taught me that the spirits of our ancestors and those we love continue to affect the living and offer us guidance and protection. Peter was the first person I knew to have left earthside into the spiritual realm because of COVID-19. I remember feeling devastated when he passed as we had planned to see each other over the summer of 2020. He has been present in my life ever since, including in the writing and rewriting of paragraphs of this manuscript. Sometimes when I write a word or a sentence that seems irrelevant or needs revision, I can smell his tobacco or hear the memory of his laughter. The point is that we are connected, and I continue to experience his influence in my life. When we both lived in Silver City, New Mexico, we would spend time together and have deep conversations about knowledge making and the ways in which Indigenous ways of knowing have been kept out of the academic realm. It was through these conversations that he introduced me to the work of Vine Deloria Jr. (Lakota) (1995, 1999, 2001), which challenges Western perspectives on Indigenous issues. His essay "Custer Died for Your Sins" (1969) had influenced Peter's formative years and informed the way he understood Indigenous sovereignty and his perspectives on the federal government. Peter also encouraged me to read Gregory Cajete (Tewa) (1993, 2000, 2015) as a way to understand how Indigenous ways of knowing could coexist with Western knowledge within educational spaces. Through Cajete's work, I discovered the work of Linda Tuhiwai Smith ((Ngāti Awa and Ngāti Porou) (1999) on decolonizing methodologies, Shawn Wilson (Opaskwayak Cree Nation) (2008) on how Indigenous knowledge is relational and based on accountability to all relations, and Lee Maracle (Stó:lō) (1988, 2019) on Indigenous women's experiences within traditional knowledge systems.

I sometimes reminisce on the conversations where Peter and I would talk about these Indigenous authors, and where he would resist my efforts to simplify or categorize the boundaries of their teachings. We would muse, without easy resolution, on how Deloria Jr. and Cajete had figured out the secret to publishing books that were accessible to Western thinkers. On occasion I would bring him questions about Tuhiwai Smith's ideas about decolonizing methodologies and if decolonization was *actually* possible—considering that education is inherently colonizing. Peter would laugh and encourage me to not essentialize my understanding of Tuhiwai Smith's teachings but rather stay within what he would call the shades of gray in the clouds. Our friendship felt like a continuous intellectual conversation, where every Indigenous scholar he would encourage me to read would result in nightlong questions as we moved through moonlit walks and laughter. I did not know it at the time, but Peter was modeling for me the potential of decolonizing education and its relational possibilities.

By emphasizing the importance of these five scholars' work, Peter taught me how to also invite others and orient them toward Indigenous scholarship and that respecting Indigenous perspectives and knowledge systems in academic and cultural discussions was possible. In 2018 when Peter found out I had accepted an offer to work at the University of Nevada, Reno, he gifted me a mixed-media collage that he had made for an event we organized in Las Cruces for International Women's Day in March of that year. He told me, "Lydia, this is for you to remember wherever you go that there are always layers, and in between those layers, there is space to travel within and resist." Today, the frame with his artwork hangs in my house. It is a reminder of how Peter and, more indirectly, Deloria Jr., Cajete, Tuhiwai Smith, Wilson, and Maracle have helped me understand that there is space to theorize about and travel within the nuances of life, death, and the afterlife as a way to push back against Western hegemonic ways of validating knowledge and also to resist the invalidation of Indigenous knowledge systems.

In addition to them, my mentor and friend Kathy Benavidez (Apache) taught me about the relationship with the dead in life through her experiences in seeking justice for the murder of one of her sons, Berto. Berto was murdered while walking the family dog on the evening of April 20, 2012, in a small mining town in Hurley, New Mexico. After his death, she wrote letters to then-Senator Howie Morales, Representative Rudy Martinez, members of the New Mexico State Police, and to the New Mexico Attorney General's Office. She requested FBI and State Police involvement. Yet there were no answers to the letters, no response from local, state, or federal authorities. In 2023 her daughter Camila, Berto's twin, tried to secure funds to buy a full page in the *Silver Daily Press* to highlight the unsolved murder, and she continues to seek justice for her brother with her mom. However, to this day Berto's murder remains unsolved. Throughout our friendship, Kathy has taught me about how she developed a relationship with both of her sons, Kahlo and Bert, after their deaths. In 2024 she gave me a sugar skull with Berto's name on it and told me to put in on my altar so that I could also talk with him because we were all interconnected. Kathy's wisdom has informed much of my thinking about the struggle of mothers to find justice for their children and the interdependent and powerful relationship between the living and the dead.

Similarly, my colleague and friend Debra Harry (Numu) (2005, 2007, 2011, 2017) shared with me when my father left earthside, that when a person dies it is not the end but a transition to another state of existence and that their presence can be felt in the natural world guiding and watching over the living. Her wisdom also guides much of my epistemological commitments. Debra introduced me to her own work on biocolonialism and colonial constructions of Indigenous identity. She also recommended the legal and intellectual work of Sarah Deer (Creek) (2004, 2015) and Beverly Jacobs (Mohawk) (2005, 2008, 2018), highlighting how their efforts have resulted in legislative awareness around missing and murdered Indigenous women and girls in the United States and Canada.

I did not know it at the time, but Debra's, Kathy's, and Peter's guidance and my learning from other Indigenous elders and scholars have greatly shaped my thinking and resulted in the main questions that drive this work: What happens when the dead speak through the living? Is grieving the dead a way in which they speak through the living? What if the dead were speaking through the living so we, the ones alive, could organize others through affects stemming from our grief to bring awareness to the structural (state impunity, economic profit, colonialism, police brutality) and the cultural factors (gender violence, transphobia, etc.) that resulted in their death?

In the following sections and chapters, I approach these questions by using the rhetorical construction *trans and nontrans women* instead of simply using the term *women* to mean both, to avoid "making transfeminist demands smaller in unifying through sameness" (Gill-Peterson 2024, 124). Also, I want to avoid the trap of white feminism of calling "feminism" inclusive when historically it has not always been the case. I want to highlight *trans* as part of and yet very often separate from the "women" category in terms of legislation, data collection, discrimination, and lived experience. When I use the terms *women* or *woman* I do so intentionally to acknowledge historical moments that excluded trans women. In this moment where the United States has increasing antigender legislation aimed at policing trans bodies and erasing trans existence and memory, and where across the continent there are still trans-exclusionary feminists, I am choosing to take a political stance in the naming of trans and nontrans women throughout this book. This deliberate language choice centers the specificity of transness and resists the tendency to subsume trans femininity and womanhood into a "generic standard" (Gill-Peterson 2024, 124) that erases their distinct experiences and realities. Furthermore, by maintaining this distinction, I highlight the systemic invisibility of trans women in research data and statistics, where trans experiences are frequently uncounted, miscategorized, or entirely absent from datasets that shape policy decisions and resource allocation. With this rhetorical and political commitment, I ground my responses to these questions primarily through the issue of the murders of trans and nontrans women by drawing from the Indigenous organizing epistemology centered on the interconnectedness of beings in this life and afterward, and through the works of critical and intersectional scholars in various disciplines.

The Gendered Killing of Trans and Nontrans Women

The gendered killing of trans and nontrans women is a phenomenon that has existed for centuries (Davis 1981; Maracle 1988; Federici 2004; Deer 2015; Gill-Peterson 2024). It has, of course, been studied by scholars across the globe and broadly understood as the result of witch hunts (Federici 2004), racial cleansing, battle tactics, Indigenous genocide, and colonialism (Maracle 1988; Jacobs 2005; Smith 2005; Lugones 2008; Rivera Cusicanqui 2020; Bejarano 2023; Fragoso 2023; Garcia Del Moral et al. 2023), female genocide (Palmater 2014, 2016; Segato 2016; Bemporad and Warren 2018), and violence toward trans women and gender-nonconforming people (Spade 2015; Messinger and Guadalupe-Diaz 2020; Stanley 2021; Valencia and Falcón 2023; Gill-Peterson 2024). There are also less explicit forms of studying the gendered killing of trans and nontrans women through issues of reproductive control (Roberts 1987; Nelson 2003; Gurr 2014; Ross and Solinger 2017; Lamb 2020), exploitation (Hill Collins 2004; Valencia 2010; Rolnik 2023), domestic violence (Jacobs 2005; Deer 2015), and police brutality (Davis 1981, 1989; Crenshaw 2016; Ritchie 2017).

The killings of trans and nontrans women are not particular to one place: Various locales around the world have records of crimes primarily against nontrans women, including the Balkans, Algeria, India, Ireland, Australia, Spain, China, Turkey, Iran, and South Africa to name a few. However, the Americas as a continent stand as a conglomerate of nations that have addressed this issue. There is an interconnectedness of the social movements in parts of the Americas dating back from the 1990s to the present, evident in the scholarship and in these movements' impact on the cultural and legal realms. In some cases, countries established laws to address the murders of trans and nontrans women in response to what was happening in other countries in the Americas.

Terminology: A Brief Note

In this book I employ three terms, *feminicide, transfeminicide,* and *Missing and Murdered Indigenous Women, Girls, and Two-Spirit* relatives (MMIWG2). These terms underscore the lack of accountability among nation-states in the Americas, and not just in Latin America. In 2005 the feminist Mexican anthropologist Marcela Lagarde y de los Ríos drew on the ideas of two feminists based in the United States, Diana Russell[4] and Jill Radford, who published *Femicide: The Politics of Woman Killing*[5] in 1992. They coined

---

4. Diana Russell had previously used the term *femicide* in her speech at the International Tribunal of Crimes Against Women in 1976 that was later published in the proceedings ((Russell and Van de Ven 1976). She claims she first heard the term *femicide* in 1974 when Carol Orlock was preparing an anthology on the topic that was never published (Radford and Russell 1992, xi). In the proceedings, *femicide* is repeatedly defined as "womanslaughter—or femicide" (93) and "the killing of females by males" (161).

5. Radford and Russell define *femicide* as "the misogynist killing of women by men" (1992, xi). In their book they claim that there are many different forms of femicide: racist femicide (when Black women are killed by white men), homophobic femicide or lesbicide (when heterosexual men kill lesbians), and marital femicide (when women are killed by their husbands). They further identify femicide committed outside the home

the term *feminicide*[6] in the same year that President Clinton signed the Violence Against Women Act as part of the Title IV Violent Crime Control and Law Enforcement Act.[7] Radford and Russell's contributions establish that femicide is part of a continuum of sexual violence, and the term was embraced in Latin America as a useful concept to describe the escalation of violent murders of women and girls in Ciudad Juárez as early as 1994. However, Lagarde felt the term *femicide* needed a dimension to capture the element of impunity and institutional violence on behalf of the state. In 2006 she added the syllable *ni* to the word femicide, resulting in a new word and concept—*feminicide*—to distinguish not only the killing of women but also to emphasize the role of the state in enabling impunity. Unlike *femicide*, which Lagarde understands as misogynistic killings in general, *feminicide* highlights crimes against women that occur within a context of institutional collapse, where the absence of the rule of law allows violence and disappearances to persist without consequence (Lagarde y de los Ríos 2006, 20). Fregoso (2023) explains that "state violence is systemic when it permeates the entire system [and] rather than referring to only the overt violent action by representatives of the state, this violence manifests itself in indifference to women's and trans people's lives on the part of the police, security forces, state prosecutors, judges, politicians, and institutions" (23). With the addition of the extra syllable *ni*, this term gained greater popularity among activists and scholars in Latin America because it underscored a lack of accountability and appropriate response on the part of the state when murdered trans and nontrans women were killed and found. The Pulitzer-winning author Cristina Rivera Garza reflects on the use of vocabulary in *Liliana's Invincible Summer* (2023), a memoir of her quest to bring her sister's murderer to justice years after the fact:

---

by a stranger; serial femicide; and mass femicide. They also argue that the concept of femicide extends beyond legal definitions of murder to include situations in which women are permitted to die because of misogynistic attitudes or social practices.

6. The first documented use of the word *femicide* was by the author John Corry in 1801 to describe the phenomenon of predatory behavior by men toward virgins, "denominated femicide" (60). The term reappears in 1974 when Orlock employs it in her manuscript.

7. In the United States the term *femicide* is relegated to the academic realm; in practice it is referred to simply as violence against women, intimate-partner violence, and in the case of murder, homicide. Sometimes the cause of death is listed as domestic violence or gunshot wound but there is no reference to the gender-motivated killing of the victim, since femicide or feminicide are not codified in the penal code (Lewis et al. 2024).

> It takes time and rage and collective effort to forge new vocabu-
> lary, concepts able to render the world anew. Labor harassment.
> Discrimination. Sexual violence. *The rapist is you.* Removing
> the veil that hides the violence afflicting and killing hundreds
> of thousands of women inside and outside their homes has
> not been easy. It takes a village to create a language precise
> enough, powerful enough, widespread enough to alert women
> of the menacing hand, the persistent whiff, of intimate partner
> violence. (47)

I use the term *feminicide* rather than femicide because Latin American feminist activists, organizations, and theorists labored to create a concept precise enough to refer not only to the killing of women for being women (femicide), often as a result of intimate-partner violence, but also to the systematic nature of the killing of women and the complicity and impunity of state institutions (Radford and Russell 1992; Lagarde y de los Ríos 2006; 2010; Toledo Vázquez 2009).

The Mexican philosopher Sayak Valencia (2019, 2023) calls on those working on feminicide to include a transfeminist perspective that underscores the ways in which trans women are murdered with impunity, excluding them from the process (postmortem) of being mourned in a dignified way (Spade 2015; Messinger and Guadalupe Diaz 2020; Stanley 2021; Valencia and Falcón 2023; Gill-Peterson 2024). She argues, by way of coining the neologism *transmortem politics* (the process of mobilization employed by trans women to protest the deaths of those in their communities to create alliances and bring attention to the struggles over feminicide in trans communities), that scholars must also include trans women in the research and theorization of feminicide. The Brazilian sociologist Berenice Bento (2016) coined the term *transfeminicide* in her essay "Transfeminicídio: Violência de gênero e o gênero da violência." Bento defines transfeminicide as the widespread political, intentional, and systematic elimination of the trans populations that is motivated by disgust and hatred. Drawing from both Valencia (2023) and Bento (2016), I use the term *transfeminicide* to name, illustrate, and implicate how trans women are also murdered at alarming rates with impunity. As Oliveros and García Marín (2021) demonstrate, I do this because "erasing" trans women "equates to a forceful re-victimization, annihilation, and violation of those who must bear the burden not only of a primitive society that eliminates anything that threatens patriarchal dynamics but also of a state that contributes to this elimination" (71). In addition, by using the term *transfeminicide* I offer an avenue to also include trans women in the research and theorization of the killing of trans women alongside and inseparable from nontrans women.

The last term I employ in this text, *Missing and Murdered Indigenous Women, Girls, and Two-Spirit* relatives (MMIWG2), originates in the work of Indigenous scholars and activists in Canada and the United States (Bourgeois 2015, 2023; Lucchesi 2019, 2022; Deer 2015); Palmater 2014, 2016; Craft 2014, 2020; Sovereign Bodies Institute 2020). These scholars and activists have each conducted research on gender-based violence in the contexts of Canada and the United States, naming it Missing and Murdered Indigenous Women, Girls, and Two-Spirit relatives (MMIWG2) to underscore the intersections of colonization, extractive industries, and capitalism with legal systems and victims' rights in the United States and Canada. Their terminology and research highlight the unique settler-colonial and environmental characteristics inextricable from this type of murder. Naming these forms of woman killing clarifies what is unique about them while also pointing to the lack of accountability among corresponding governmental bodies.

Affective Postmortem/Transmortem Politics

In this section I detail a series of events that for me connected the affective dimension to political mobilization. During my time in New Mexico (2013–2018) I got to know Adrien Lawyer, who was then the executive director of the Transgender Resource Center of New Mexico, and Gael Hernandez, who was the executive director of the nonprofit New Mexico Dream Team. As codirector of the Center for Gender Equity and Social Justice in Silver City, I often invited them to lead programming. At the same time, they would let me know how to support them, including through letter writing and being at protests that were happening in Albuquerque centered on seeking dignity for transmigrants housed at the Cibola Detention Center in Milan, New Mexico.

On June 2, 2018, Gael sent me a message about a protest scheduled for June 6 to call attention and demand justice for Roxsana Hernández, a trans woman from Honduras who died in the custody of US Immigration and Customs Enforcement (ICE) on May 25, 2018.

She was one of four asylum seekers who died under ICE custody that year at the Cibola Detention Center, which is privately owned by CoreCivic, formerly Corrections Corporation of America ("Detainee Death Reporting"

Figure I.1. Poster of Roxsana Hernández. *Source:* Photo by the author.

2021). After Roxsana's death, Trans Queer Pueblo, the Transgender Resource Center of New Mexico, Equality New Mexico (EQNM), and other organizations held actions to call attention to the abuses toward the trans women housed there. The Transgender Law Center worked diligently to seek justice for these asylees and filed a wrongful-death claim against the responsible parties in the case of Roxsana Hernández. Family members had obtained an independent autopsy revealing that "she had deep bruising, and severe dehydration and suffered from complications related to untreated HIV" (Transgender Law Center 2024).[8]

In 2019 another trans-woman asylee from El Salvador, Johana Medina Leon, died due to complications caused by the abuse she endured at New Mexico's Otero Detention Center and the medical neglect she experienced there (like Roxsana, she also had HIV and had been refused treatment).

---

8. The case is still ongoing according to the dossier on the Transgender Law Center website.

In March that year, the American Civil Liberties Union (ACLU) of New Mexico issued a letter calling for an investigation of detention-center abuses at the Otero Detention Center and for an end to the mass detention of migrants and asylum seekers who do not pose a security risk to the United States. In 2020 a group of trans women (#Cibola29) who were detained at the Cibola Detention Center organized and wrote letters to media outlets such as *USA Today* that exposed ICE abuses toward trans-women detainees.[9] This campaign and previous abuses led ICE to close the transgender unit at the Cibola Detention Center and transfer all trans women who were detained there.

I recount these stories to illustrate what I call affective postmortem and transmortem politics. Affective politics refers to how emotions, or affective states, play a significant role in the shaping of political attitudes, behaviors, processes, and the creation of policies.[10] We see affective politics in play all around us. Political actors such as those running for office, interest groups, or political parties all use emotional appeals such as fear and anger to connect with voters and gain their support. Affective politics can also be seen in how public support for policies and political decisions affects political decision-making. When journalists talk about polling public opinion, they are also addressing the public's often strong responses to the emotions these policies may elicit. These reactions can be related to health care, immigration, environmental issues, and other political decisions—and may shape the way a leader supports or implements a specific political agenda. In the case of Roxsana's death, family members, activists, and trans advocates' affective states (grief, anger, rage, sadness) played an essential role in the transmortem process to bring justice and dignity to Roxsana's death. Roxsana and Johana's deaths, and other abuses and deaths of trans-women migrants detained in ICE facilities, played a role in both the *affective postmortem politics* of family members and the organizing that led to engaging with the Transgender Law Center. Similarly, the *affective transmortem politics* of organizations and trans-women detainees at the Cibola

---

9. As of 2025, the Cibola County Correctional Center is still operated by ICE; however, the trans unit has been closed since January 2020.

10. I draw from psychology to refer to emotions as feelings stemming from reactions to singular stimuli. In this manuscript I draw from affect theory and affect studies to refer to affects as nonlinguistic effects, such as mood, atmosphere, feelings, disgust, surprise, or enjoyment. Finally, I refer to affective states as extended mood states not caused by a single stimulus, but rather an accumulation of experiences such as anxiety, rage, fear, hope, and so on.

and Otero detention centers resulted in letter-writing campaigns led by the #Cibola29, the subsequent closure of the Cibola Detention Center, and the involvement of the ACLU of New Mexico.

The stories of Roxsana Hernández, Johana Medina Leon, and #Cibola29 exemplify the role of emotions in our political life and political judgments. They demonstrate how ethical judgments can influence us in the pursuit of justice so that we are moved to act, protest, advocate, and call for change (Nussbaum 2001, 2013, 2019; Marcus 2010; Hochschild 2016). The outrage surrounding Roxsana's death called attention to a broader issue of ICE abuses toward trans-women asylees. The outrage and grief, as affects, became a force that shaped activism and political discourse, and implicated the power dynamics of the US immigration system in ways that had direct material consequences (Ahmed 2004, 2017, 2021, 2023; Gould 2009; Moïsi 2008; Clemens 1997; Butler 2004, 2021; Scheper-Hughes 1992, 2008; Berlant 2011, 2012; Pedwell 2014). The death of Roxsana Hernández, while felt subjectively, was politicized by communities. For example, when ICE recognized Roxsana by her birth name instead of her chosen name, ICE, and by extension the US government, denied her dignity in death; when the independent autopsy report came back to reveal she had been beaten up and denied medical treatment, it showcased how Roxsana was denied basic rights; and when surveillance footage that was part of the Cibola Detention Center's internal review of Roxsana's death was deleted (Cho et al. 2024) it denied her family and the public the right to know what happened to Roxsana when she died under custody of the US government. These actions compelled many, including myself, to join efforts to call attention to abuses under ICE and seek justice for Roxsana. The decision to participate in the transmortem process to seek justice for her was affective, because it was not only made through rational choices, but also through the felt compulsions of our feeling bodies. In other words, affect is political and the political is affective.

Emergent Critique

Scholarship on feminicide and femicide has continued to emerge since Carol Orlock and Diana Russell began to use the term femicide in the 1970s. This scholarship has defied the constraints of academic disciplines and taken up space not only in academic journals but also in legal briefs, news articles, and social media. Generally, scholarship on feminicide seeks to understand a pattern of violence that arises out of a multiplicity of what can be perceived as simple interpersonal interactions that result in the murder of trans and nontrans women. Its emergent nature impels us to tear down historical structures and academic critiques and build them up differently by emphasizing critical interconnections, as we train our minds to listen with all our body's senses so that we can notice the ways that small actions and connections can lead us to imagine and enact change.

In the following paragraphs I offer a small overview of some of the scholarship that animates my analysis throughout this book. I offer this brief section to document how the scholarship has been inherently interdisciplinary and emergent as well as how scholarship often did not include space for an analysis of the murders of trans women, Black women, and Indigenous women. For example, early pioneers in feminicide scholarship such as the Chicana feminist scholar Rosa-Linda Fregoso (2010, 2023) have written expansively on mothers whose daughters were murdered, witnessing, and cultural factors of feminicide, also calling attention to what Fregoso terms *contra-feminicide movements*, an assertion that inspires my work. Other scholars focus on the relationship to capitalism and culture (Monárrez Fragoso 2007, 2010, 2023; Rodríguez 2009; Domínguez Ruvalcaba 2011; Domínguez Ruvalcaba and Ravelo Blancas 2003, 2010, 2011), labor and neoliberalism (Wright 2006; Ravelo Blancas 2011; Ravelo Blancas and Domínguez Ruvalcaba 2006), human trafficking (Altman 2001), and human rights and representation (Staudt 2008; Driver 2015). Their scholarship, importantly, examined the relationship between the killing of nontrans women and broader systems of power specific to Ciudad Juárez and Mexico.

Non-Mexican scholars, journalists, and activists began to observe parallels between the murders of nontrans women in Ciudad Juárez and Mexico and the murders of nontrans women in their own countries. For example, Argentinian feminist scholars contributed cultural (Segato 2003, 2013, 2016; Segato and Vitenti 2023), economic (Gago 2017, 2020), and political (Pia López 2020) critiques on the killings of nontrans women in Argentina. Similarly, Brazilian feminists Débora Diniz (2011, 2012, 2015, 2019, 2020) and Adriana Piscitelli (2014, 2017, 2022) added interpersonal critiques of gender violence and its sociolegal implications in Brazil. In addition to their work, the Brazilian psychoanalyst Suely Rolnik (2023) anchors her critique of feminicide in the colonial logic that makes us mistrust the knowledge of our bodies. Rolnik develops an emergent critique of what she calls "the pimp-colonial-capitalist regime" (63), a dynamic that results in the accumulation of capital over life itself. She argues that "what the regime appropriates is the essence of life, its potency of creation of new forms, at the exact moment that the impulse of this potency emerges" (3). She asserts further that "what gets pimped here, what gets expropriated and corrupted, is the vital force of all the elements that constitute the biosphere: plants, animals, humans, and so forth" (63). These and other feminist scholars from the Global South have expanded the analytic framework of feminicide by connecting it to neoliberalism, colonial legacies, and capitalism in the Latin American context, thus offering an emergent critique of how these systems expropriate life's vital forces through structural and cultural mechanisms of gender violence that extend beyond interpersonal dynamics.

While scholars in the United States and Canada have not fully embraced the term *feminicide*, Black and Indigenous scholars examined gender-based killing through various disciplines using the often-intertwined lenses of race (Crenshaw 1991, 2016; Hill 2024), gender (Amuchie 2016; Roberts 1997; Ritchie 2017), colonialism (Bourgeois 2014, 2015, 2023; Lucchesi 2019, 2022; Deer 2004, 2015; Deer et al. 2008; Palmater 2014, 2016; Craft 2014, 2020; Betasamosake Simpson 2016), immigration (Correa-Cabrera and Keck 2022; Sabri et al. 2018), and intimate-partner violence and the criminal justice system (Davis 1981, 1999; Hill Collins 2004; Tyree and Niles Goins 2021). Collectively, this scholarship situates gender-based killings of Black and Indigenous nontrans women (and more recently trans women and two-spirit relatives) as occurring in connection to systems of power related to colonialism, race, class, capitalism, immigration, and carceral institutions.

This emergent scholarship emphasizes that feminicides occur at the intersection of multiple oppressions, with victims being those marginalized by nationalists and colonial systems. According to Federici et al. (2021), Afrodescendant and Indigenous women are disproportionately affected as "globalization is a project of recolonization" (63). Building on this analysis of the uneven impacts of globalization, Monárrez Fragoso (2023) explains that "poor women, Black women, First Nation women, trans women, and immigrant women are at greater risk than elite white women . . . because nonwhite women's existence is impacted by multiple vulnerabilities derived from intersecting structures of power in their lives" (40). Similarly, Rangel Oliveros and García Marín (2021) note that racialization, social class, and immigration status are "as shown by the crimes perpetuated, intersections that influence how transfemigenocide is carried out" (71). Feminicide, transfeminicide, MMIWG2, and contra-feminicide movements are nuanced and unique to their sociopolitical contexts and yet interconnected by global economic processes.

My contribution to this emergent scholarship is situated in the commitment to highlight how murders of trans women, Indigenous women and two-spirit relatives, and Black trans and nontrans women have existed in parallel to the murders of white or mestiza[11] nontrans women and must be included in the scholarship. Recognizing the presence of trans women, Indigenous women and two-spirit people, and Black trans and nontrans women, and their activism in contra-feminicide movements, offers an opportunity to explore the distinctive affective dimensions of their protagonism and contributions to enacting cultural and legislative change. More broadly, I hope to model how scholarship on feminicide, transfeminicide, and MMIWG2 can extend beyond the boundaries of academic critique through praxis and accountability to all relations.

In this book I draw from Indigenous ways of knowing, scholars of feminicide, transfeminicide, and MMIWG2, Black feminists, theorists of affect, and Sayak Velencia's concept of postmortem and transmortem politics to argue that the affective is indispensable to understanding the emergence of social mobilizations against feminicide, transfeminicide, and MMIWG2—and the interconnectedness of these mobilizations—across the Americas. Specifically, I argue that grief and mourning mobilized by activists' responses to the killing of women in Ciudad Juárez opened an affective hemispheric dialectic with other responses by activists in the Americas. Grief, often understood as an emotional response to loss, manifests through a mix of emotions including but not limited to sadness, anger, guilt, denial, fear, loneliness, and numbness. Grief, and by extension mourning, pulses in a way that reminds us of our interconnectedness to all beings. Thus, I see grief stemming from feminicide, transfeminicide, and MMIWG2 as a way for the dead to speak through the living and as a transformative affective force that has resulted in a transnational struggle.

Overview

Overall, the manuscript comprises four chapters that, taken together, reveal how mourning the murder of trans and nontrans women transmuted grief into postmortem politics that then transformed into a struggle for legislative change and sociocultural awareness in the Americas. Specifically, I highlight the work of activists, scholars, artists, writers, and influencers from 1994 to

---

11. A woman of mixed race, usually of Indigenous and Spanish descent.

2023 to chronicle the intersection between their activism and the development and rise of social media, and the eventual implementation of legislation and codification of feminicide/femicide as a crime in countries across the Americas. Individually, each chapter attends to the question of the affects produced in the living by the murders of trans and nontrans women, and MMIWG2, as expressed through literature, art, social media, and other cultural texts in addition to the resulting postmortem or transmortem politics that influenced specific activism, legislation, and public discourse. The title of each chapter represents affects that were either named by activists and scholars themselves, that I identified in their social media, or through direct conversations. Naming the chapters after affects in no way suggests that these affects are universal, or that they are felt and understood the same way by people across the globe. Rather, I chose to name the chapters after named affects within specific geopolitical contexts to honor the work of activists in those regions. After discussing the activism that emerged in Ciudad Juárez in the first chapter, I turn toward the rest of social media activism in Latin America to examine how the rise of social media allowed activists to express their emotions, organize, and share strategies and resources in succinct and interconnected ways with other activists across the Americas through the #NiUnaMas, #NiUnaMenos, #MMIW, #MMIWG2, and #Sayhername movements. I then interrogate how these highly affect-driven mobilizations have affected legislative and cultural responses in Brazil, Canada, and the United States. At the heart of this transcultural analysis is a reading of grief as an embodied affect that connects our bodies to our communities not as a rational choice, but rather as a felt compulsion with political power.

In chapter 1, "Impotence and Frustration," I analyze how pain, impotence, and frustration play a part in the postmortem politics of a group of women in Ciudad Juárez, Mexico—a crucial catalyzing site for postmortem politics across the Americas. Writers Rohry Benítez, Adriana Candia, Patricia Cabrera, Guadalupe de la Mora, Josefina Martínez, Isabel Velázquez, and Ramona Ortiz would get together and write on Saturdays in what they called S Taller. They became increasingly concerned about how murdered women's lives were slandered and shamed in the press. Their commitment to bring dignity to seven murdered nontrans women led them to create vignettes for each based on interviews with the dead nontrans women's family and friends. The resulting work, *El silencio de la voz que todas quiebra*,[12] (1999), was born out of impotence and frustration. I trace how

---

12. The book has not been translated into English; the title per my translation is The Silence That the Voice of All Women Breaks.

these women's postmortem politics and collaborations with other activists inspired a plethora of cultural artifacts including but not limited to novels, nonfiction books, documentaries, feature films, murals, and performances. I argue that this initial affective response from activists underscored problematic discourses and government responses around the killing of nontrans women in investigations, inclusion of trans women's deaths, recordkeeping, monument building, and eventual legislative change. I examine how the birth of social media coincided with major efforts to call attention to the murdered women in Ciudad Juárez and how this resulted in the digital nationwide movement #NiUnaMas. I conclude this chapter by claiming that affects of impotence and frustration stemming from the continuous killing of trans and nontrans women in Ciudad Juárez keep activists fighting for justice. With the rise in popularity of social media platforms such as MySpace, Facebook, and Twitter, this activism furthered its reach through other states in Mexico and ignited interest in the feminicides of Ciudad Juárez nationally and ultimately globally.

In chapter 2, "Fear and Rage," I trace how the rise of social media allowed activists to express their emotions, organize with others, and share strategies and resources in succinct and interconnected ways with other activists across the Americas through the #Niunamenos, #MMIWG/ #MMIWG2S, and #Sayhername movements. Drawing from the named affects of fear and rage by activists on Twitter, I examine how the #niunamas movement turned the localized phenomenon of the feminicides of Ciudad Juárez into #niunamenos, a Latin American interconnected struggle against feminicide that influenced the creation of laws against feminicide in sixteen Latin American countries from 2002 to 2017. I conclude by portraying how #NiUnaMenos became intertwined with the #MMIWG/#MMIWG2S and #Sayhername movements by creating a coalitional digital conversation around the murders of Indigenous and Black, and trans women.

Chapter 3, "Determination and Tension," is a case study that centers on how the Brazilian state and activists have addressed the issue of gender violence and feminicide, particularly given that according to data from the *Atlas of Violence 2025*, produced by the Institute of Applied Economic Research (IPEA) and the Brazilian Forum on Public Security, from 2013 to 2023 47,463 women were murdered in Brazil (Cerqueira et al. 2025, 49). In 2023 alone 3,903 homicides of women were recorded, a 2.5% increase over 2022 (Cerqueira et al. 2025, 49). More recently, data from the TGEU's (Trans Europe and Central Asia) Trans Murder Monitoring (TMM) project reveals that 350 trans and gender-diverse people were reported murdered around the globe in 2024, and of those 73% occurred in Latin America and the Caribbean, with 105 or nearly one-third of the cases reported in Brazil (for the seventeenth year in a row) (TGEU 2024). I trace how in Brazil, mechanisms such as the Inter-American Commission on Human Rights along with mobilizations made of survivors, families, activists, and NGOs all helped to put pressure on governments to legislate gender violence, including feminicide. They also launched social media campaigns that intersected with efforts to pass legislation. I then discuss the state-sponsored murder of politician and activist Marielle Franco in 2018 and the postmortem politics that ensued after her death, which underscored the tension between legislative and cultural changes. I conclude by questioning how the affects of determination and tension in the face of grief continue to organize activists to fight for the life of trans and nontrans women in a country where one trans woman is murdered every three days and where a nontrans woman is murdered every six hours.

In chapter 4, "Indignation and Persistence," I examine how the indignation of Indigenous activists has resulted in persistent efforts to legislate protections for these communities amid inaction by the governments of Canada and the United States in the face of increasing numbers of missing and murdered Indigenous women. First, I chronicle the legislative efforts of both the United States and Canada to address gender violence broadly, underscoring how settler-colonial violence legally allowed gender violence toward Indigenous communities as an extension of the ideology of Manifest Destiny and expansion. By anchoring the Indigenous knowledge of violence toward women as an extension of violence toward the earth, I argue that there is an inextricable relationship between the colonial logics of conquest, extractive industries, and increasing numbers of MMIWG2. I conclude by examining how Indigenous activists' persistence informs their grassroots organizing, efforts to educate within their communities, and their activism to influence lawmakers. It is this persistence that is creating a roadmap toward naming femicide as a crime and legally changing how gender violence is understood in both the United States and Canada.

The concluding chapter offers reflections on how mourning transmutes grief into a process of postmortem and transmortem politics, and how it is a way for the dead to speak through the living. Grief is a multidimensional pulse—and by extension through mourning, it becomes an embodied mobilizing force. Grief also offers an analytical framework useful for understanding other global movements. Here I offer an analytic of grief and public mourning as frameworks and tools that result in post- and transmortem politics throughout the book.

I hope this book contributes to comparative and interdisciplinary projects discussing the affective dimensions of grief and mourning and their impact on mobilizations for legislative and sociocultural change in the Americas. It expands the central concerns of human rights frameworks regarding the responsibility of the state to prevent and combat gender-based violence. It also broadens the central questions of the intersectionality of race, class, sex, gender, and documented status with a transnational framework that looks for points of interconnection across the Americas. Through this analytical lens, we can better understand how grief stemming from the murders of trans and nontrans women and missing and murdered women, girls, and two-spirit relatives was foundational to the launch of a series of interconnected social movements in Canada, the United States, Latin America, and the Caribbean.

Chapter 1

Impotence and Frustration

Breaking the Silence in Ciudad Juárez

Esto ocurrió en 1993. En enero de 1993. A partir de esta muerta comenzaron a contarse los asesinatos de mujeres. Pero es probable que antes hubiaera otras. . . . Aunque seguramente en 1992 murieron otras. Otras que quedaron fuera de la lista o que jamás nadie las encontró, enterradas en fosas comunes en el desierto o esparcidas sus cenizas en medio de la noche.

—Roberto Bolaño[1]

In the early 1990s, the members of S Taller, a creative-writing group in Ciudad Juárez, met weekly on Saturday mornings to dream, discuss, and create other universes through writing literature, and to be in community through creativity (Benítez et al. 1999; Báez 2006).[2] By 1993 their joyful and imaginative space to write on Saturday mornings shifted into a space to voice their frustration and impotence over an increasing number of news reports of murdered young women in Ciudad Juárez. They became increasingly concerned with the way these women's lives were slandered and shamed in

1. *t.* This happened in 1993. January 1993. From then on, the killings of women began to be counted. But it's likely there had been other deaths before. . . . Although surely there were other girls and women who died in 1992. Other girls and women who didn't make it onto the list or were never found, who were buried in unmarked graves in the desert or whose ashes were scattered in the middle of the night. (Bolaño 2008, 444)

2. The members of S Taller included Rohry Benítez, Adriana Candia, Patricia Cabrera, Guadalupe de la Mora, Josefina Martínez, Isabel Velázquez, and Ramona Ortiz.

the press. The members of S Taller felt indignation and embarrassment at how the women were becoming a spectacle through sensationalist accounts in newspapers and TV programs (Báez 2006; Driver 2015). Their Saturday mornings became a space to find a way to change these sensationalized narratives; they felt these reports not only tarnished these dead women's lives but often were overtaken by salacious details. The members of S Taller wanted to bring dignity to the dead women. Eventually, these discussions led them to write a book—a counternarrative—that could capture "la imagen humana de las víctimas, el rostro y el alma, por lo menos de siete de ellas" and would include "datos hechos consignados que por sí mismos reflejaran el verdadero entorno en el que ocurrieron los asesinatos de mujeres en Ciudad Juárez" (Benítez et al. 1999, 5).[3]

In this chapter, I employ a mixed methodological approach involving the analysis of archival material, participant observation, and cultural critique to trace the story of S Taller's resulting manuscript, *El silencio de la voz que todas quiebra:Mujeres y víctimas de Ciudad Juárez* (1999),[4] the authors' struggle with publishing it, the text's subsequent distribution, and how its impact illustrates a process of postmortem politics (Valencia and Zhuravleva 2019) that suggests how the affects of impotence and frustration influenced their activism and ultimately contributed to later cultural narratives (material, digital, film, art) of feminicide in Ciudad Juárez. Cultural critic Hector Domínguez Ruvalcaba and sociologist Patricia Ravelo Blancas explain that the publication of *El silencio* was "groundbreaking" as it "is the first book addressing the problem of disappearances of girls in this city [Juárez]" (Domínguez Ruvalcaba et al. 2015, 544). In the introduction to *El silencio*, Benítez, Candia, Cabrera, de la Mora, Martínez, Velázquez, and Ortiz write in the book's opening sentence that it was born out of "la impotencia y la frustración" (1999, 5).[5] I named this chapter "Impotence and Frustration" to honor their affects in this specific context. In the following sections, I provide a brief context of feminicides in Ciudad Juárez and the discourse that had been circulating before the publication of *El silencio*. Then, I trace how these women's affective postmortem politics influenced the publication

---

3. *t.* the human image of the victims, the face and soul, at least for seven of them. Recorded facts that in themselves reflected the true environment in which the murders of women in Ciudad Juárez occurred. See Benítez et al. (1999).

4. *t.* The silence of the voice that shatters every woman: women and victims of Ciudad Juárez

5. *t.* impotence and frustration

of their manuscript and set the stage for other activists, scholars, writers, and artists to organize and produce scholarship, novels, nonfiction books, documentaries, feature films, murals, songs, and performances that eventually had a hemispheric reach. Finally, I examine how this increase in the cultural representation of feminicide coincided with the rise of social media, specifically with the birth and widespread use of Facebook and Twitter.

Postmortem Politics:
S Taller and the Murders of Ciudad Juárez, 1993–1998

On January 23, 1993, the body of Alma Chavira Farel was found on the outskirts of Ciudad Juárez. She had been raped, and evidence did not point to a specific perpetrator. The investigation that followed yielded contradictory, inconclusive results. Forty-eight hours later, Angélica Luna Villalobos's body was found. She was six months pregnant and had been strangled; similarly to Alma, the evidence did not point to a specific perpetrator. These women were two out of eighteen nontrans women and girls who had been counted as murdered, described as mestizas and poor by local authorities, and reported about in the Ciudad Juárez and Mexican press in 1993 (CNDHM 1998; Benítez et al. 1999; Medellín 1999; Pérez-Espino 1999; Bertrán 1999; *Washington Post* 2000; Monárrez Fragoso 2000; González Rodríguez 2002).

With the number of dead nontrans women rising, and accurate numbers unobtainable from diverse governmental offices, Esther Chávez Cano organized a group of women named Grupo 8 de marzo.[6] Supported by public intellectuals, artists, and academics, they questioned the lack of governmental recordkeeping (Esther Chávez Cano Collection, n.d.).[7] In addition, the group compiled news articles relating to crimes against nontrans women to keep count of the number of nontrans women murders

---

6. March 8 Group

7. Esther Chávez Cano was one of the pioneers in questioning the impunity of the authorities, taking to the streets and plastering the city with pink ribbons representing the dead women. In 1999 she also established the first rape crisis center, Casa Amiga, which became known for its community outreach. Beatriz Lozoya was one of the civilian volunteers involved in Casa Amiga. In 2008 Chávez Cano was given Mexico's National Human Rights Award. She died of cancer in December 2009. Her extensive archive is housed in the New Mexico State University Special Collections and includes newspaper clippings, magazine articles, and personal emails related to organizing marches, actions, and legislative testimony.

occurring in order to categorize how and why these nontrans women had been murdered (Domíngez Ruvalcaba et al. 2015).[8] Throughout the 1990s this categorizing and recordkeeping would consistently challenge the numbers and narratives produced by the governmental entities. The discrepancy between these unofficial numbers kept by nongovernmental civilians and the ones sanctioned by governmental officials established a pattern that in the Juárez public sphere was referred to by activists as la guerra de los números[9] (Domínguez Ruvalcaba 2011), which I will discuss at a later moment in this chapter.

By 1995 the Chihuahua Attorney General's Office had found their suspect and claimed that Abdul Latif Sharif, a US-born citizen and chemist, was responsible for the murders of the nontrans mestiza and poor women (Ortega 1999). However, after his capture, the murders continued. In 1996 the same office declared that the murders were also being perpetrated by a gang called the Rebels who were copycats inspired by Sharif. The general attitude of government officials toward the murdered nontrans women was accusatory; they blamed the victims for their deaths, claiming some of them were sex workers or irresponsible maquila (low-wage export factories) workers, or that their family dysfunction had caused their misfortune.[10] The coverage of these murders was slanderous at worst and sensationalist at best (CNDHM 1998; Benítez et al. 1999; Ravelo Blancas and Domínguez Ruvalcaba 2006; Fernandez and Rampal 2007; Fregoso and Bejarano 2010; Driver 2011, 2015).

These victim-blaming narratives constructed by government officials were often validated through their dissemination by the local press, official church sermons, and schools (Driver 2011, 2015). It was against these heavily circulated narratives that the members of S Taller, united by their frustration and impotence, organized themselves and participated in a process to save "la dignidad de esas muchachas, laceradas hasta después de su muerte" (Benítez et al. 1999, 5).[11] This process of postmortem politics,

---

8. These murders of women in Ciudad Juárez were legally referred to as homicide of females. Popularly they were known as "asesinatos de mujeres." It was not until the 2000s that the term *femnicidio/feminicide* was popularized and used for this category of extreme violence.

9. *t.* the war of numbers

10. There is an opportunity for future researchers to excavate whether trans women, especially those who were sex workers, were not included in these figures because they were counted in figures representing their sex assigned at birth.

11. *t.* these young women's dignity even after their death

Figure 1.1. Postcard included within *El Silencio de la voz que todas quiebra* (Benítez et al. 1999). *Source:* Photo of postcard by the author.

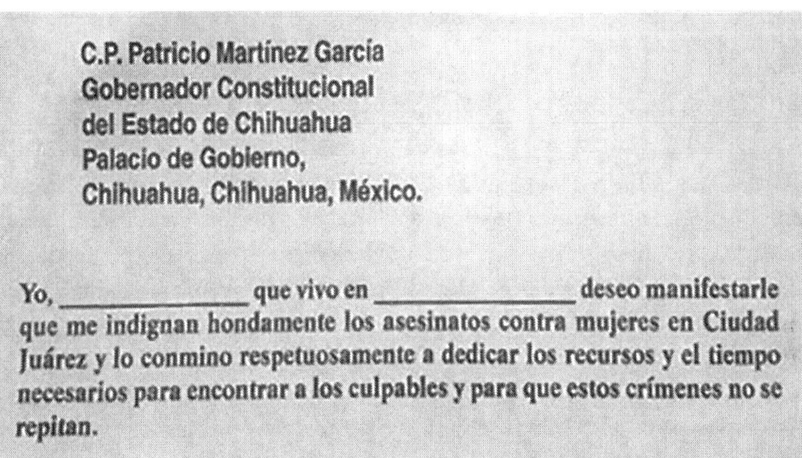

intended "to confront the necropolitics that murder trans and cis women every day, with impunity, and that excludes them from the possibility of being read in a socially dignified way even after their death" (Valencia and Zhuraleva 2019, 181), led the members of S Taller to create the text *El silencio de la voz que todas quiebra*. Their objective was to find "la imagen humana de la víctimas, el rosto, el alma"[12] (Benítez et al. 1999, 5) and to provide a collage of texts ranging from fictional recreated testimonies and investigations to chronicles of their experiences while attempting to investigate the matter. They believed this work would allow "al lector acercarse tanto al drama humano de las mujeres asesinadas como a esa realidad de la que todos somos reponsables" (Benítez et al 1999, 5).[13]

In summary, these authors sought to change the general perception of some of these women from sexually commoditized and marginalized maquila workers to humans—nontrans women with dreams and hopes of their own—by personalizing their individual stories. The women of S Taller hoped that giving a fuller picture of some of the murdered nontrans women would enable the public that read their book to make connections

---

12. *t.* the human image of the victims, the face, the soul

13. *t.* the reader to get close to the human drama of the murdered women as well as the reality that we are all responsible for

between the events taking place and consider the lives of the murdered nontrans women, and then choose to exercise their political citizenship by mailing a pre-filled-out postcard to the governor of the State of Chihuahua.

Breaking the Silence from Ciudad Juárez

The women of the S Taller collective created a manuscript that was composed of an introductory essay and seven sections. The authors crafted testimonies based on the interviews and diary entries of Silvia Elena Rivera Hernández, Elizabeth Castro García, Olga Alicia Carrillo Pérez, Sagrario González Flores, Argelia Irene Salazar Crispín, Adriana Torres Márquez, and Eréndira Ivonne Ponce Hernández—7 out of the 137 murdered nontrans women between 1993 and 1998.[14] Each of the sections contained either a testimony, an essay, or a study that reflected on social problems that could be considered contributing factors to the murders of these nontrans women, as well as a chronicle of the authors' experiences—specifically with the impunity and complicity of the police, government, and public—that they consider a consequence of the systemic patriarchal social structures. In a sense, these authors employ what Saidiya Hartman (2008) describes as critical fabulations, which involve creating a plausible story to rescue or bring to life those lives (in her case, the lives of slaves and Africans) that are left out of the archives. These critical fabulations to rescue and bring dignity to the lives of the women in *El silencio* are an example of one of the strategies of postmortem politics.

Once their manuscript was ready, they sent it to several publishing houses in Mexico City. After being turned away by these, the writers of S Taller, through feminist networks, were referred to one of Mexico's top public intellectuals, Elena Poniatowska, to seek help in publishing their manuscript.[15] On March 29, 1999, the authors met with her, but she refused

---

14. This number was corroborated through a rigorous investigation by Rhory Benítez et al. (1999) that took information from two sources: *Homicidios en prejuicio de mujeres que han causado indignación en los diferentes niveles sociales de la comunidad 1993–1998*, published by la Subprocuaduría de Justicia del Estado, and journalistic investigations researched by Universidad Autónoma de Ciudad Juárez (UACJ), el Comité Independiente de Chihuahua Pro-defensa de los Derechos Humanos, and Grupo 8 de Marzo.

15. The editor at Editorial Planeta Mirta Ripol wanted the story told a different way and commissioned the writing of the book from Victor Ronquillo, who as a result wrote *Las muertas de Juárez*. This book was released nationally on September 9, 1999. It was

to help them get the work published. She later explained her reasoning in the second part of a three-part essay published as "Las ciudades fronterizas son hoteles de paso":

> Cuando me visitaron en el DF, yo misma tenía tantísimo trabajo y el tema de las muchachas muertas me pareció tan feo que las relegué para más tarde, decepcionándolas. Hoy, les pido una disculpa. Estoy segura de que involuntariamente contribuí al clima de misoginia con el que se toparon en la ciudad de México al presentar su manuscrito. Los temas del aborto, del maltrato a la mujer, del asesinato son dolorosos, y casi todos preferimos darle vuelta a la hoja. (Poniatowska 2002)[16]

Poniatowska's indifference was indicative of the difficulty in getting Mexico's top public intellectuals to address the issue of the murdered women and consequently the general population. This was despite the fact that she had written several novels that are considered feminist attempts to call attention to the patriarchy and Mexico's structural investment in male-dominated values, and had collected important testimonies from one of Mexico's most traumatic events on the evening of October 2, 1968, the Tlatelolco Massacre, when government forces opened fire just days before the 1968 Olympics on thousands of peaceful protesters in the Plaza de las Tres Culturas in Mexico City. Even though she later apologized to the authors of S Taller, she initially showed disregard toward these women who sought to impart dignity to an increasing number of dead nontrans women. Her attitude also reflected a centralist ideology that promotes the lack of engagement regarding violence toward trans and nontrans women, youth, men, and marginalized groups in Mexico, especially those who live outside the confines of Mexico City

---

then showcased internationally at la Feria International del Libro on October 16, 1999. Shortly after its publication, there were accusations in prominent newsprint sources like *Universal, Proceso, Reforma, El Angel, and Al Margen* that Ronquillo and Editorial Planeta had co-opted material from *El silencio*. Ronquillo dismissed these accusations in the *Reforma* and *Proceso* issues of October 31, 1999.

16. *t*. When they visited me in Mexico City, I had so much work and the topic of the dead girls was so ugly to me that I simply relegated them for later, disappointing them [S Taller]. Today I ask them for forgiveness. I am sure that I unintentionally contributed to the climate of misogyny that they encountered in Mexico City when they submitted their manuscript. The issues of abortion, mistreatment of women, and murder are painful, and almost all of us prefer to turn the page.

and who are not read as middle- or upper-class or non-Indigenous (Castillo and Tabuenca Córdoba 2002).[17]

Following the dismissal of their manuscript, with the help of the rape crisis center Casa Amiga and Ediciones Azar A.C., a small publishing division of Universidad Autónoma de Chihuahua, the women of S Taller were able to publish the manuscript in November 1999 and titled it *El silencio de la voz que todas quiebra: Mujeres y víctimas de Ciudad Juárez*.[18]After its release, the book had little immediate impact on the public at large. Most of the national attention it received came before its release, specifically in the 1190 and 1198 issues of the newspaper *Proceso* (Ravelo 1999). These articles do not mention *El silencio* by name, but they report that the manuscript that had been submitted to and rejected by Editorial Planeta was plagiarized, adapted, and published as *Las muertas de Juárez* by Victor Ronquillo, and published by none other than Editorial Planeta. Later, in response to these accusations made by José Manual Garcia, Ronquillo wrote an op-ed published in the newspaper *Reforma* defending himself against the allegations of plagiarism (Ronquillo 1999a). Despite this public controversy in national newspapers, *El Silencio* remained largely overshadowed in public discourse, illustrating how institutional power, access to cultural capital, and mainstream media shaped how S Taller's grassroots testimonial work was amplified in Mexico. However, *El silencio* did receive some attention in articles written in English (Molloy 2002; *Washington Post* 2000). The authors also appeared at several promotional book readings in the United States (Burciaga 2000).

As more academics became involved in studies about the murders of nontrans women in Ciudad Juárez, *El silencio* became better known. More than two decades later, it is cited and considered one of the most reliable "nonacademic" sources by academics and journalists working on the issues involving Ciudad Juárez (Washington Valdez 2005; Domínguez Ruvalcaba

---

17. For events and cultural productions originating in the provinces, it is difficult to achieve notoriety in publishing houses, theaters, and scholarship. In Debra Castillo and Socorro Tabuenca Córdoba's *Border Women: Writing from La Frontera* (2002), the literary scholars offer an in-depth critique on border theory, including a discussion of these centralists' ideologies and their resulting gendered and marginalized politics (7). In the same text, the authors quote Rosario Sanmiguel, who says that "the day that a large press publishes [her] work and it is distributed like that of Campbell or Gadea is the day that [she] will stop being from the border and begin being from the center. The border and borderness means being outside the exercise of power" (20).

18. *t.* The Silence of the voice that shatters every woman: women and victims of Ciudad Juárez

et al. 2015; Fregoso 2023). For example, Susana Báez, a professor at Universidad Autónoma de Ciudad Juárez, says of *El silencio*: "Se nos muestra como un documento de gran valor social, pues denota el compromiso ético de las autoras y busca propiciar el mismo entre sus lectores; sus enunciatarios principales son la sociedad civil y las instituciones del Estado" (2006, 186).[19]

Although a full PDF version of the text is now available on the Internet, it is difficult to find an actual hard copy in Mexican bookstores, including the book markets of its three largest cities, Mexico City, Guadalajara, and Monterrey. In part, obtaining a hard copy is difficult because it was out of print by 2001, and also because it was "distributed mainly through the authors' networks and by a few dedicated booksellers who provide materials from publishers outside Mexico City to academic libraries," including fourteen libraries in the United States (Molloy 2002). *El silencio* is the result of postmortem politics by S Taller. Almost two decades later its reach can be traced in the ongoing war of numbers, cultural representations of the feminicides of Ciudad Juárez that flooded the public sphere throughout the 2000s, and calls to action that have gained traction with social media.

War of Numbers

One of the resulting practices of S Taller's postmortem politics was documenting the numbers of deaths of murdered nontrans women. S Taller and Casa Amiga's effort to document these murders (Monárrez Fragoso 2000, 2009, 2023) was a way to keep a record of them since the Mexican federal and state authorities were not keeping a record of these murders as motivated by gender. In their book *Sex, Drugs, and Body Counts* (2010), the political scientists Andreas and Greenhill (2011) argue that in political terms "if something is not measured it does not exist . . . if there are no 'data,' an issue or problem will not be recognized, defined, prioritized, put on the agenda, and debated" (1). Therefore, by quantifying a phenomenon, in this case the murders of nontrans women, S Taller and Casa Amiga recognized its existence, transforming an abstraction into a tangible metric of quantifiable importance to call forth potential action from the government. These nonstate communities of women were documenting numbers

---

19. *t.* It is shown to us as a document of great social value because it denotes the ethical commitment of the authors and seeks to promote the same among its readers. Its main enunciators are civil society and state institutions.

that the state did not conceive as having a gendered dimension. Casa Amiga's recordkeeping forced the state to also participate in the practice of documenting these murders outside of labeling them as "homicides." This practice of independent recordkeeping was also adopted by the Division of Gender Studies at the Universidad Autónoma de Ciudad Juárez, Voces sin Eco, and the Independent Committee of Human Rights of Chihuahua who joined Grupo 8 de marzo.

In addition to keeping track of nontrans women's bodies, these community organizations and scholars began to analyze these deaths and categorize their possible causes. The reports compiled by activists, NGOs, and human rights officials identified broader patterns in the deaths of these women.[20] The victims were described as young women between 17 and 28 years old, from poor working-class families; some were identified as maquila workers, students, sex workers, and shoe store clerks. Their race was noted as mestiza, but recent scholarship suggests that many were and continue to be primarily of Indigenous origin (García Del-Moral 2020; Frías 2021). According to these reports, the murdered nontrans women were usually found in vacant lots within Ciudad Juárez or on ranches and other areas of the desert on the outskirts of the city. They were primarily found bound, raped, maimed, and strangled. In terms of possible causes, a seminal qualitative survey published by Héctor Domínguez Ruvalcaba and Patricia Ravelo Blancas (2003) asked locals in Ciudad Juárez why they thought these nontrans women were murdered. Their results compiled a total of 32 different theories collected from their fieldwork.

Among the top theories were those related to the complicity of policemen, messages from drug lords to the authorities, trafficking of organs, precarity of women and prepubescent girls, a serial killer, and the porn industry—especially the branch related to the elaboration and marketing of snuff films (Domínguez Ruvalcaba and Ravelo Blancas 2003).

The collaboration between community organizations and scholars began to shed light on the problem through the lenses of gender, migration, and

---

20. See *Informe sobre los homicidios de mujeres en Ciudad Juárez* (1998) by la Comisión Nacional de Derechos Humanos de México; *Muertes Intolerables* (2003) by Amnesty International; *Informe sobre Ciudad Juárez* (2003) by la Comisión Interamericana para los Derechos Humanos; *Homicidios y Desparaciones de Mujeres en Ciudad Juárez* (2004) by Instituto Nacional de Ciencias Penales; the 2005 *Country Reports on Human Rights Practices* by US Department of State; *Feminicidio* (2009) by Oficina en México del Alto Comisionado de las Naciones Unidas para los Derechos Humanos.

the economic dynamics of the maquila industry (Tabuenca and Aguilar 2000; Monárrez Fragoso 2000, 2006; Padilla 2002; González Rodríguez 2002; Ravelo Blancas and Domínguez Ruvalcaba 2006; Wright 2006; Monárrez Fragoso et al. 2010; Iturralde 2010; Fregoso and Bejarano 2010; García and Coutiño Osorio 2011; Gayón 2018; Guerrera 2018; Finnegan 2021; Fregoso 2023). Their activism, recordkeeping, and research also pressured state and federal Mexican authorities into appointing a special task force that resulted in the establishment of la Fiscalía Especial de Investigación de Homicidios contra Mujeres (Special Prosecutor's Office to Investigate Homicides Against Women) in 2004. Furthermore, this collaboration enabled a shift in terminology to describe these types of crimes: from "murders of women" and "homicide of women" in the 1990s to "feminicide" in the later 2000s (Lagarde 2006, 12). When the state began to record and conduct investigations of homicides of nontrans women, a war of numbers began and has continued between the official counts of homicides provided by the state and those provided by independent community organizations in Ciudad Juárez (and more broadly, in the rest of Mexico). Today, the numbers reported by communities, NGOs, and Amnesty International are still higher than those reported by the Mexican state.

The use of numbers is often presented as an objective metric. However, numbers are anything but neutral. They are powerful argumentative tools, persuasive rhetorical devices, that are strategically mobilized to persuade, convince, and shape policy discourse (Wynn and Reyes 2021). In the case of Mexico, the discrepancy between state and nonstate figures initially situated state numbers as official and the numbers produced by NGOs and other communities as unofficial. By branding their numbers as "official," the state strategically delegitimized competing numerical representations, characterizing them as unreliable indicators produced by the collective hysteria of these nontrans women-run groups. Also, the state's strategy systematically transformed individual murdered persons into decontextualized and subjective data points.

The state's embrace of statistical abstraction became a mechanism of narrative suppression that not only rendered these murdered nontrans women fundamentally invisible but also influenced public perception. For example, the increasing concern with drug-related violence in the 2000s diverted the government's attention from the murdered nontrans women. The cultural critic and scholar Héctor Domínguez Ruvalcaba explains:

> . . . las ONG manejaban un número (que era el que manejaba Amnistía), el gobierno otro. Luego empezaron especulaciones

sobre que había muchas más asesinadas que las reportadas y que el número de desaparecidas era mucho mayor. Por esas razones nosotros no podemos asegurar ningún número. Muchas muertes recientes se asocian al narco, lo cual es un problema de clasificación, pues mientras que el feminicidio se ve como causa de muerte por el hecho de ser mujer, en este caso puede considerarse una muerte más relacionada con el crimen organizado. (2011)[21]

The state strategically obfuscated feminicide statistics by conflating them with broader categories of nontrans women's murders linked to organized crime. This rhetorical move artificially suppressed the apparent scale of gender-motivated murders. In the book *Trafficking Rhetoric* (2024), Hill examines the use of speculative figures to explain how the state manipulates numbers for its own ends. Specifically, Hill explains that "numbers function as pathetic appeals by eliciting public feelings on a sensitive issue, thereby satisfying the dual desires for rational policy making and passionate crusades" (32). In the case of Mexico, by blending statistics on gender-motivated killings with murder rates, the state used numbers to shape a powerful narrative that enabled policymakers and the public to justify then-Mexican President Felipe Calderon's militarized approach to fighting organized crime under the pretext of crime reduction. The strategy precipitated the Operativo Conjunto Chihuahua, a comprehensive military intervention that saw Ciudad Juárez transformed into a zone of state-sanctioned martial control.

Confronted by the numerical invisibility rendered by the state's strategy, activists and community organizations fought back by transforming cold numbers into powerful, personal testimonies that amplified the lives of each murdered nontrans woman through storytelling in public spaces that included reunions, marches, and interviews. The shift in strategy by these independent actors from recordkeeping through numbers alone, to individualizing the numbers, changed the potential of their political impact. These nonstate actors resisted and continue to resist the attempts by the state to

---

21. *t.* the NGOs managed one number (which was the one Amnesty managed), the government another. Then speculation began that there were many more murdered women than was reported and that the number of missing people was much higher. For these reasons we cannot guarantee any number. Many recent deaths are associated with drug trafficking, which is a classification problem, because while feminicide is seen as a cause of death due to being a woman, in this case it can be considered a death more related to organized crime.

make these murders less. By focusing on bringing dignity to the life that these murdered women lived, these nonstate actors continue to make these women's lives count in death—much as in the postmortem politics of S Taller. This strategy also provided an outlet for family members, community organizations, and NGOs to voice their grief and feelings of impotence and frustration by participating in a process of postmortem politics. By letting the stories of the dead speak through them, these independent actors continue to counter the necropolitics of the state.

One of the most emblematic examples of how the war of numbers and postmortem politics by families of murdered women resulted in transnational accountability was the case *Campo Algodonero v. The United Mexican States* (Inter-American Court of Human Rights 2009). The case was brought before the Inter-American Commission on March 6, 2002, and presented before the commission on November 4, 2007, against Mexico for the murders of Claudia Ivette González, Esmeralda Herrera Monreal, and Laura Berenice Ramos Monárrez. The murders of these women occurred in Ciudad Juárez; they were three of eight women who were discovered in an abandoned cotton field known as Campo Algodonero on November 6, 2001, by two boys who were playing soccer and stumbled across one of the bodies. In documents provided to the court, part of the case consisted of illustrating the structural causes of violence and discrimination against women through institutional prejudices, inconsistencies in recordkeeping (war of numbers), severe failure by the Mexican government to protect women's rights, and lack of accessible processes for the families to obtain justice. Through consistent activism and pressure, the victims' families and other community groups played an essential role in calling for justice to the point that this case made it to the Inter-American Court of Human Rights.

After two public hearings on April 28 and 29, 2009, on November 16, 2009, the Inter-American Court of Human Rights found Mexico guilty of violating the human rights of the three murdered women and their families under the American Convention of Human Rights and the Convention of Belém do Pará (Inter-American Court of Human Rights 2009, para. 539). Some of the expert witnesses included leading community experts, psychologists, criminologists, and scholars on the now-named crime of feminicide. These included Marcela Lagarde y de los Ríos (who coined the word *feminicidio*), Julia Monárrez Fragoso (who coined different typologies of feminicide), Servando Pineda Jaimes, Marcela Patricia María Huaita Alegre, Ana Lorena Delgadillo Pérez, Rosa Isela Pérez Torres, Elizabeth Lira Kornfeld, Jorge de la Peña Martínez, Fernando Coronado Franco, Elena Azaola Garrido, and

Clara Jusidman Rapoport (para. 83). Their expert witness testimonies provided context and established a history of impunity by the state.

Mexico was ordered to comply with a series of sixteen measures, including financial compensation to the families of the victims (Inter-American Court of Human Right 2009, sec. 6); publishing the results of the trial "so that Mexican society is aware of the facts that are the purpose of the instant case" (para. 455); creating a website listing of all the women and girls who had disappeared in Chihuahua since 1993 and who were still missing (para. 468); building a monument to commemorate the victims with their next of kin (sec. 4.1.3); conducting investigations that include a gendered perspective (sec. 4.2.2); "continue standardizing all its protocols, manuals, prosecutorial investigation criteria, expert services, and services to provide justice that are used to investigate all the crimes relating to the disappearance, sexual abuse and murders of women" (order 18); and providing appropriate and effective medical, psychological, or psychiatric treatment, immediately and free of charge, through specialized state health institutions to all the next of kin (order 22).

S Taller's legacy and the strategy of family members, community organizations, and NGOs to voice their grief and feelings of impotence and frustration by actively participating in postmortem politics resulted in this case reaching the Inter-American Court of Human Rights, making this ruling possible. The ruling itself was unprecedented and had a significant impact. First, the ruling was directed at the entire Mexican state, not just Ciudad Juárez, which meant that changes needed to be implemented at all governmental levels: federal, state, and municipal. Second, the ruling also provided guidelines and obligations that transcended the boundaries of Mexico, which meant that the *Campo Algodonero* case would influence future rulings for other Latin American countries.[22] These guidelines also advised that investigations should examine the role of stereotypes, culture, and discrimination, and their connection to violence against women (Inter-American Court of Human Right 2009, para. 531). Finally, the ruling also included a series of measures aimed at preventing future disappearances, such as publicly available and updated web pages and databases—which indirectly led other Latin American and Caribbean countries to also participate in feminicide recordkeeping.

---

22. After this ruling, a wave of Latin American countries added *femnicidio* as a crime in their penal codes with a wide range of respective sentencing. Also, the operational guidelines for investigating feminicide were explicitly developed and approved in accordance with the judicial recommendations from the *Campo Algodonero* case.

Cultural Representations:
Feminicides in Ciudad Juárez Take Center Stage

Published at the end of the twentieth century, S Taller's *El silencio* (1999) inspired, both directly and indirectly, other researchers, artists, and creators who wanted to represent or investigate the topic of the murdered women of Ciudad Juárez. Since the year 2000, there have been a plethora of cultural representations related to or about the feminicides in Ciudad Juárez that have flooded the public sphere, including films, documentaries, fiction and nonfiction books, songs, performance arts, visual arts, murals, and digital maps.[23] There has also been significant scholarship analyzing some of these representations (Alcalá Iberri 2004; AMDOC 2002, 2012; Araluce 2011; Arteaga Botello 2010; Báez 2006; Bowden 1998; Castillo and Tabuenca Córdoba 2002; Delgadillo and Maldonado 2003; Driver 2011, 2015; Domínguez Ruvalcaba and Ravelo Blancas 2023; Domínguez Ruvalcaba and Corona 2010; Domínguez Ruvalcaba et al. 2015; Finnegan 2021; Fregoso 2023; Fregoso and Bejarano 2010; García et al. 2016; Herrera et al. 2010; Huerta Moreno 2015; Lozano 2019; Monárrez Fragoso 2000; Padilla and Pérez 2002; Ravelo Blancas et al. 2000; Segato 2013; Staudt 2008; Wright 2006).[24] Perhaps the three that are the best known for their international reception are Lourdes Portillo's documentary *Señorita Extraviada* (2001),[25] Roberto Bolaño's novel *2666* (2004), and Gregory Nava's movie *Bordertown* (2007) featuring Jennifer Lopez, Antonio Banderas, and Martin Sheen. However, extensive cultural artifacts were created to bring awareness to the issue of feminicides in Ciudad Juárez. In this section I analyze two representations, *Cruz de los Feminicidios*[26] (Voces sin Eco 1998) and *Póker de damas* (Margolles 2016b), because they represent processes of postmortem and transmortem politics, respectively.

The first of these representations is the *Cruz de los Feminicidios*: a visual symbol of a simple black cross against a pink backdrop, a white cross against a pink backdrop, or a pink cross against a black backdrop. In informal discussions with several feminist activists in Ciudad Juárez, including

---

23. For an extensive personal database, please email me.

24. Many other scholars have researched feminicides in Ciudad Juárez through lenses other than representation; these are only a few that specifically focus on the representation of feminicides and their impact.

25. *t.* Missing Young Woman

26. *t.* Feminicide Cross

Figure 1.2. Cruz de los Feminicidios: Black-on-pink-background graffiti on lamppost. *Source:* Photo by the author.

Beatriz Lozoya, I was told that the first *Cruz de los Feminicidios* was painted as graffiti around 1998, and from there the cross never stopped appearing in different areas of the city. Today, crosses in varying stages of decay can still be seen painted on lampposts down Avenida 16 de Septiembre, Eje Vial Juan Gabriel, Blvd. Zaragoza, and Avenida Abraham Lincoln, the main roadways leading to the Attorney General Offices for the Mexican Republic, the State of Chihuahua, and the Specialized Prosecutor's Office for Women. They can also be seen in other parts of the city or on murals honoring the victims of feminicide. The creation of the *Cruz de los Feminicidios* was claimed by a collective of grieving mothers and family members who in 1998 established the community organization Voces sin Eco[27] (Esther Chávez Cano Collection, n.d.). For them, the *Cruz de los Feminicidios* was a symbol to make the lives of their murdered daughters seen throughout the city and a way to demand an end to the murders of nontrans women.

---

27. *t.* Voices without Echo

Figure 1.3. Cruz de Clavos (2001) at the US–Mexico Paso del Norte border crossing in Ciudad Juárez. *Source:* Photo by the author.

The cross has also taken different iterations, including as a monument called *Cruz de Clavos* (2001). The original cross was installed in Plaza Hidalgo in front of the Palacio de Gobierno by activists from the feminist community organization Grupo 8 de marzo and ex-workers of the company Aceros de Chihuahua. This cross had 260 nails, which correspond to the number of feminicides that had been accounted for up until that date. A couple of months later the cross was removed by government officials. Today, a version of the *Cruz de Clavos* stands on the Mexican side of the international bridge Paso del Norte.

The *Cruz de los Feminicidios* has also taken the shape of wooden pink crosses with victims' names written on them. These have been erected as clandestine monuments in places where mass graves have been found including in Campo Algodonero, Lomas de Poleo, and Arroyo el Navajo, and then substituted by state-sponsored monuments per the Inter-American Court of Human Rights decree. In addition to these iterations, since 1998 the *Cruz de los Feminicidios* has gained international attention and has been used as a symbol of struggle against feminicide globally among activists. According to Julia Monárrez, one of the earliest researchers of feminicides in Ciudad Juárez, "Las cruces que se convierten en murales públicos se han convertido en una demanda de justicia internacional por el feminicidio, las ponen en todas partes como demanda de justicia" (Martínez Prado 2023).[28] *Cruz de los Feminicidios* has come to embody the postmortem politics of mothers, families, and activists both in Ciudad Juárez and transnationally. In Latin America and the Caribbean, it has been adopted by those who are active in calling attention to transfeminicides. This cross has also come to represent a way of bringing dignity and justice to trans-women victims because it underscores that trans women, as femme-identifying people, also suffer from targeted misogyny and violence because of their gender.

The second work I will discuss in this section that is pertinent to trans-mortem politics is *Póker de damas* (Margolles 2016b)[29] by the Mexican visual artist Teresa Margolles. She is a founding member of SEMEFO (Servicio Médico Forense/*Forensic Medical Service*), and also the name of an artist collective in Mexico City that creates visceral artworks using materials found in morgues. In 2004, in an interview with Santiago Sierra in *BOMB Magazine*, Margolles explained: "The power of art scares me so much. I realized that I didn't know how to talk about human loss, human pain. I thought my own pain was the most important, but then I discovered that there is collective pain. I am frightened by death, by what's happening in the world" (*BOMB Magazine* 2004). In 2005 she traveled to Ciudad Juárez to explore what was the role of the artist in situations of violence (TV UNAM 2020).

Influenced by her research in Ciudad Juárez, Margolles came to be known for multiple works of art that address feminicide including *Lote Bravo* (2005), first exhibited by the Museum of Fine Arts, Houston, from November 5, 2005, to April 23, 2006. *Lote Bravo* (2005) is a large-scale installation of four hundred adobe bricks handmade from sand and collected in different areas of Ciudad Juárez where the bodies of murdered women were found. Another early work was *Ciembra Formwork* (2006), which was also a

---

28. *t.* The crosses that turned into public murals have become a demand for international justice against feminicide, they are now placed everywhere as a demand for justice.

29. *t.* Ladies' poker

large-scale installation that consisted of 546 pieces of clothing belonging to women from Ciudad Juárez who were beaten, threatened, lived in fear, or were murdered, first shown in the group exhibition *Frontera 450+*. It was the first full exhibition on feminicide in the United States and was presented from October 21, 2006, to January 28, 2007, at the Station Museum of Contemporary Art in Houston (Driver 2011).[30] In 2010 Margolles created a single-channel video projection called *Irrigación,* commissioned by Ballroom Marfa, an internationally recognized noncollecting contemporary-art museum, for their exhibition *In Lieu of Unity.* The video shows an irrigation truck from behind as it dispenses five thousand gallons of water mixed with blood, excrement, and other bodily matter that Margolles collected from multiple places in Ciudad Juárez where more than five hundred people had been found murdered in the first four months of 2010.

That year Margolles also began to consider the disappearance and destruction of nightclubs in Ciudad Juárez and the impact this had on the workers of these spaces. The resulting work titled *Pistas de baile*[31] (Margolles 2016a) is a series of photographs of trans-women sex workers at recently demolished nightclub dance floors in Ciudad Juárez. In these photographs, the trans women reclaim life in what is visually represented as a dead landscape. These trans women embody life by standing proudly in power-stances and reaffirming themselves against the violence and destruction of the Ciudad Juárez landscape. In *Póker de damas* (Margolles 2016b), a parallel project to *Pistas de baile* (2016a), she explores how those left alive deal with death and the memories of their loved ones ("Sala10: Teresa Margolles" 2020). *Póker de damas* was first exhibited from June 11, 2016, to September 18, 2016, at Manifesta 11 in Zurich, the European biennial of contemporary art, as part of the conference theme "What People Do for Money." More recently it was exhibited virtually at MUAC Contemporary Art Museum in Mexico City from July 13, 2020, to July 26, 2020, which is how I first experienced it—at the height and uncertainty of the COVID-19 lockdowns.[32] In what follows I will discuss both exhibitions of *Póker de damas.*

For Manifesta 11, the curator Christian Jankowski commissioned several artists and asked them to choose a partner in the host city of

---

30. The Museum of Fine Arts, Houston, purchased *Lote Bravo* as part of their permanent collection.

31. *t.* dance floors

32. Portions of the exhibition survive on MUAC's official website, Facebook, and YouTube pages, and Mor Charpentier's gallery on Facebook ("Póker de damas" 2020).

Zurich, Switzerland, based on a list of one thousand different professions. Margolles initially wanted to invite Karla, a trans woman and a sex worker she befriended in 2010 and whom she featured in *Pistas de baile*, to travel to Zurich to play a game of poker with Sonja Victoria Vera Bohóruqez, an Ecuadorian trans woman and sex worker who lived in the Swiss city, to highlight the violence experienced by trans sex workers through a transnational conversation. However, on December 22, 2015, Karla was viciously murdered in Ciudad Juárez by being beaten to death ("Sala10: Teresa Margolles" 2020). She was sixty-four years old at the time, a survivor, and a sister to her chosen family of other trans-women sex workers. Upon her death, corresponding local authorities issued her birth certificate negating her identity as a trans woman and transferred her remains to her biological family—making it impossible for her chosen family to say goodbye and mourn her loss. Karla's assassination, which is still unresolved today, affected Margolles and she decided to modify her original idea ("Sala10: Teresa Margolles" 2020).

For the final *Póker de damas*, Margolles invited Sonja to travel to Ciudad Juárez. In an interview with Laura Gutknecht while promoting Manifesta 11, Sonja explains that Margolles wanted her to be the "voice of Karla" because "all of us working for money, all of us are Karla" (Jankowski 2020). Sonja traveled to Ciudad Juárez to play poker with Valeria, Berenice, and Vivian—some of Karla's chosen family. While the names of the women are included in the exhibition explanation, in the video the women do not introduce themselves. This strategically keeps their names separate from the bodies on the screen. In a sense, this allows them to safely express themselves without specific words being attributed to them. The game took place for three hours in room 10 at Hotel Bombín in Ciudad Juarez on May 11, 2016. The first installation of *Póker de damas* took place in room 104 at Hotel Rothaus in Zurich. They chose this location for the installation because Sonja used to work there. She explains to viewers of the promotional video: "Ten years ago when I came to Switzerland, here was a place where the girls they were working, the owner, well I mean, the chief of the girls here was Beatrice, she was a Brazilian transexual that already made the operation, she is already dead, two years ago, she was a good friend of mine" (Jankowski 2020).

In the Manifesta 11 promotional video, the camera follows Sonja and Laura into the room where the audio from the video *Póker de damas* can be heard. The clip is of Sonja describing how Karla died. At the same time, the camera captures the three things visible in the room: a piece of brick from a wall that Sonja brought back from the site where Karla's body was found, an enlarged portrait of Karla's photograph, and a copy of Karla's death certificate. According to art critic Pablo Larios, there was also "a video in which a group of sex workers speak about their friends' lives, including a violent murder" (Heiser and Larios 2016).[33] *The Guardian* also reported that Margolles "organised a further *Póker de damas*, including Bohorquez, in a Zurich hotel, where Manifesta visitors [are able] to ask questions and chat" (2016). This in-person exhibition of *Póker de damas* was recognized as powerful by critics. *The Guardian* remarked that it was "one of the best, and toughest" (2016) at Manifesta 11. In their review of Manifesta 11, *Ran Dian*, a contemporary art magazine, lauded Margolles's work for being "the only piece to thematize the risks inherent in labor" (2016). Jörg Heiser, director of the Institute of Art in Context at the University of the Arts in Berlin, described it as "very moving and powerful," and Pablo Larios called it "a moment of solid value in an exhibition that was too often filled with flippant schtick and cartoonish gimmicks" (Heiser and Larios 2016).

This in-person exhibition of *Póker de damas* was very different from the exhibition I experienced virtually in July 2020, not only because it was online but also because it had other complementing material. The virtual exhibition put on by MUAC in their virtual Sala 10 included a curatorial page written by Alejandra Labastida, with a few photographs of Karla and two videos.[34] The first was *Póker de damas* and the second, titled *Trans-Migrantes-Trans* (2020), documented a conversation between the curator Alejandra Labastida and Grecia Herrera. A practicing nurse, Grecia Herrera is also featured in *Pistas de baile* and is the founder of Respettrans, the trans migrant shelter in Ciudad Juárez.

I have only seen *Póker de damas* twice in its entirety, both viewings in July 2020. What struck me the most at the time were Karla's friends Berenice, Valeria, Vivian, and Sonja reclaiming "Karlita" as a trans woman, and the life she lived. The excerpts shown on the nine-minute, 33-second video capture moments where the women discuss their friend Karla, the violence they experience daily, and how they resist the fact that "ni siquiera

---

33. The video Larios is referring to is *Póker de damas* (Margolles 2016b).

34. The surviving landing page simply has four squared stills taken from *Póker de damas* (2016). Labastida's curatorial text is interspersed with two squared photographs of Karla (the one from *Pistas de baile* and a second one where she appears against a graffitied wall with two waterfalls; under one is a naked woman's silhouette and under the other Karla stands powerfully with left hand on her hip, sassily looking at the camera).

mañana nos pertenece."[35] Throughout the entirety of the video, the camera angle (of the room in which the trans women are being filmed) shows four single-pane mirrors behind the trans women, centering the poker game and capturing those whose backs are toward the camera. It is as if Margolles built a safe space—a material ellipsis from the rest of the world—that allowed these trans women to see all that was happening in the room. In one excerpt, Karla's friends notice the mirrors and one of them melancholily says, "Karla no tuvo un espejo en frente para ver lo que estaba pasando detrás."[36] This moment exemplifies the reflexivity and the construction of the room. The camera angle allows this for both the protagonists and the viewers by blending the act of remembering with the affects of impotence and frustration against a life of unpredictable violence. Karla's friends name what the mirrors allow them to see—the unforeseen forces that may be a threat to their survival—both concretely in the poker game and abstractly in life.

By documenting this conversation, Margolles captures and represents how the feelings of frustration and impotence manifest themselves between Berenice, Sonja, Valeria, and Vivian, humans who share vulnerability on the level of their identity, their profession as sex workers, and their grieving processes. In a way, the space of the poker game enables an unfurling of these different layers of vulnerability. According to Alejandra Labastida, associate curator at MUAC, the poker game symbolizes that: "Incluso para aquellas cuyo oficio es una elección, el precio a pagar es habitar un ambiente predatorio y sumergido en el consumo de drogas y alcohol, lo que convierte cada encuentro en un juego de supervivencia. La capacidad de las trabajadoras sexuales trans para interpretar correctamente distintas situaciones y modificar su comportamiento es esencial, así pueden evitar agresiones, no sólo de sus clientes, sino de sus familias, de las autoridades e incluso de sus propias compañeras" ("Sala10: Teresa Margolles" 2020).[37] Labastida's interpretation of the game of poker in Margolles's *Póker de damas* establishes an analogy between poker as a game of survival and the lives of trans sex workers. *Póker*

---

35. *t.* not even tomorrow belongs to us

36. *t.* Karla did not have a mirror in front of her to see what was happening behind [her]

37. *t.* even for those whose job is a choice, the price to pay is to live in a predatory environment immersed in the consumption of drugs and alcohol, which turns every encounter into a game of survival. Trans sex workers' capacity to correctly interpret distinct situations and modify their behavior accordingly is essential, as this is how they can avoid aggression, not only from their clients, but also from their families, authorities, and even other sex workers.

de damas is also a representation of the creation of transmortem politics; the content of the video establishes a genealogy of grief that takes the form of strategies of survival by trans sex workers in response to the frustration and impotence felt in the face of inevitable daily violence.

In tandem, the existence and the experience of witnessing the content of the video also create a transmortem process for the viewer, whereby Karla comes to life through the conversations of her friends as a trans sex worker who is vibrant and wise; Karla takes up the conversational space of the video. For example, in one of the excerpts, Berenice, Valeria, and Vivian are discussing how some sex workers are attacked by their clients, and then pause and remember:

-En el caso de Karla. . . .

-Si, por ejemplo si . . .

-Hasta ahorita su muerte, pues hasta ahorita esta impune, porque hasta ahorita no sabemos que pasó, ni quien hizo eso. (*Póker de damas* 2020)[38]

This conversation brings Karla to life, as the words and the silence in the pauses all imply that she has the right to an investigation of her murder, to be valued, and for her killer to be punished. While acknowledging that Karla is dead, Berenice, Valeria, and Vivian claim the right to know what happened to their friend, thereby helping the viewer to connect to their frustration and impotence over their friend's death.

The 2020 virtual exhibition reaffirms this reclamation of Karla's life with the other video *Trans-Migrantes-Trans* (2020), a twenty-two-minute interview featuring Labastida and Grecia from the COVID-19 era. The video documents Grecia's friendship with Karla and sheds light on the lives of trans migrants in Ciudad Juárez by discussing how and why Grecia founded Respettrans, the first LGBTQI+ shelter in the city (MUAC 2020; Smith 2023). In *Trans-Migrantes-Trans* (2020) Grecia discloses to Labastida that she posted items related to the struggle against transfeminicides on Repettrans's

---

38. *t.* -In Karla's case . . .
-For example, yes . . .
-Her death is still unpunished, we still don't know what happened, nor who did it . . .

Facebook page, and that she had to make the page private because of the backlash and hate she received. She explains that she now posts mainly about

> cómo rescatar estos cuerpos de nuestras hermanas que se van a un SEMEFO, para darles de perdida una Cristiana sepultura digna . . . ya que en vida no lo logramos . . . y así mínimo tener al termino de nuestra vida pues . . . digno . . . un lugar donde vaya a quedar ese cuerpo pues digno . . . un lugar de respeto minimo y también cómo nos trataban las autoridades con cualquier cosa—que si no eres familiar, o que si no eres . . . pues . . . cualquier cosa que nos obstaculiza . . . pues ahi en la página no puedo poner mucho bonito porque en realidad no nos pasa mucho bonito, pero estamos hablando de transmigrantes y los transfemnicidios de estas mujeres transmigrantes que vienen desde sus paises y pues con ellas en la caravana viajo con ellas el VIH, la muerte, el crimen organizado, en fin un sinfin de problemas que duelen que dañan a nuestras vidas . . . los gobiernos dijeron que eso no importaba, que no era valido, que no podian tener un albergue exclusivo—que cualquier albergue las iba a agarrar pero pues . . . la realidad fue otra . . . empezaron a morir las chicas . . . ("Sala10: Teresa Margolles" 2020)[39]

Grecia's transmortem politics not only involve reclaiming the bodies of trans women, but also engaging with Mexican authorities to return these bodies to the deceased's chosen families instead of their biological families, and trying to convince the authorities to issue death certificates with the trans women's

---

39. *t.* how to rescue these bodies of our sisters that go to the SEMEFO [the morgue] to give them dignity at least through a Christian burial . . . given that if in life we are not able to achieve it [living with dignity as trans women], at least at the end of our life . . . well . . . having a place . . . with dignity . . . a place where their body can remain . . . a place of respect, at least . . . and also how the authorities were treating us with anything—that if you were not a family member, or that if you are not . . . well . . . anything that produces obstacles in claiming their bodies . . . well there on the page I can't post nice things because in reality we don't really have many nice experiences, but like we are talking about trans migrants and the transfeminicides of these women who come from their countries and well in the caravans, HIV, death, organized crime, a never-ending number of problems traveled with them, problems that hurt and harm our lives . . . the government said that that is not what mattered, that it wasn't valid, that they could not have a shelter exclusive to them because any shelter would take them but well . . . the reality was another one . . . girls started to die.

chosen names so that they can be given that dignity. Grecia understands that dignity extends beyond life. For her, dignity means providing trans women with a final resting place that honors and celebrates their true identity, offering in death the respect and recognition they were denied through systemic disregard and disrespect during their time alive. While Grecia advocates for their dignity in death, she also explains how that very death is what led her to continue advocating for the establishment of a shelter so that these trans migrants can live their life free of violence, or at least have a space to live while they await news of their asylum cases, thereby also illustrating the transformative potential inherent in transmortem politics.

These two films, *Póker de damas* (Margolles 2016b) and *Trans-Migrante-Trans* (2020), also illustrate what I conceptualize as *trasnsurority*.[40] I think of transurority as a shared affective solidarity created by experiences of survival and violence unique to trans women. This transurority fosters a shared affective solidarity against colonial legacies such as borders, the patriarchy, and trans-exclusionary feminism. Such transurority is a type of solidarity that is beyond what the concepts of survival, sorority, and sisterhood can offer. Thus, transurority involves a way of knowing that is an embodied and enfleshed epistemology, one that is uniquely anchored in a genealogy of trans women's experiences of survival that include (but are not limited to) pain, suffering, anger, joy, and happiness. Sonja, Berenice, Valeria, Vivian, and Grecia's transurority is best represented in Sonja's words: "All girls like us . . . all we are Karla, all in one day can be Karla" (Jankowski 2020).

Another aspect of both exhibitions in 2016 and 2020 (aside from their representations of impotence, frustration, transmortem politics, and transurority) is that they also illustrate Margolles's desire for her work to inspire its viewers to "get a reflection and start to do something about it" (Jankowski 2020), much in the same spirit that S Taller intended for readers of *El silencio*. In the 2016 promotional video for Manifesta 11, Sonja responds to the question: "Is this work a memorial for Karla?":

> No, no—that is also what I thought at the beginning—because of course Teresa was very touched about what happened, you know? Look at what happened in Orlando, for example—just right now—the same feeling was with us when we lost one piece of us, a human. That is why Teresa said no. She said: I want

---

40. I developed this concept inspired by the concept of *dororidade* developed by the Brazilian scholar Vilma Piedad.

> people to get a reflection and start to do something about it. It is not to be sorry. Tribute? For what? . . . Teresa told me she is dead. . . . For what? To be sorry for what? No. It's like . . . she wanted people to get a reflection and start to do something about it—that is what is really important. (Jankowski 2020)

In *Póker de damas* (Margolles 2016b), Margolles represents the reclamation of Karla's life through her friends while also mirroring an invitation to those outside the film to reflect on what they have witnessed and sit with the emotions and thoughts the work evokes for them—because as Sonja emphasizes, "That is what is really important" (Jankowski 2020).

In the 2016 exhibition, attendees of Manifesta 11 had the opportunity to sit and talk with Sonja over a game of poker, allowing them to interact with her as a multifaceted trans woman who is not just a sex worker, thereby embodying Margolles's goal to have audiences reflect and do something, even if it is as simple as sitting across a poker table and getting to know Sonja. In the 2020 virtual exhibition, Margolles's goal for people to reflect is amplified not only by the intrinsic format of the exhibition, but also by the complementarity of *Trans-Migrantes-Trans* (2020) where there is modeling for what that "Start to do something" could be. It could include, for instance, working with local authorities to provide shelter to trans women and trans migrants, issuing death certificates that impart dignity to trans women, stopping transphobic attacks, and participating in supporting trans women's efforts, among other things. Margolles's call to action transcended national boundaries through her exhibition in Manifesta 11, and the virtual exhibition hosted by MUAC over the pandemic, creating a transnational opportunity for audiences to not only reflect on their prejudices about trans women, migration, and sex work, but also on the sociopolitical implications of grief and the literal and epistemic transfeminicide.

Calls to Action on Social Media
and the #Niunamas Movement

The birth of social media coincided with major efforts to call attention to the murdered women in Ciudad Juárez in the spirit that S Taller intended in *El silencio* (1999), by including a postcard that could be mailed to the General Attorney's Office of the State of Chihuahua. Social media enabled activists to create a digital space for postmortem and transmortem politics that connected what was happening in Chihuahua with other areas of Mexico. This, with the rapid spread of information, launched the national movement Ni Una Más.

The rise in popularity of messaging platforms such as ICQ (1996), Yahoo Messenger (1999), MSN Messenger (1999), MySpace (2003), and email allowed activists in Ciudad Juárez to work as a network by quickly communicating digitally and sharing resources with other women in the state of Chihuahua. These included distributing scanned copies of S Taller's *El silencio* (1999), organizing strategies, and ideas about how to get issues of gender violence on the political agendas of politicians in Chihuahua (Ravelo Blancas et al. 2000; Instituto Chihuahuense de la Mujer 2015). These collaborations resulted in the visibility of these organizations' postmortem politics, specifically characterized by the very public wearing of black clothing (culturally reserved for funerals). Luz Esthela Castro Hernández, coordinator of the Center for Human Rights of Women, explains: "Como en aquel entonces nuestra vestimenta era una túnica negra, entonces nos bautizaron como 'Las mujeres de negro.' Este colectivo de organizaciones tuvo mucho impacto porque coincidió con las denuncias internacionales" (Instituto Chihuahuense de la Mujer 2015, 37).[41] In 2002 Mujeres de Negro (see below) organized a walking procession from the city of Chihuahua to Ciudad Juárez.

Around this time, activists from Ciudad Juárez associated with the pilgrimage took the first portion of the phrase "Ni una más"[42] from a poem written in 1995 by Susana Chávez, a poet and early contra-feminicide activist from Ciudad Juárez, and used it as a slogan for the pilgrimage, thus giving birth to the Ni Una Más movement (Monárrez Fragoso 2023, 85).[43] In *The Force of Witness* (2023), Rosa Linda Fregoso recalls how Cynthia Bejarano

---

41. *t.* Given that at that time our clothing consisted of a black tunic, we were known as "the Women in Black." This group of organizations had a lot of impact because it coincided with international complaints.

42. *t.* Not one more

43. The original phrase in the 1995 poem was "Ni una menos, ni una muerta más" (Not one less, not one more woman dead). In the postmortem collection of Susana's poems *Primera Tormenta*, named after her blog by the same name, Hilda Sotelo explains that Susana wrote "Ni una más" on the *Cruz de Clavos* that was placed on the Santa Fe bridge in 2002 as the final point of the Mujeres de Negro pilgrimage. She explains that after this march the phrase gained popularity (Chávez Castillo 2020).

and she chose the photograph for the cover of their book *Terrorizing Women* (2010). Fregoso explains:

> The photograph pays homage to these mother-activists at the forefront of the Ni Una Más movement, first launched in 2002 as a campaign, slogan, and chant taken up by an internationalist network to end feminicide and gender/sexual violence. "Ni una más" are three words appearing in various forms on the cover of our book, as in the background, embossed on the large wooden cross that is fastened on a pink placard bearing 268 soldered nails each representing a woman murdered in Ciudad Juárez between 1993 and 2002. Next to the cross, the slogan "Ni una más" is printed on the poster held by a woman activist. "Ni una más" adorns the pink hats of members of the Mujeres de Negro (Women Dressed in Black) feminist group that spearheaded the contra-feminicide campaign. It is these courageous women, compelled to act by the life-altering trauma of personal loss, whose lives are now threatened by the terror of feminicidal violence. (2023, 85)

For Fregoso and Bejarano, this photograph represented the role of these women as political actors. This photograph, captured during the procession by Mujeres de Negro, not only expressed public mourning by modeling a funerary procession; it also made the murdered women come to life by sharing their stories and saying their names. For Melissa Wright (2006), "Mujeres de Negro face the paradox that by exercising their democratic voices through public protest, they are dismissed, by their detractors, as 'unfit' citizens, based on their contamination as 'public women,' whose causes are equally contaminated by their public presence" (154). Yet, by adopting the slogan "Ni una más" and making their mourning public, they explicitly denounced the intolerance for leading to one more death and demanded concrete action. The Ni Una Más movement created a public space to express the frustration and impotence felt as a result of the murder of the women and subsequent government inaction, thereby making the pain of collective mourning a public issue.

The many forms of public mourning also gave the dead life by demanding that the lives of both dead and living nontrans women be counted and that they take up physical and discursive public and political spaces. Maria Pia López explains, "Making mourning a public event, sharing this fragility and exposing it, questioning who we are in the wake of each death, establishes a new notion of political community, sustained by the recognition of what we have in common and not by the illusion of individual competition and solipsistic autonomy" (2020, 18). After 2002 the impact of this procession resulted in state-level governmental discussions about policies, practices, and laws related to gender violence (Quintana 2009). The phrase "Ni una más" became visible, constant, and inescapable for both the public and governmental officials alike.

Between 2005 and 2009, the social media platforms Orkut (2004), Facebook (2004), YouTube (2005), and Twitter (2006) began to be used in Ciudad Juárez and other places in Mexico. Activists learned how to use these platforms to conduct different forms of activism from sharing resources (such as *El silencio*), posting news articles, making public denunciations, connecting with others who wanted to organize for the same cause, to posting calls to action to pressure government officials to pass legislation. During this time, contra-feminicide activists also developed other social media tactics such as the formation of closed Facebook groups by and for trans and nontrans women. For example, I was invited by friends in Ciudad Juárez to join these groups around 2009.[44] These closed Facebook groups emphasized the necessity of being "private" to ensure the safety of the members and the prevention of hateful comments being left on the page. Mostly, however, these closed groups shared experiences involving various levels of violence perpetrated by specific individuals. Often these posts ended by expressing sentiments about the uselessness of the Mexican authorities and how they were sharing to simply alert others of predators so that members could avoid places where these men socialized, including their places of work, clubs, gyms, and the bars they frequented. Sometimes there would be suggestions about what routes to take if there increased danger in areas of the city, with reminders of how many feminicides had occurred that year. These closed groups created a sense of action and gave the illusion of being able to control the ability to feel safe. They also became a place where testimonies of violence were shared and received with compassion, with comments expressing gratitude for sharing the story and the name of the predator, with blessings and well-wishes. On public Facebook pages, some would share resources, news articles, and statistics, or post about their frustration and felt impotence, which resonated with others including other community groups across Mexico, who took it upon themselves to

---

44. Later in 2014 my cousins and colleagues in Guadalajara, Cuernavaca, Queretaro, Veracruz, and Mexico City invited me to join groups specific to these cities.

mobilize nontrans women and call attention to the issue of feminicide and trans and nontrans women's right to a life free of violence.

The existence of both public posting and closed-group posting allowed for digital organizing that, in combination with consistent and in-person marches, culminated in another pilgrimage from November 10, 2009, to November 23, 2009. Organized by Mujeres de Negro and called Éxodo por la vida de las mujeres,[45] it proceeded from Mexico City to Ciudad Juárez to call attention to the increased murders and disappearances of women. Their slogan, "Ni una más," was the same as in their first pilgrimage and their digital presence was marked by the hashtag #niunamas. This pilgrimage was widely covered by the press. One report in *La Jornada* describes the pilgrimage: "Por ahí van marchando las Mujeres de Negro. Con su nuevo éxodo quieren que la nación entera las acompañe a transitar de la realidad de muerte, opresión y violencia de género, a una nueva realidad construida por todas y todos, de plenitud de derechos, de plenitud de vida. A eso llama la campana que van cargando y haciendo repicar por media República" (Quintana 2009).[46] This haunting of the national consciousness by the demands and physical, mourning presence of Las Mujeres de Negro was compounded by the decree issued by the Inter-American Court of Human Rights on November 16, 2009, against the Mexican state, thus making postmortem politics central to the fight against feminicide.

The legacy of the affects of impotence and frustration first expressed in S Taller's text *El silencio de la voz que todas quiebra* (Benítez et al. 1999) can be traced in the processes of postmortem and transmortem politics of community organizations, artists, and activists. These affects also had unforeseen reverberations due to the rise of social media. Activists were able to connect with others who also shared experiences of impotence and frustration in the face of increasing numbers of murders of women, and this emotional bond facilitated a process of organized postmortem politics that pushed for a national political agenda that defined feminicide as a violation of human rights in Mexico. Furthermore, the feminicides of Ciudad Juárez grew in visibility both nationally and globally with the rise of social media and access to the Internet.

---

45. *t.* Exodus for the life of women

46. *t.* There go the Women in Black marching. With their new exodus, they want the entire nation to join them on their journey—from a reality marked by death, oppression, and gender violence, to a new reality, one built collectively, where rights are fully realized and life can be lived in its fullness. That is what they are calling for with the bell they carry and ring throughout half the Republic of Mexico.

Chapter 2

Fear and Rage

Legislating Feminicide Across the Americas

Sangre mía,
de alba,
de luna partida,
del silencio.
de roca muerta,
de mujer en cama,
saltando al vacío,
Abierta a la locura.
Sangre clara y definida,
fértil y semilla,
Sangre incomprensible gira,
Sangre liberación de sí misma,
Sangre río de mis cantos,
Mar de mis abismos.
Sangre instante donde nazco adolorida,
Nutrida de mi última presencia.[1]

—Susana Chávez Castillo

---

1. Poem by Susana Chávez Castillo, published on her blog Primera Tormenta (2001) and titled "Our Blood": Blood of my own / blood of sunrise / blood of a broken moon / blood of silence / of dead rock / of a woman in bed / jumping into nothingness / Open to the madness / Blood clear and definite / fertile seed / Blood the unbelievable journey / Blood as its own liberation / Blood, river of my songs / Sea of my abyss / Blood, painful moment of my birth / Nourished by my last appearance.

Susana Chávez Castillo had been participating in the many marches, public-mourning events, organizing of meetings, and cultural events in Ciudad Juárez from the time she was twenty years old (Ramos 2012; Chávez 2020). Often she would read a poem or two, and in 2002 she wrote the phrase "Ni una más" on the "Cruz de Clavos,"[2] alluding to the line in one of her poems: "Ni una menos, ni una muerte más"(Chávez 2020).[3]According to contra-feminicide activists Beatriz and Adela Lozoya Gutiérrez, and graffiti artists who were heavily involved in the Ni Una Más movement (with whom I had informal conversations in 2009 during my third visit to Ciudad Juárez), the line came from one of Susana's poems that she read in 1995 at a march protesting the murders and disappearances of nontrans women in Ciudad Juárez. Scholars have also documented this fact (Ramos 2012; López 2020; Monárrez Fragoso 2023).

Unfortunately, on January 6, 2011, she went out dancing with some friends and met three young men who ended up cutting off her hand and strangling her to death in a bathroom, leaving her body outside on the cross streets of Cristóbal Colón and Ramón Corona (Excélsior 2011). The men were eventually captured and sentenced to fifteen years in prison in 2013; however, they only served five years of their sentences because they were minors when they committed the crime (Sáenz 2022). The poem in the opening epigraph of this chapter was written by Susana as an ode to feminicides, published on her blog, and inscribed on her tomb by her family. In a way, Susana's poem foresaw the violent nature of her death and the possible fuel her death would impart to the contra-feminicide movement, when she wrote, "Blood, painful moment of my birth / Nourished by my last appearance." Susana's murder became another feminicide statistic in Mexico (Monárrez Fragoso 2023, 85; Ramos 2012) and her activism and poetry inspired and nourished the growth of transnational networked feminism (Fotopoulou 2016) and the digital rise of the intersectional social movements #NiUnaMas, #niunxmenos, and #NiUnaMenos (the most recognized of the various contra-feminicide movements worldwide today). Family members' and activists' use of social media has helped these movements build a collective identity (Gerbaudo and Trer 2015) that at its root advocates for trans and nontrans women, and femme-identifying people's right to life, as well as propagating the emotions associated with their grief in the public space (Castells 2012; Gravante 2016).

---

2. See fig. 1.3 in chapter 1.

3. *t.* Not one less, not one more woman killed

To map the impact of Susana's phrase "Ni una menos, ni una muerte más" (Chávez 2020), I analyzed 60,139 tweets between January 1, 2007, and December 31, 2014, to discuss how the phrase propelled a series of reports and legislative efforts in Latin America, first from 2007 to 2009 and then from 2010 to 2017.[4] I chose to focus on messages on the platform Twitter, now X, because research on the function of Twitter in mobilizations shows that it serves as a real-time communication tool for organizational purposes, for eyewitness communication, for gaining public visibility (Castells 2009; Bruns and Stieglitz 2014; Kurian et al. 2015; Laudano 2016; Bruns 2019), and for cultural expression and community building—as is the case with Black Twitter (Brock 2020), and to circumvent mainstream media and create autonomous spaces (Florini 2019). In their book *#Hashtag Activism: Networks of Race and Gender Justice* (2020), Jackson et al. examine how disenfranchised communities (women, Black people, and transgender people) "repurposed Twitter . . . to make identity-based cultural and political demands, and in doing so have forever changed national consciousness" (xxv). Through an interdisciplinary mixed-methods approach (communication studies, digital humanities, and network science), Jackson et al. analyze the digital and social signature of hashtags specific to the context of the United States. They

---

4. A brief methodological note: Most of the online data cited here is from my own digital archive of collected screenshots of posts on Facebook, Orkut, Twitter, and Instagram since 2008. I have also used the accessible data generator Google Trends for searched terms on the web and YouTube. Facebook and X (formerly Twitter) allow users to search data but do not provide tracking analytics for the public like Google does. I would like to note here that Facebook and X generate large amounts of data that the general public does not have access to. Access to data on this platform was made possible by developing coding skills to "scrape" the platforms and/or paying third parties to do so. Although some researchers were able to conduct detailed research on the #NiUnaMenos movement as it relates to feminicide, little can be found about the #NiUnaMas movement between 2009 and 2014. While researchers can request an API key on X, access to historical data has been restricted to users who can pay the $5,000 price tag of the API Enterprise membership. While I taught myself to use Tabs and Twint, coding-based programs that allowed bypassing the API key to access and analyze data, they stopped working when Twitter became X in 2023. Furthermore, free programs such as Hashtagify that allowed anyone to track a hashtag also stopped working after Twitter became X. Because of these complications and because I am not a coder, I used the service "Trackmyhashtag" to buy data related to the hashtag #NiUnaMas from January 1, 2007, to December 31, 2014, based on the dates of some of the legislative efforts on feminicide in some countries of the Americas and because it was what I could afford. For example, if I had wanted to purchase data on tweets mentioning #niunamenos (which number in the millions from January 1, 2015, to the present), the cost of that data would be $3,000 per one million tweets.

argue that the online activism implicated in the hashtags #BlackLivesMatter, #YesAllWomen, #MeToo, #SurvivorPriviledge, #WhyIStayed, #YouOKSis, #SayHerName, and #GirlsLikeUs "leads to material effects in the digital and physical sphere . . . [by] moving debates about identity politics, inequality, violence, and citizenship from the margins to the center and into places as crucial as presidential agendas" (xxxii). Similarly to Jackson et al.'s work, I approach hashtag activism "as a networked activity, focusing not only on the attributes of individual tweeters or activists but also on the connections between them" (Jackson et al. 2020, xxxv) because I see this method as complementary to Indigenous epistemologies that value the interconnectedness between all beings and storytelling as a methodology and a means of knowledge transmission and resistance (Smith 2012).

In terms of being able to manage the data I collected and paid for, I focused on coding the tweets, retweets, and mentions by the theme of recurring counterpublic conversations. I included retweets and mentions because as Jackson et al. explain:

> When someone authors a tweet, by default that tweet will be visible to anyone on Twitter. Someone else can choose to retweet that tweet, broadcasting it to their own followers, either in its original form or with some commentary attached. The act of retweeting signals at least passing attention to, and often an endorsement of, the original content. Users may also mention one another by using a particular conversational syntax (@user) within the body of a tweet. . . . By means of these conventions, a stream of tweets can be reconfigured as a network, with Twitter users connecting with one another via retweets and mentions within the text of their tweets. (2020, xxvi)

By analyzing the tweets beyond their quantified characteristics, I used coding and critical technocultural discourse analysis (Brock 2020) to develop a genealogy that highlighted the lives of Maricela Escobedo, Susana Chávez, Adriana Marisel Zambrano, Chiara Perez, and Rosa Elvira Cely. Their deaths were undertaken by hashtag activists to tell their stories and drive counterpublic narratives implicated as forms of resistance as well as legislative efforts throughout Latin America and the Caribbean between 2010 and 2017.

Ultimately, I argue that the mothers, family members, and activists became engaged in postmortem and transmortem politics stemming from the feminicide of their loved ones and adapted on-the-ground activist strategies into digital spaces. While contemporary mobilizations embody the logic of a participatory process "based on personalised content sharing across media networks" (Bennet and Segerberg 2012, 739), mothers, family members, and activists also activated forms of witnessing and public mourning inextricably interconnected with the hashtags #NiUnaMas and #NiUnaMenos and forged a powerful commonality with others unaware of feminicidal violence. In doing so, they transformed the localized phenomenon of the feminicides of Ciudad Juárez into an interconnected struggle (Caballero and Gravante 2017; Chen et al. 2018) that led to a series of legislative achievements in Latin America and the Caribbean that resonated with the contra-feminicide activism across the Americas including those involved in the #MMIWG/#MMIWG2S,and #Sayhername movements.

Early Efforts to Legislate Feminicide

A search on Google Trends indicates that web searches related to the term "Ni una más" began to rise in Mexico and the world since 2004 (it is worth noting that this is when Google started to track term searches) (figs. 2.1 and 2.2). Similarly, Google Trends illustrates that YouTube searches related to "Ni una mas" have shown relatively consistent interest over time, with peak interest in 2008, 2009, 2010, and 2014 (Google began tracking searched terms on YouTube in 2008) (fig. 2.3). From 2007 to 2014, searches for "Ni una mas,"[5] "femicidio," and "feminicidio" had a significant presence in Latin America (fig. 2.4). As we see in what follows, this increased interest in searching the term "Ni una mas" corresponds to on-the-ground and hashtag potential impression, reach, and activism that pushed for states to introduce legislation to address gender violence specifically (fig. 2.5).[6]

---

5. Originally I searched for "Ni una más" with the accent over the a, but because spelling in the digital world often excludes accents I searched for "Ni una mas" without an accent to get the most representative data.

6. Trackmyhashtag offers analytics of a specific hashtag. In the case of #NiUnaMas, the service provided analytics for the "potential impression" and "reach" of #NiUnaMas. Although an "impression" means that a tweet has been delivered to a Twitter user's timeline, an impression is always considered a potential because not everyone who receives a tweet will read it, but it is possible that they will. An impression tells us the expansion and reach of a Twitter campaign. Thus, in the case of #NiUnaMas, the potential impression metric is 2,778,627,313 between 2007 and 2014. In contrast to a hashtag's potential impression, "reach" refers to the total number of Twitter accounts that the tweet/hashtag/Twitter campaign has reached. In the case of the hashtag #NiUnaMas, the potential reach is 260,175,790 between 2007 and 2014.

Figure 2.1. Screenshot from Google Trends of interest over time in Mexico since 2004 in the term "Ni una mas" (May 2024). *Source:* Screenshot by the author.

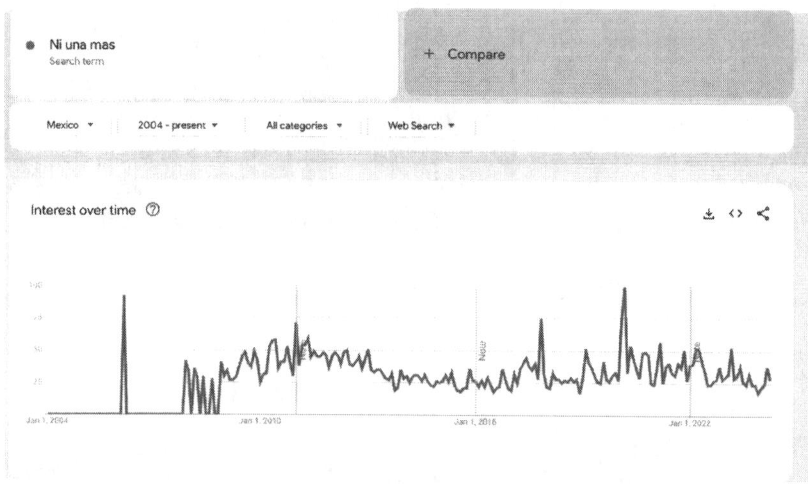

Figure 2.2. Screenshot from Google Trends of interest over time worldwide since 2004 in the term "Ni una mas." *Source:* Screenshot by the author.

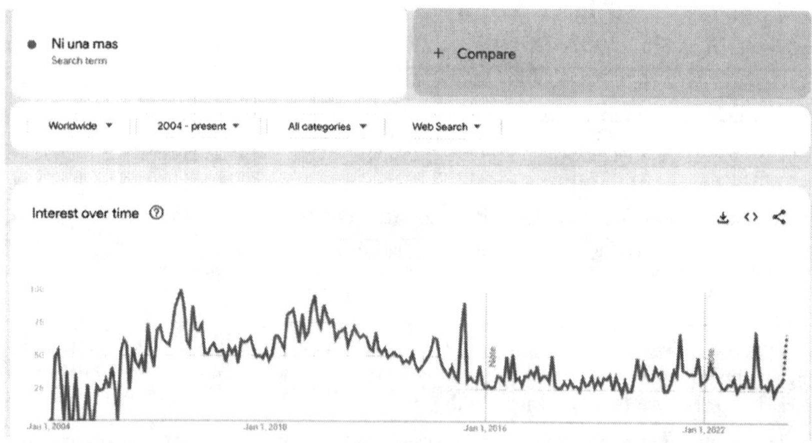

In February 2007, Mexico passed the General Law on Women's Access to a Life Free of Violence (Secretaria de Relaciones Exteriores 2007, 12–13), becoming the first country in the Americas to identify feminicide as a violation of a woman's human rights, specified in Articles 21 through 26, and proposing that feminicide be classified as a crime. The law also addressed the state's tolerance of this crime (García Del Moral 2020); however, despite proposing it, this did not reform the country's Criminal Code to include feminicide as a crime (Toledo

Figure 2.3. Screenshot from Google Trends of interest over time since 2008 in YouTube searches for the term "Ni una mas" worldwide. *Source:* Screenshot by the author.

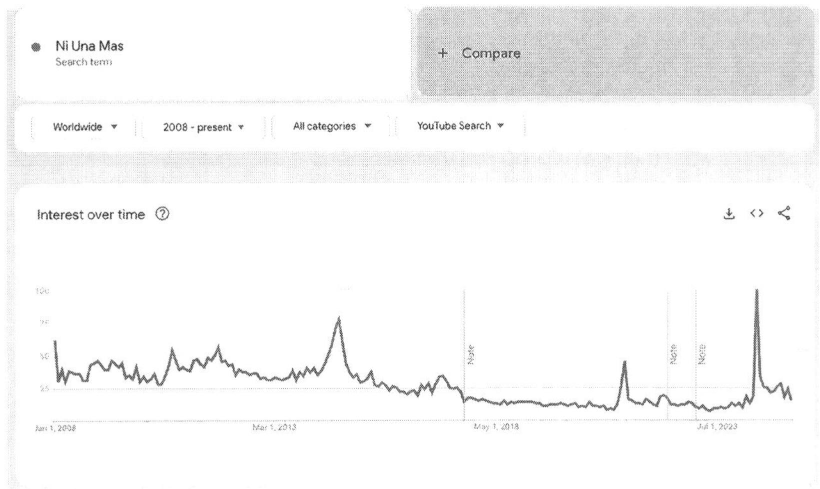

2009). While Mexico did not introduce this classification in its Criminal Code in 2007, it did delineate what could be done to reform criminal codes.

In the rest of the Americas, Costa Rica introduced the Law to Penalize Violence Against Women in 2007 (Ley n8.589 25 2007), which condemned perpetrators to anywhere from twenty to thirty-five years in prison, with eligibility for a reduced sentence within a year. With this legislation, Costa Rica became the first country to classify femicide (not feminicide) as a crime. The Chilean attorney Patsilí Toledo (2009) explains that both terms, feminicide and femicide, refer to the same criminal act: the gender-based killing of women. Toledo claims that the theoretical differences between the terms are outweighed by the areas of agreement, including that the terms arise as a feminist response to the lack of gender perspective in crimes committed against women. Hence, beginning in 2007, in Mexico and in Costa Rica we see both "femicido" and "feminicidio" used in legislation. Furthermore, in October 2007, the Economic Commission for Latin America and the Caribbean (CEPAL) published a comprehensive interdisciplinary report on gender violence titled: *¡Ni una más! El derecho a vivir una vida libre de violencia en América Latina y el Caribe.*[7] The title of this report, which was disseminated throughout Latin America and the Caribbean, enunciated Susana Chávez's slogan, which had become the slogan of public-mourning mobilizations against feminicides in Ciudad Juárez (Blanco 2019).

---

7. *t.* Not One More: The Right to Live a Life Free of Violence in Latin America and the Caribbean

Figure 2.4. Screenshot from Google Trends of web searches of the term "Ni una mas" worldwide with map of the world showing heavy interest in the Americas, India, Japan, and parts of Europe. The image also shows the top five regions for searching the term as: Venezuela, Puerto Rico, Paraguay, Uruguay, and Honduras. *Source:* Screenshot by the author.

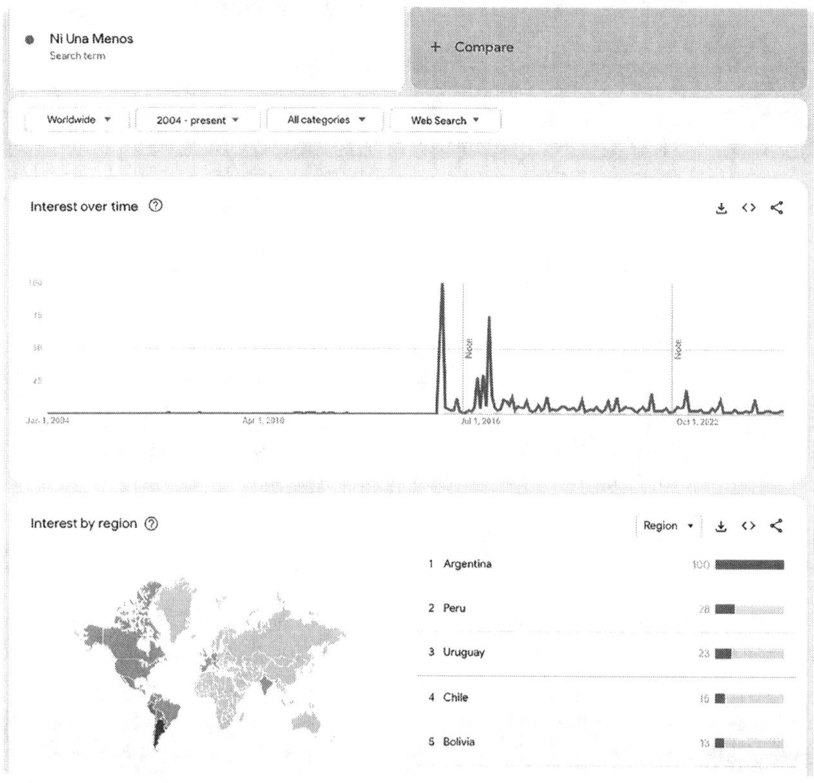

Figure 2.5. Overview analytics for the hashtag #niunamas provided by Trackmy hashtag. *Source:* Screenshot by the author.

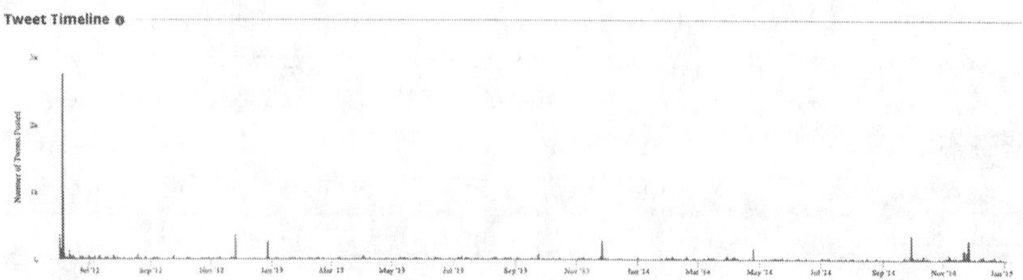

In 2008 Guatemala passed the Law Against Femicide and Other Forms of Violence Against Women, which went into effect on May 15 that year. The law prescribes a prison sentence for those guilty of crimes of violence against women, including feminicide, of twenty-five to fifty years. In that same year, Colombia enacted Law 1257, which established community standards by promoting awareness of women's rights and addressing gender-based violence against nontrans women in multiple contexts: within families (including domestic violence and marital rape), within communities (including sexual violence and sex trafficking), and in relation to women's reproductive rights. Colombia also modified Article 104A of their Criminal Code, which established that: "Whoever causes the death of a woman, due to her condition of being a woman or for reasons of her gender identity or where any of the following circumstances have occurred or preceded, will incur a prison sentence of two hundred and fifty (250) months to five hundred (500) months" (Artículo 104A). This modification made Colombia the third country after Costa Rica and Guatemala to criminalize feminicide in the Americas. Colombia's modification of its Criminal Code was innovative in that it defined violence toward women as a gender-based offense that inherently included trans women. As a result, Colombia has seen a broad interpretation of the classification of gender violence, applying the same norms and sanctions to the violence experienced by transgender women (Sánchez Avella and Arévalo Mutiz 2020).

The legislative achievements of Mexico, Costa Rica, Guatemala, and Colombia would not have been possible without the efforts of activists, legal scholars, and nonprofit organizations in these countries since the 1994 Belem do Para Convention, which defined gender violence as a violation of human rights and established the right for women to live a life free of violence (Blanco 2019). Granted, the efforts to legislate gender violence and feminicide/femicide of Mexico, Costa Rica, Guatemala, and Colombia were also in part due to the visibility of the press coverage, which became more readily available online and was shared through emails[8] (Esther Chávez Cano Collection), Facebook,[9] Twitter, Instagram, and other platforms. Between

---

8. The Esther Chávez Cano archive has an extensive collection of newspaper and magazine articles from different parts of the world covering the feminicides, sent directly to Esther by people who supported her work, as well as email printouts of articles sent to her.

9. By 2007 Facebook had evolved as described by Mark Zuckerberg's infamous words, "We're actually producing more news in a single day for our 19 million users than any other media outlet has in their entire existence" (Pariser 2011, 380), thus suggesting that the sharing of other websites and news articles had wider dissemination. By 2009 Facebook had three hundred million users.

2004 and 2009, web and YouTube searches for terms like "Ni una mas," "feminicidio," and "femicidio" increased significantly (figs. 2.6 and 2.7).

This surge reflected how the growing availability of online content across platforms (websites, social media networks, and YouTube) amplified the visibility of contra-feminicide postmortem activism led by mothers, relatives, and civil associations. Their postmortem politics moved seamlessly between physical and digital platforms, strategically occupying online spaces to advance their advocacy around gender-based murders and other forms of violence (Boyd 2011). Their activism resonated with other contra-feminicide activists across the Americas who used these networks to facilitate a more accessible exchange of information.

The Rise of #NiUnaMas and Digital Postmortem Politics

In Mexico, after the 2009 pilgrimage *Éxodo por la vida* from Mexico City to Ciudad Juárez organized by Mujeres de Negro, Susana's slogan "Ni una más" was everywhere from signs, chants, graffiti, radio and TV interviews, and printed press (Esther Chávez Cano Collection). From the first march organized by Mujeres de Negro, the slogan "Ni una más" developed a prominent, consistent presence in the digital spaces, especially in blogs and social media platforms such as Facebook and YouTube. In what follows,

Figure 2.6. Graph produced from Google Trends data of web-search interest worldwide, 2004 to 2009, in the terms "femicidio," "feminicidio," and "Ni una mas." *Source:* Created by the author.

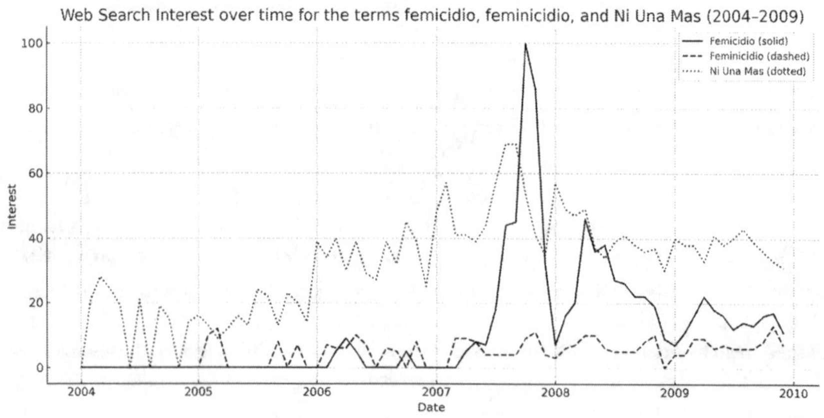

Figure 2.7. Graph produced from Google Trends data of YouTube searches world-wide, 2008 to the present, of the terms "femicidio," "feminicidio," and "Ni una mas." *Source:* Created by the author.

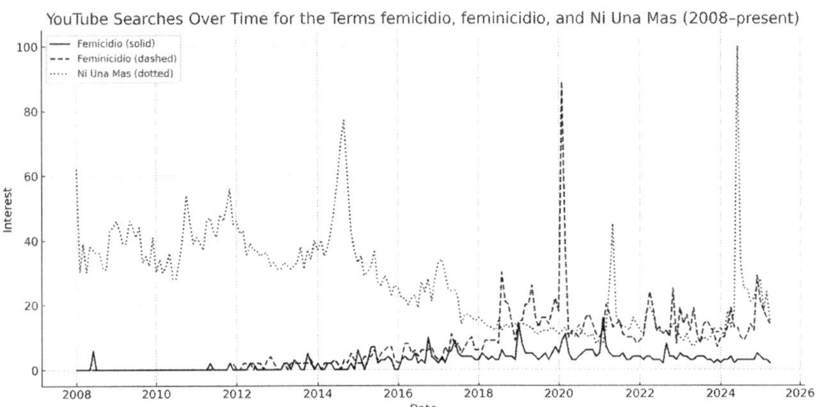

I first register the direct connection between community-driven online mobilizations stemming from feminicides. Then, I examine how these virtual mobilizations produce awareness in others and a denunciation of the state that drives legislation. Lastly, I trace the logic of public mourning. By examining the relationship between the cause and effect of the virtual and tangible spaces, I highlight how a crime such as feminicide simultaneously revolutionizes the virtual space and transforms the material space. I argue that postmortem politics are created when the affect of mourning a death publicly takes up space as both physical and virtual complaints that in turn propel legislation.

The slogan "Ni una más" developed as the hashtag #NiUnaMas on Twitter in November 2009.[10] Within days of its first use, the hashtag became discursively and visually associated with the on-the-ground movement. The hashtag #NiUnaMas articulated a form of public mourning defined by rage-filled denunciations and on-the-ground demands that not one more woman be killed. For example, the following tweet from November 20, 2009, refers

---

10. In their article *"Femitags* for Feminist Connected Crowds in Latin America and Spain," Guiomar Rovia Sancho and Jordi Morales-i-Gras (2022) claim that "#NiUnaMas (#NotASingleWomanMore) trended in Mexico around 2020 to denounce every new victim [case] of rape or femicide"; however, data from Twitter and Facebook suggests #NiUnaMas was trending as early as 2010 (see fig. 2.8 in this chapter).

to the feminicides by posting a picture of the *Cruz de Clavos* cross on the International Bridge:

> Jesús Robles Maloof @roblesmaloof Nov 20, 2009
>   #NiUnaMas! Cruz que recuerda los feminicidios. Pte. International Paso del Norte frontera México-EU http://pic.gd/cc7e9f[11]

The use of the hashtag #NiUnaMas in the tweet in combination with the word "feminicidio" and the *Cruz de Clavos* where the Mujeres de Negro ended their 2002 and 2009 marches—and which Rosa-Linda Fregoso describes as "one of the most potent and visible symbols of vernacular resistance culture" (2023, 129)—discursively associates and weaves #NiUnaMas to the process of postmortem politics of mothers, activists, scholars, collectives, civil associations, and nonprofits. It also introduces the hashtag with the exclamation point as an affective enunciation of rage in the digital space of public mourning.

Similarly, the second tweet from December 11, 2009, connects the use of the hashtag to macropolitical processes by pointing to the role of governmental entities in all matters concerning feminicide. For instance, the tweet below calls out Mexico's Secretariat of the Interior (SEGOB) and its brief response to the Inter-American Court of Human Rights sentence.

> adrián@chalalu Dec 11, 2009
>   En escueto comunicado, la SEGOB responde a sentencia de la CIDH, sobre caso de muertas del Campo Algodonero en Cd. Juárez #NiUnaMas[12]

In this case, the use of #NiUnaMas at the end of the tweet in combination with the message serves to call out the government. The tweet's discursive gesture becomes a form of public shaming of the governmental institution. Moreover, #NiUnaMas becomes a coded phrase whose implicit meaning is to demand that political institutions stop acting with impunity and address

---

11. *t.* #NiUnaMas! Cross that reminds us of feminicides. International Bridge Paso del Norte. Mexico–US border.

12. *t.* In a brief communiqué, SEGOB responds to the CIDH ruling on the case of the dead women from the place known as the Cotton Field in Juárez. #NiUnaMas

the killing of women.[13] Ultimately, the use of #NiUnaMas became more popular in Mexico as the rate of feminicides grew across the country.[14]

In December 2010 and January 2011, the use of the hashtag #NiUnaMas rose across Mexico. This increase coincides with the murders of mother and activist Marisela Escobedo Ortiz, who was murdered in front of the Government Palace in Chihuahua on December 16, 2010, and poet and activist Susana Chávez, who was murdered exactly three weeks later on January 6, 2011.[15] The on-the-ground and digital postmortem politics after their deaths centered on the failures of the Mexican legal system and the impunity on behalf of the Mexican state permeating both cases.

Marisela was a mother and activist whose daughter, Rubi Marisol Fraire Escobedo, disappeared in Ciudad Juárez in 2008. Since Rubi's disappearance, Marisela and her family members had participated in protests and marches seeking resources and information about Rubi's whereabouts. Through their diligence, they were able to locate Rubi's ex-boyfriend, Barraza Bocanegra, who eventually confessed to her murder, and as a result her family members were able to find what remained of her body in 2009. According to his confession, as told by Marisela, he had dismembered and burned Rubi's body at a pig ranch on the outskirts of Ciudad Juárez (Pérez Osorio 2020). On April 29, 2010, Barraza was acquitted for lack of evidence and released, despite his in-court confession. *La Jornada* reported: "Sin embargo, los jueces consideraron que la declaración autoinculpatoria de Barraza Bocanegra y las de los testigos fueron insuficientes para demostrar su responsabilidad, por lo que esta duda razonable les permitió dictar una sentencia absolutoria" (2010a).[16] The lack of legal recourse to obtain justice

---

13. See appendix, table 1: Sample Tweets Related to #niunamas in Mexico 2009–2010.

14. While the following statistics were provided by the Special Commission for Feminicides, 61st Legislature, in ONU Mujeres (2012) as official numbers, some of these numbers document only feminicides that were reported and exclude the murders of trans women who in Mexico are classified by their sex assigned at birth. In 2009 and 2010, Ciudad Juárez registered 469 feminicides, more than 50% of those committed over the last sixteen years (La Jornada 2011). The rate in the rest of the country came to 2,335 registered feminicides (ONU Mujeres 2012).Granted, during the presidency of Felipe Calderón there was an increase in killings of both men and women related to criminal organizations (narco-violence), which is also a factor in these numbers.

15. In 2020, ten years after her murder, Netflix released a documentary portraying Marisela's life, *The Three Deaths of Marisela Escobedo*.

16. *t.* However, the judges considered that Barraza Bocanegra's self-incriminating statement and those of the witnesses were insufficient to prove his responsibility, so this reasonable

for her daughter impelled Marisela to lead a series of marches in Ciudad Juárez to protest against the Mexican state's collusion with organized crime and the lack of legal recourse for families affected by feminicide.

In her postmortem politics, especially after the State of Chihuahua's verdict on her daughter's case, Marisela consistently advocated for a reexamination of the verdict that released her daughter's murderer and reminded reporters that she had nothing left to lose and therefore no longer was afraid (Pérez Osorio 2020). Having lost her fear, Marisela kept asking for an audience with the then Governor José Reyes Baeza Terrazas and later with the new governor of Chihuahua, César Duarte Jáquez. She even asked for an audience with then–Mexican President Felipe Calderón. In December she began another protest in the form of an encampment in Plaza Hidalgo in front of the Government Palace of Chihuahua, demanding to be heard by Duarte Jáquez. On the evening of Thursday, December 16, 2010, she was shot in the head in front of the Government Palace (La Jornada 2010b; Excélsior 2010).[17]

In the days following Marisela Escobedo's death, #NiUnaMas began to trend. The tweets ranged in content and sentiment. A thematic analysis of the content of 1,587 tweets and retweets containing #NiUnaMas generated from December 16, 2010, to January 31, 2011 (a little over a month after Marisela's death) illustrates the following: (a) public denunciation of the Mexican state's connection to organized crime; (b) the uselessness of the judicial branch; (c) naming feminicidal violence as responsible for her death; (d) a demand for justice; (e) calling out the Secretariat of the Interior; (f) a call to protest in Chihuahua and Mexico City; and (g) emotional appeals. For example, the following tweet alludes to the legal language in Article 26 of the General Law on Women's Access to a Life Free of Violence, which in Mexico passed in 2008:

> Lamatria @a_YO_tzinapa Dec 16, 2010
> ARTÍCULO 26.- Ante la violencia feminicida, el Estado mexicano deberá resarcir el daño #escobedo #marisela #NiUnaMas[18]

---

doubt allowed them to issue an acquittal.

17. *The Three Deaths of Marisela Escobedo* made her life and fight for justice available for global audiences to witness her story.

18. *t.* ARTICLE 26.- In the face of femicidal violence, the Mexican state must compensate the damage

This tweet engages in digital postmortem politics by bringing past legislation into this digital conversation to give dignity to Marisela's death, thereby reminding other users of this commitment of the Mexican state to its citizens.

Similarly, other tweets engaged in the production of digital postmortem politics by calling for the materialization of an on-the-ground protest in the state of Chihuahua and Mexico City:

José Merino@PPmerino Dec 16, 2010
    protesta el 17dic, a las 10AM,a las puertas de palacio de gobierno Chihuahua x asesinato de #mariselaescobedo #NiUnaMas #feminicidio[19]

Martha Tagle@MarthaTagle Dec 17, 2010
    Hoy a las 5pm DF manifestación en Gobernación, repudio a asesinato de Maricela Escobedo #Chihuahua #NiUnaMas[20]

These two tweets are examples of national-level digital organizing for on-the-ground action. Other tweets ask for the call for protest to be retweeted. These micropolitical calls to action allowed for information to spread among activists concerned with the contra-feminicide struggle. While at the time these on-the-ground protests consisted of about two hundred to four hundred people, it is important that this mobilizing on Twitter and the resulting on-the-ground efforts were propelled by digital forms of public mourning that had now reached nationwide supporters willing to organize in their respective cities.

Three weeks later, the murder of Susana Chávez heightened the use of the hashtag #NiUnaMas, which by then was inextricably associated with denouncing the complicity of government officials, calling out governmental institutions, calling for protests across Mexico on January 15 and 26, 2011, and calling for Mexicans to engage with the contra-feminicide struggle. I consider these tweets and retweets to be examples of these invitations for engagement through a call for people to show up in front of the Attorney General's Office in Mexico City and light a candle for Marisela and Susana

---

19. *t.* protest on December 17, at 10 a.m., at the doors of the Chihuahua government palace x murder of #mariselaescobedo

20. *t.* Today at 5 p.m., Mexico City demonstration in the Government, repudiation of the murder of Maricela Escobedo

as part of the on-the-ground protest organized by Agenda LGBT, la Liga de Trabajadores Socialistas, the feminist collective Pan y Rosas, and the collective Mujeres Libres en Resistencia (La Jornada 2011):

> Nadine Kerr C. @Nadinepink Jan 15, 2011
> #Niunamás #16Enero enciende una luz por #México afuera d la #PGR Av. P/Reforma 211-2132 #DF #Feminicidio #SusanaChávez #MariselaEscobedo[21]

> Mauricio Ayala Torres@Mawicio·Jan 15, 2011
> Replying to @SonReflexiones@triquisorg "#NiUnaMás #Enero16,18hrs,Cruz d veladoras a fuera d la #PGR,Av P/Reforma 211-2132 #feminicidio #SusanaChávez #MariselaEscobedo"[22]

The organizers' goal for this protest was to give visibility to the issue of violence against women and the targeting of contra-feminicide activists as in the cases of Marisela Escobedo and Susana Chávez, which the Mexican government refused to address. In a sense, the organizers created a "space of convening" (Chávez 2013, 8) that invited other people to turn their attention to the killing of women. Through an invitation to witness the public mourning of Marisela and Susana, the organizations that materialized the march partook in what Karma Chávez (2013) describes as a coalitional moment that "occurs when political issues coincide or merge in the public sphere in ways that create space to reenvision and potentially reconstruct rhetorical imaginaries" (8). In this case, their concerns centered on the impunity and the killings of Marisela and Susana, bridged issues of misogyny as a patriarchal pattern affecting seemingly distinct interest groups (women, socialists, LGBTQI+), which then united in fighting a common phenomenon: intersectional, gender-based violence and killing, first locally and then in tandem across the Americas. By combining on-the-ground activism with digital activism, these organizations aligned with specific subjectivities and ideological agendas that were able to engage a significant number of people and call attention to the impact of feminicides across

---

21. *t.* January light a light for #Mexico outside #PGR Av. P/Reforma 211-2132 #DF #Feminicidio #SusanaChávez #MariselaEscobedo

22. *t.* Mauricio Ayala Torres@Mawicio·Jan 15, 2011
Replying to @SonReflexiones@triquisorg "#NiUnaMás #Enero16,18hrs,Candlelight cross outside the #PGR,Av P/Reforma 211-2132 #feminicidio #SusanaChávez #Marisela Escobedo"

Mexico and the Americas.

Another relevant observation about the tweets is that those generated after January 6 name Marisela Escobedo or Susana Chávez or both. Accordingly, the practice of naming the murdered women in the digital space as well as in marches and rallies became an emerging strategy to give the dead women life and dignity amid consistent government-sponsored smear campaigns. Naming Marisela and Susana is a form of postmortem politics that reclaimed their lives and forced social media users to witness their lives, producing emotions in people such as sadness, fear, pain, and indignation. These emotions were then expressed via tweets and posts resulting in a collective vulnerability where users saw themselves in others and, by sympathizing with others they did not know, suddenly found themselves interconnected with other people regardless of class, gender, race, or nationhood, all through publicly mourning the loss of these women who had been murdered fighting the very malady that killed them. This public mourning created a coalitional space where people who had not been called to participate in the contra-feminicide movement felt compelled to witness and join by creating or reproducing posts and tweets and disseminating them in their social media networks. For example, the pain expressed in the tweet below names both women and notes that their deaths are painful not only because they were daughters, sisters, mothers, and friends, but also because they were women and activists. The tweet thereby implies that their deaths were part of the necropolitics of the Mexican state, specifically then-President Calderón's strategy to suppress activists:

> Sandra Amé@Sandraame Jan 11, 2011
>   Duele #MariselaEscobedo Duele #SusanaChávez porque
> no sólo eran hijas, hermanas, madres, amigas . . . eran Mujeres
> y eran Activistas #NiUnaMás[23]

#NiUnaMas produced digital postmortem politics through the memory of the murdered women's lives, allowing their lives to speak through us in the collective consciousness. Tweets about Marisela and Susana that emerged from social media users throughout Mexico displayed a form of public mourning that called into question the commitment of the patriarchal, necropolitical Mexican state to its constitutional amendments (positing a right to a life free of violence and the right to protest) and its citizens.

---

23. *t.* It hurts #MariselaEscobedo It hurts #SusanaChávez because they were not only daughters, sisters, mothers, and friends . . . they were Women and they were Activists

The tweets after Marisela and Susana's murders also produce an affective shift from indignation and frustration to a loss of fear and a demonstration of rage. Much in the same way Marisela expressed that she had nothing left to lose, Twitter users began to express themselves more bluntly by calling out the press for not covering the deaths of these activists and for instead engaging in smear campaigns against them. For instance:

> Tania Morgendorffer@TanitusRaritus Jan 16, 2011
>   Si los medios callan, que hablen las redes sociales. #niunamás #prohibidoolvidar[24]

Twitter users pointed to the mediatic silences and encouraged others to take to social media and create visibility of other murders. In a way, these users fostered resistance by taking the means of journalistic production into their own hands in the face of a silenced press.

Similarly, other tweets called for public reflexivity propelled by rage and a loss of fear. This emergent strategy stems from public mourning with the discourse surrounding the hashtag #NiUnaMas. For example, the tweet below asked users if they were going to wait for the next murdered woman to be their mother, sister, friend, companion, or colleague:

> Volga de Pina@pulgarebelde Jan 19, 2011
>   ¿Qué pues? ¿Van a esperar que la próxima sea su madre,
> su hermana, su amiga, su compañera, su colega? #NiUnaMas

The affective dimension of this appeal rests in the use of "Qué pues," which can loosely be translated as a defiant "What's up?" This affective appeal challenges users to self-reflect and invites them to see the interconnectedness between these women and the women in their own lives. By 2014, with the murder of forty-three male students in Ayotzinapa and rising Black Lives Matter protests, the hashtag #NiUnaMas began to be linked to the hashtags #Los43 (the forty-three), #Ayotzinapasomostodos (We are all Ayotzinapa), and #JusticiaparaAyotzinapa (Justice for Ayotzinapa) (fig. 2.8).

These hashtags sought to condemn the state's role and shameless cover-up of the disappearance and murder of forty-three male students from the Ayotzinapa Rural Teachers College in tandem with #Blacklivesmatter, which condemned racial and police violence toward Black bodies. It is at this intersection of increasingly visible state-sponsored violence toward

---

24. *t.* If the media is silent, let the social networks speak.#niunamas #forbbidentoforget

Figure 2.8. Word cloud of hashtags associated with #NiUnaMas in the 60,139 tweets analyzed. *Source:* Screenshot by the author.

marginalized and mostly poor bodies that the hashtag #NiUnaMas produced postmortem politics from a micropolitical attempt to connect subjectivities through personalization and the potential for coalitional moments.

Tracing the rise of the use of #NiUnaMas after Marisela Escobedo's and Susana Chávez's murders illustrates how digital postmortem politics played a role in calling for protests and demanding that the legislation truly be put into practice both legally and culturally. Strategies such as calling out the practice of impunity in the Mexican government and inviting reflexivity from Mexican citizens about the alarming rates of feminicidal violence in Mexico coalesced in digital and physical spaces for people to participate in public mourning and to mobilize to demand justice and dignity for Marisela, Susana, and other murdered women in Mexico. In the following section, I will examine how these online strategies employed by mourning family members and activists were adopted by contra-feminicide activists in other countries in the Americas.

#NiUnaMas: Legislating Feminicide
Across the Americas from 2010 to 2015

A search of the term "Ni una mas" on Google Trends from 2009 to 2023 illustrates that web searches for the phrase were prominent throughout Latin America and the Caribbean with an increase in searches after 2009 and a decrease in 2015 (when there is a surge in searches for "Ni una menos," which became the term associated with the contra-feminicide and reproductive-justice movements in Latin America and the Caribbean as of 2015) (fig. 2.9).[25] Searches for "Ni una mas" were especially relevant in

---

25. Even though searches for the term "Ni una mas" decreased in 2015, the term continues to be searched until today.

Figure 2.9. Graph produced from Google Trends data of web-search interest worldwide, 2009 to 2024, in the terms "Ni una mas" vs. "Ni una menos." *Source: Created by the author.*

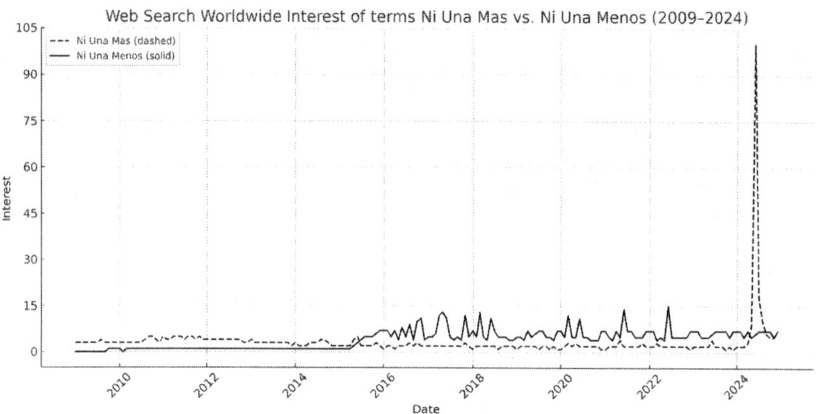

countries in Latin America and the Caribbean such as Venezuela, Puerto Rico, Paraguay, Uruguay, Honduras, Guatemala, Argentina, Nicaragua, Dominican Republic, Panama, Bolivia, Mexico, Costa Rica, El Salvador, Colombia, Ecuador, Peru, Chile, and Brazil. There was also an increase in searches based in Canada and the United States. The increase in searches in all these countries suggests an awareness of the fight against feminicide throughout the Americas.

During this same period, countries in the Americas named laws or classified feminicide in their criminal codes by naming the crime as "feminicidio" or "femicidio." In this section, I will primarily discuss the countries that passed legislation between 2010 and 2014 through the evidence of on-the-ground mobilizations, documented through the press and social media campaigns that mention either Ni Una Mas or #NiUnaMas, thus suggesting a preemptive interconnected struggle that would lay the groundwork for the now global #NiUnaMenos movement launched in Argentina in 2015.

In 2010 Chile passed Law 20.480, which reformed Law 20.066 about interfamily violence. They reformed their Criminal Code by classifying "femicidio" as a crime in Article 390, increasing the sentencing for the crime and reforming the procedures (Ley 20480). Similarly in 2011, Peru followed suit by passing Law 29.819, which reformed their Criminal Code under Article 107 *Parricido/Feminicido,* sentencing those guilty to a minimum of twenty-five years in prison. In 2012 Nicaragua and El Salvador both passed integral laws focusing on violence toward women that sought reforms of their criminal codes as well. On February 20, 2012, Nicaragua passed the Law Against Violence Towards Women. It has two sections, Título II and Título III, which specifically explain what constitutes a crime of violence against women and also prescribe preventive measures. In contrast to other criminal codes, Nicaragua's Article 9 titled "Femicidio" states that sentencing varies depending on whether the femicide occurred in public or in private—a detail that other criminal codes do not explicitly mention. In 2013 Bolivia, Honduras, Mexico, and Panama all classified femicide or feminicide as a crime in their criminal codes and stipulated minimum sentencing of twenty-five years. Along the same ethos, Ecuador, the Dominican Republic, and Venezuela also classified feminicide as a crime. However, Venezuela, similarly to Nicaragua's 2012 legislation, recommended a minimum sentencing of fifteen years.

Eight countries (Chile, Costa Rica, Ecuador, Guatemala, Honduras, Nicaragua, Panama, and Venezuela) identified the crime as femicide, while four identified it as feminicide (Peru, Bolivia, El Salvador, and Mexico).[26] Patsilí Toledo Vásquez wrote a report for the Mexican office of the High Commission of the United Nations for Human Rights that evaluates the differences and repercussions of the use of femicide vs. feminicide. Toledo Vásquez explains that in countries like Guatemala, where the women's movement uses the term *feminicide,* the adopted legislation chose to use *femicide* instead. She argues that "esto refleja las resistencias que políticamente puede encontrar el uso de una expresión que—en su construcción teórica—alude a la impunidad y al quiebre de Estado de Derecho que ella supone, quiebre que, por cierto, pocos países tendrían la voluntad política de reconocer" (2009, 87).[27] Thus, countries that use "femicide" in their criminal codes instead of "feminicide" do not acknowledge the impunity often present in these cases, nor the state's responsibility that "feminicide" implicitly recognizes (Toledo Vásquez 2009).

Posts and tweets on platforms such as Facebook, Twitter, and Instagram that name specific countries in the Americas along with #NiUnaMas and the

---

26. See appendix, table 2: Legislative Efforts in Latin America and the Caribbean 2007–2024 and 2015–2024.

27. *t.* this reflects the political resistances that can be found in the use of an expression that—in its theoretical construction—alludes to impunity and the state of law that it supposes, a matter that by the way very few countries would have the political will to recognize.

words "ley" (law) with "femicidio" or "feminicido" suggest that there was a hemispheric awareness among women, feminists, and allies of the struggle against feminicide. Their central concern was legislating feminicide as a crime by reforming criminal codes. This was an attempt to reduce (if not eliminate) the widespread killing of women through the creation of legal pathways for nation-states to hold those who killed women accountable—for the law to change the cultures that turned a blind eye to gender violence, even in its more extreme manifestation. Even though these efforts to legislate feminicide were localized by country, they illustrate the use of social media as a consciousness-raising tool that invited citizens of respective countries to participate in on-the-ground postmortem politics that also migrated to digital platforms. These hybrid mobilizing efforts shared an affective dimension of contra-feminicide activists that was galvanized by rage and a loss of fear in the face of respective regional governments' lack of action toward women killings. This resulted in the creation and classification of feminicide/femicide as a crime in twelve countries between 2010 and 2014.

The Postmortem and Transmortem Politics of *#NiUnaMenos*

The #NiUnaMenos movement is the most recognized of the various worldwide contra-feminicide movements today. Among social media and feminist scholars, it has also been well studied because of how it transformed feminism (Revilla Blanco 2019; Bedrosian 2022; Salvatori 2022; Rovira-Sancho and Morales-i-Gras 2022; De Maio 2023); as an example of how trans and nontrans women and feminist movements in the Global South use technology and hashtag activism for political action (Acosta 2018; Giraldo-Luque et al. 2018; Belotti et al. 2020; Belotti et al. 2024); its on-the-ground impact (Chenou and Cepeda-Másmela 2019; Gayles and Muñoz-Muñoz 2022; Gayles 2025); and its sustainability (Piatti-Crocker 2021). Building on these studies, in this section I argue that the rise of #NiUnaMenos and the sustainability of the movement form a modality of witnessing and participating in postmortem and transmortem politics that not only stand on the groundwork laid by the efforts of previous mobilization efforts, parallelisms, overlappings, and continuities with #NiUnaMas—including the momentum of legislating feminicide/femicide throughout the Americas after 2010—but also by hashtag activism that is inherently self-reflexive and adaptive.

Similarly to Casa Amiga in Ciudad Juárez, which was established in 1999, La Casa del Encuentro was established in 2003 as a space to provide support to victims of gender violence in Buenos Aires, Argentina. The staff at La Casa del Encuentro began to keep track of the number of feminicides in Argentina covered in national and regional medias, as well as through the news agencies DYN and Télam, as a response to a lack of official government data on the issue. In 2008 La Casa del Encuentro produced the first report on feminicide in the country (La Casa del Encuentro 2020). In 2009 they created the Adriana Marisel Zambrano Feminicide Observatory in Argentina; Adriana Marisel Zambrano was murdered by her husband in 2008. Her case was not covered in the press and her family, having heard of La Casa del Encuentro, reached out about the case and the organization advocated to obtain justice for Adriana (La Casa del Encuentro 2020). Naming the observatory after Adriana is another manifestation of postmortem politics because it consistently reminds people of the injustice surrounding her death while at the same time keeping her memory alive through the production of monthly and yearly reports on the numbers of feminicides and transfeminicides/transvesticides[28] that La Casa del Encuentro began tracking in 2013 shortly after Law 26.743 was passed in 2012 (La Casa del Encuentro 2020, 90).

The production and dissemination of these reports helped lobby the Argentinian government. In 2012 they passed Law 26.743 giving citizens the right to have a gender identity (while the law does not explicitly name trans people, it does include language about the right to dress however the person sees their gender) and modified Article 80 in the Criminal Code through Law 26.791, which criminalized homicides because of hatred toward race, religion, gender, or sexual identities, or both of those, and their expressions, and classified crimes of men against women as "femicidio vincluado" (linked femicide) (Ley 26.791 2012). Note that this was not a change in the Criminal Code to include femicide as a type of crime as in other countries in Latin America, nor did it classify transfemicide/transvesticide as a crime; rather, Argentina limited itself to defining femicide (and transfemicide/transvesticide) as a type of variant of homicide motivated by hatred toward gender or sexual identities or both and their respective expressions. Despite the passage of this law, from 2013 to the beginning of 2015 La Casa del Encuentro (2020) reported 563 feminicides and nine transfeminicides/transvesticides during that period (90). La Casa del

---

28. Transvesticide or travesticidio is a term particularly used in countries like Chile and Argentina to describe the gender-based killings of what locally are referred to as "travesties" (transgender people).

Encuentro (2020) describes the inclusion of transfeminicides/transvesticides being made possible by Law 26.743:

> los asesinatos de personas trans, travestis y transgénero siempre existieron en nuestro contexto heterocisnormativo. No obstante, no se visibilizaban en los medios de comunicación y recién comienzan a publicarse a partir de la Ley de identidad de género. Es por ello que el Observatorio de Femicidios en Argentina "Adriana Marisel Zambrano" puede llevar el monitoreo de los mismos a partir de la primera publicación de un transfemicidio/travesticidio el 29 de marzo de 2013, a casi un año de la sanción de la Ley. (66)[29]

The inclusion of transfeminicides and transvesticides in these reports in 2013 suggests a shift in feminist circles, who interpreted the gendered killing of women to be inclusive of trans bodies whose bodies and personhoods also experience the impact of patriarchal violence, despite these crimes not being classified in Argentinian law.

By March 16, 2015, La Casa del Encuentro and the Argentinian press had reported eight feminicides: Florencia Magali Torres, Julia Benítez, Mirta Turra Gutiérrez, Clorinda Bustos, Elsa Romina Ojeda, Isabel San Martín, Leydi Meneses, and Daiana Ayelén García (La Casa del Encuentro 2020, 502–3). The last of these reported deaths, Daiana Ayelén—who was nineteen and was found half naked in a trash bag on March 16—mobilized feminist groups. According to María Pía López, this string of deaths resulted in a street performance and a reading marathon by writers and journalists (López 2020, 8). This reading marathon was convened through Twitter under the hashtag #NiUnaMenos at the Argentine National Library's Museum of the Book and Language to make gendered violence visible in the public sphere and to express the rage against femicides. Mariana Carbajal (2019) explains that "en esa convocatoria se usó por primera vez la consigna 'Ni Una Menos.' Se tomó de una frase acuñada por la poetisa y defensora de derechos humanos mexicana

---

29. *t.* the harassment of trans, transvestite and transgender people has always existed in our heterocisnormative context. However, it was not visible in the media and began to be published based on the law of gender identity. This is why the Observatorio de Femicidios en Argentina "Adriana Marisel Zambrano" can begin monitoring them from the first publication of a transfemicide/transvesticide on March 29, 2013, a year after the sanction of the law.

Susana Chávez" (200–201).[30] Here, Carbajal is referring to the now infamous first part of the line in Chávez's poem: "Ni una menos, ni una muerta más." Mariana De Maio (2023) notes that the digital form of this call on Twitter was "the first time the hashtag #NiUnaMenos was used" (58). For Carbajal (2019) the use of the hashtag #NiUnaMenos emerged as a collective scream from the rage produced by being fed up with patriarchal violence and its cruelest practice: feminicide (199).

On March 26, 2015, at the Argentine National Library's Museum of the Book and Language reading marathon, María Moreno tried to bring dignity to the women found in trash bags by stating, "We are all the woman in the bag, and we are coming out of it so that there will be not one less" (Lopez 2020, 8). Lopez reflects on this reading marathon as a shifting moment, explaining that: "Not One Less is the outcry against the growing horror: it says that lives matter and that each body counts, should be valued, counted—one of the movement's initial demands was the creation of a public register of femicide—but also that their stories should be recounted" (8). For Lopez, the collective narrative centered on creating meaning and keeping the memory of the murdered women alive through acts of public mourning. By the beginning of May 2015, there had been three more femicides: Laura Elizabeth Vázquez Provoste, Zully Alamanni, and Blanca Escalante Olima. Then on the morning of May 11, 2015, the body of fourteen-year-old Chiara Páez had been found buried in her boyfriend's backyard. She was beaten to death and was three months pregnant (Acosta 2018; Carbajal 2019; López 2020; Belotti et al. 2020; De Maio 2023). In response to Chiara's feminicide and the other eleven murdered women in the first five months of the year, the journalist Marcela Ojeda tweeted:

> Marce Ojeda@Marcelitaojeda·May 11, 2015
> Actrices, políticas, artistas, empresarias, referentes sociales . . . mujeres, todas, bah . . . no vamos a levantar la voz? NOS ESTAN MATANDO[31]

Within a matter of hours, the tweet was retweeted and the call to organize spread among journalists, writers, and activists. The most active accounts

---

30. *t.* It was through this call that the slogan "Ni Una Menos" was used for the first time. It came from a phrase coined by Mexican poet and defender of human rights Susana Chávez.

31. *t.* Actresses, politicians, artists, businesswomen, community leaders, women, all of you, bah . . . are we not going to raise our voices? THEY ARE KILLING US.

following Ojeda's tweet included: @soyingridbeck (Ingrid Beck), @solevallejos (SoledadVallejos), @claudiapinieiro (Claudia Piñeiro), @ mercedesfunes (Mercedes Funes), @fetcheves (Florencia Etcheves), @gabrielagrosso (Gabriela Grosso), and @hindelita (Hinde Pomeraniec). In threaded conversations between these accounts, they proposed a march for June 3, 2015, under the demand "Ni una menos" (Not one less).

As #NiUnaMenos became a trending topic, the issue of feminicide and gender violence transgressed the barrier of only being addressed in feminist circles to gain the support of the general public, including unprecedented support from soccer players, actors, artists, athletes, journalists, political and union leaders, and cartoonists whose illustrations went viral on social media (Carbajal 2019). Scholars who have studied #NiUnaMenos in depth (Giraldo-Luque et al. 2018; Acosta 2018; Revilla Blanco 2019; Chenou and Cepeda-Másmela 2019; Urzúa Martínez 2019; Piatti-Crocker 2021; Belotti et al. 2020, Belotti et al. 2024; Bedrosian 2022; Salvatori 2022; De Maio 2023) recognize that the wide reach of the mobilization would not have been possible without the tradition of previous feminist activism by the Mothers of the Plaza de Mayo.[32]

On June 3, 2015, more than three hundred thousand people took to the streets mobilized by rage, and displaying a coalitional moment, they engaged in postmortem politics that articulated nine clear demands from the state as described by Carbajal (2019):

1. Implementation in its entirety and with the corresponding budget allocation of Ley No. 26485/2009 "Comprehensive Protection Law to Prevent, Punish and Eradicate Violence against Women in the areas in which women develop their interpersonal relationships." As described in the National Plan where it was established.

---

32. The Mothers of the Plaza de Mayo emerged during a period of state-sponsored terrorism during the Argentinian dictatorship (1976–1983). This group of mothers of disappeared children began to publicly protest the military government and demand their children be returned to them. Their efforts garnered worldwide attention. They are still active today, gathering every Thursday in front of the Casa Rosada (the equivalent of the White House in Argentina) to demand justice for their children and other intersecting causes. They are recognized in #NiUnaMenos's mission statement for laying the groundwork for the success of #NiUnaMenos.

2. Compilation and publication of official statistics on violence against women including femicide rates.

3. Opening and full operation of the Domestic Violence Offices of the Supreme Court of Justice in all provinces, to expedite precautionary protection measures. Making "Linea 137," Argentina's 24-hour, free, confidential helpline for victims of gender-based violence, available throughout the entire country, not just in Buenos Aires and other metropolitan areas.

4. Guarantees for the protection of victims of violence. Implementation of electronic monitoring of perpetrators to ensure that they do not violate the restrictions of approach imposed by Justice.

5. Guarantees for victims' access to Justice. Staff attention trained to receive complaints in each prosecutor's office and each police station. Linking the cases of civil and criminal jurisdictions. Free legal sponsorship for victims throughout the judicial process.

6. Guarantees for compliance with the rights of children with the sponsorship of legal specialists trained in the subject matter.

7. The creation of more emergency Homes/Shelters, Day Homes for victims, and housing subsidies, with interdisciplinary assistance from a gender perspective.

8. Incorporation and deepening in all the educational curricula of the different levels of comprehensive sexual education with a gender perspective, the topic of sexist violence and workshops to prevent violent courtships.

9. Mandatory training on the topic of sexist violence for State personnel, security agents and judicial operators, as well as professionals who work with the issue of violence in different official agencies throughout the country.

Evident in these demands is an ethical commitment to fight against a neoliberal state that on the one hand performatively claims to care for the rights of its citizens to live a life free of harm, but on the other, perpetuates injuries against marginalized bodies in the name of gore capitalism (Valencia 2010, 2018)[33] through a lack of funding and implementation of the laws that are supposed to guarantee those rights.

#NiUnaMenos made this paradox evident through these demands and coalesced around the message that "gender violence is your business" (Belotti et al. 2020) resulting in immediate actions on behalf of the Argentinian state. Two days after the march, the Supreme Court announced the establishment of an official Feminicide Registry. Four days after the march on June 7, 2015, the news outlet *Página 12* reported that the free national emergency line 144 had gone from receiving one thousand calls a day related to gender violence before the march, to 13,700 calls after the march. Also, at the end of 2015, the Argentinian National Congress passed Law 27.210 to create the Corps of Lawyers for Victims of Gender Violence to guarantee access to justice for victims of gender violence; it was implemented in 2019. They also passed Law 27.234, which stipulated that the educational campaign "Educate in Equality: Prevention and Eradication of Gender Violence" be taught at all education levels in Argentina in both public and private schools.[34]

#NiUnaMenos and Its Coalitional Possibilities

The hashtag #NiUnaMenos was used in efforts to pass legislation spurred by specific cases of feminicide that rattled the countries of Colombia, Peru, and Brazil.[35] For example, in Colombia, despite the passage of Law 1257 in 2008 and the criminalization of feminicide through Article 104A, the responsibility on behalf of the state was not enough. On March 23, 2012, thirty-five-year-old student Rosa Elvira Cely was raped, tortured, and impaled in the Parque Nacional by one of her classmates. Rosa made a series of calls to the emergency line 123, and two hours later was found alive by firefighters and the police. She died from her injuries four days later. It

---

33. Valencia defines gore capitalism as a form of capitalism where extreme violence, particularly against vulnerable populations, has become both normalized and economically profitable.

34. However, under the recent Milei administration, many of these achievements have been undermined or are under threat.

35. See appendix, table 3: Sample Tweets from Across the Americas Using #NiUnaMas 2010–2024.

took police three months to locate her attacker; he was later tried in the Colombian justice system and ultimately sentenced to forty-eight years in prison. In 2014 Rosa's family decided to sue the City of Bogotá for failing to provide an adequate response after her death. This then prompted the city attorneys to claim that Rosa had put herself at risk by associating with the type of people she did (Alsema 2016)). The response by city officials implying that Rosa was responsible for her own rape, torture, impalement, and subsequent death sparked rage and indignation throughout Colombia, with calls for Mayor Enrique Peñalosa to resign. Rosa's family and feminist groups organized marches with the chant, "No more feminicides, we're all Rosa Elvira" (Palomino 2016) and used the hashtag #NiUnaMas to gather support. However, by 2015, after Argentina's usage of the hashtag #NiUnaMenos, the call for legislation in Colombia was likewise accompanied by the hashtag #NiUnaMenos. To honor Rosa Elvira Cely, in 2015 the Colombian Congress passed Law 1791 and named it after her. This law, Ley Rosa Elvira Cely, classifies feminicide as an autonomous crime to guarantee the investigation and punishment of violence against women for reasons of gender discrimination, to prevent and eradicate said violence, and to implement strategies to raise awareness in Colombian society. That same year, Peru and Brazil also passed legislation classifying feminicide. In the next chapter, I will discuss the case of Brazil in detail.

By 2016 #NiUnaMenos organizers, "a diverse group of women seeking to build transversal forms of activism that move beyond non-inclusive and masculinized organizational practices" (Gayles and Muñoz-Muñoz 2022), had a website presenting their values, manifestos, and mission.[36] The group's central objectives were to call out the government for defunding the established Femicide Registry, call out their failure to implement the educational programs, and to form coalitions with activists in other countries like Mexico, Peru, and other territories where discrimination against trans and nontrans women's bodies takes place (Ni Una Menos 2018). Postmortem politics were implemented by referencing the previous marches organized by Mujeres de Negro in Mexico. For example, María Pia López (2020) explains:

> Not One Less called for women to march—during the first National Women's Strike—in black or to dress in black if they were unable to strike or march. Everyday life was disrupted by

---

36. See https://niunamenos.org.ar/quienes-somos/carta-organica/.

> the appearance of black clothes in all public spaces. . . . It was pouring rain that afternoon, but a crowd of furious women dressed in black marched anyway. Some women of African ancestry objected to the use of the color black as a symbol of tragedy, although, for the organizers, the most powerful resignification was the color black as emblematic of battle and recovery of the Black Power movement. In Brazil after the murder of Marielle Franco, a new chant spread: "luto e luta"—mourning is fighting. (19)

Through this account, López underscores how different identities were also negotiated and allowed to exist because of the collectivity in public mourning. It also underscores the interconnected awareness of other struggles in the Americas by referring to how specific subjectivities negotiated the politics of mourning, and in the case of Brazil, as we will see in chapter 3, turned mourning into a fight.

Furthermore, in 2016, #NiUnaMenos expanded to other countries in Latin America, Africa, Asia, Europe, and some places in North America and became more inclusive of other subjectivities. Additionally, a global march on November 25, 2016, also known as 25N, sought to bring awareness to issues of gender violence using #NiUnaMenos as one of their referents, thus associating feminicide with a global issue (Giraldo-Luque et al. 2018). Galvanized by the #NiuNaMas movement and calls from citizens, Paraguay also passed legislation criminalizing femicide in 2016.

On June 3, 2017, #NiUnaMenos organized their third march; that year they also included the hashtag #Vivasnosqueremos (We want ourselves alive). Their central concern and consistent mention of femicide were associated with social, political, and economic forces (Belotti et al. 2020). As the movement became more visible and global, the online conversation developed a harsher tone with calls to confront the colonial and racist legacies of feminist movements in Latin America. This was evidenced by signs at the marches as well as tweets and posts (Belotti et al. 2020). In that same year, amid mounting pressure from its citizens, Uruguay criminalized feminicide.

The movement seemed to be adapting its ideological structures and adopting a more intersectional approach. In their 2018 manifesto for a strike organized for March 8, the Ni Una Menos (2018) organizers state:

> Paramos contra el racismo, la discriminación y xenofobia hacia
> las mujeres indígenas, negras afrodescendientes y afroindígenas.

Paramos para exigir la libertad de las mujeres de la comunidad Wichi de juárez basta de persecución, criminalización y judici-alizaciòn a las mujeres y comunidades mapuche.

Paramos contra el genocidio y femicidio de mujeres que tiene su origen en la trata esclavista y en la violencia colonial. Paramos contra la justicia clasista, blanca y patriarcal. Paramos por el buen vivir de nosotras y nuestras comunidades.[37] (121).

This shift in their platform demonstrates an adaptive shift to be inclusive of Black and Indigenous communities in the Americas. Granted, although this antiracist and anticolonial ethos was expressed, it did not mean it "reached the level of interpersonal exchanges" (Gayles and Muñoz-Muñoz 2022, 210). In her pivotal book on Black activism in Argentina, *Pain into Purpose* (2025), Prisca Gayles describes how Black women organizers from Argentina's Afro-Argentine movement showed up at #NiUnaMenos meetings to voice their concerns about "the hyper-sexualization of Black women's bodies, how they are assumed to be prostitutes, about how even at feminist gatherings White women strangers touch their skin and hair without permission, about how one Black woman was filmed in a communal shower at a feminist retreat in La Plata" (141). Gayles explains that "the efforts of Black women, along with efforts of Indigenous women, resulted in the antiracist rhetoric present in the more recent official platform of #NiUnaMenos" (141). Similarly, by 2021 #NiUnaMenos had incorporated an inclusive transfeminist aspiration and started using gender-inclusive language in their manifestos and the #NiUnxMenos.

In a sense, the #NiUnaMenos opened the possibilities of coalition across women, LGBTQI+, and men (López 2020). This intentionally interconnected endeavor allowed for a coalition described by María Lugones (2003) as being "always the horizon that rearranges both our possibilities and the conditions of those possibilities" (ix). The coalitional possibility is relevant in the case of #NiUnaMenos when we consider that after 2014, other hashtags began to circulate in the digital spheres. For example, in

---

37. *t.* We strike against racism, discrimination, and xenophobia toward Indigenous, Afrodescendant, and Afro-Indigenous women. We strike against the genocide and femicide of women who trace their origin to the slave trade and colonial violence. We strike against classist, white, and patriarchal justice. We strike for the well-being of ourselves and our communities.

2014 in the United States #Blacklivesmatter and #SayHerName began to call attention to the systematic racialized killings of Black men and women at the hands of police. The hashtags #MMIWG and #MMIWG2S began in Canada in 2014 and were adopted in the United States to call attention to the unbearable rates of missing and murdered Indigenous women, girls, and two-spirit relatives, and to highlight their connection to extractive industries and ongoing colonial legacies. Similarly, the hashtag #translivesmatter also began to circulate during this period in response to attacks against trans bodies. These movements have many points in common with #NiUnaMenos. Still, perhaps the most evident is their use of postmortem and transmortem politics, which uses the power of publicly mourning a single life to demand the right to life. By honoring the lives of those murdered, disappeared, or both, these movements find transversal resonance in other struggles.

The #NiUnaMenos had a trending presence across platforms including but not limited to Twitter, Facebook, Instagram, and TikTok in countries across Latin America.[38] This interconnected network of people in digital and physical spaces became vested in the right to demand the right to life in the wake of necropolitics[39] (Mbembe 2003, 2019) and gore capitalism (Valencia 2010) by witnessing and participating in postmortem/transmortem politics. This awareness and visibility in the public sphere have enabled the sustainability of #NiUnaMenos marches every March 8 and made the marea verde (green tide)—the abortion-rights movement in Latin American countries—possible. As of 2024, all countries in the Americas have some form of legislation either by law or in their criminal codes that classify feminicide/femicide as a crime except for Haiti, Cuba, the United States, and Canada.

Both #NiUnaMas and #NiUnaMenos were fueled by the participatory process (Bennet and Segerberg 2012) of publicly mourning the deaths of many women. In this chapter, I centered the role of social media as a form of witnessing by highlighting the cases of Maricela Escobedo, Susana Chávez, Adriana Marisel Zambrano, Chiara Perez, and Rosa Elvira Cely to argue

---

38. As of April 2024, Instagram had 2,252,381 posts with the hashtag #NiUnaMenos, 605,850 posts with #NiUnaMas and #niunamás, and 448,382 with #vivanosqueremos; X had over two million tweets with #NiUnaMenos; YouTube had 3,600 videos with #NiUnaMas vs. 17,000 videos with #NiUnaMenos. The digital footprint of these movements continues to create spaces of public mourning.

39. This term refers to the use of social and political power to dictate how some people may live and how others must die, thereby determining who is disposable and under what conditions death is allowable or even beneficial to those in power.

that postmortem politics are created when the affect of mourning a death publicly transforms physical and digital platforms into spaces that allow others to witness their lives and to denounce the impunity of the state and other actors, in turn propelling legislation. In the next chapter, I will focus on Brazil as a case study of how the Inter-American Commission on Human Rights and on-the-ground and digital mobilizations by survivors, families, activists, and NGOs continue to hold the Brazilian state accountable for the legislation meant to reduce gender violence, including feminicide and transfeminicide.

Chapter 3

Determination and Tension

The Continuous Struggle for Recognition

Nos expulsam dos banheiros, das escolas, de casa, do trabalho e, mesmo assim, não conseguem nos explusar do mundo. Estamos encardadas. Mesmo se nos matassem a tudas. Uma a uma. É possível exterminar as travesties. Jamais as travestilidades.

—Caia Coelho[1]

On July 25, 2023, Julia Nicolly Moreira da Silva was found dead in her house by her neighbors in the neighborhood Baixada Fluminense of Rio de Janeiro. She had been gagged, beaten, and stabbed several times in the neck, chest (lungs), and ribs (G1 2023). Julia was a nurse and worked for Ideas, a national nonprofit subsidized by the Brazilian state that provides public health services to marginalized communities. Two years earlier she had been stabbed by a man who had been arrested, charged, and convicted of attempted murder. In Brazil, like in other places in Latin America, trans women are excluded from Lei do Feminicido (the law on feminicide) because the language in the law classifies womanhood based on their sex not their gender. A year after his arrest, Julia received a death threat that, her family said afterward, was from that man. However, according to the

---

1. *t.* They expel us from the bathrooms, from schools, from home, from work and even so, they cannot expel us from the world. We are embodied. Even if they killed us all. One by one. It is possible to exterminate *travestis* (transgender people). Never transvestisms/transgenderisms (Benevides 2023b, 10).

criminal investigation conducted by the Baixada Fluminense Homicide Police Station, Julia's murder was committed by a nineteen-year-old man and his seventeen-year-old friend (who were arrested a month later).

Julia's death was one of the 145 murders of trans people in Brazil recorded by the nonprofit organization Associação Nacional de Travestis e Transexuais[2] (ANTRA) in 2023.[3] Julia's murder exemplifies Berenice Bento's (2016) argument that transfeminicide is a widespread political, intentional, and systematic elimination of the trans populations that is motivated by disgust and hatred. Bento's definition of transfeminicide points to the excessive use of violence and displays of cruelty, including in Julia's case, in trans murders in Brazil, where trans women under the age of twenty-nine are, on average, up to five times more likely to be murdered (Benevides 2025, 69). Julia's story makes evident that despite the passage of *Lei do Feminicidio* in 2015, the language of the law compared to other countries in Latin America, such as Colombia, is transexclusionary. Moreover, the case also underscores the impunity that characterizes police and judicial practices in the murders of femme bodies through a lack of rigor in the investigations and a noted delay in the time involved in identifying and arresting suspects.

According to the Observatory for Gender Equality in Latin America and the Caribbean, Brazil has the second highest number of laws in the Americas (twenty-four) addressing gender violence. Yet despite this robust legal framework, gendered violence persists at alarming rates. In 2023, ANTRA documented 145 transfeminicides, and in 2024, the Ministry of Public Safety in Brazil also reported 1,467 cases of feminicides—the largest number recorded by the Brazilian state since passing the Lei do Feminicidio in 2015. Further illustrating this trend, the 2025 report "Visível e Invisível: A Vitimização de Mulheres no Brasil" (Visible and Invisible: The Victimization of Women in Brazil), published by the Fórum Brasileiro de Segurança Pública (Brazilian Public Security Forum), identified a sharp

---

2. *t.* National Association for Transvestites and Transexuals

3. A note on terminology: In Brazil the use of the words *travesties* (transvestites) and *transexuais* (transexuals) stems from a historical popularization of medical–psychiatric vocabulary in the 1990s (Carvalho and Carrara 2015) that was adopted by the trans community. Thus, in this section, I will use the word *trans* rather than *transgender* so as not to impose a gender category that is not commonly used in Brazil. By using the word *trans* to refer to trans populations, I broadly refer to those who identify as *travesties* and *transexuais*, per the increased use by Brazilian scholars of the terms *trans* or *pessoas trans* (Carvalho and Carrara 2015, 386), and recognize that there are classed and raced differences between these categories.

increase in severe forms of violence against women and girls based on national surveys in 2023 and 2025. According to the document, 37.5% of respondents, approximately 21.4 million nontrans women, reported experiencing at least one act of violence in the previous year. This marks the highest prevalence recorded in the survey's eight-year history (Fórum Brasileiro de Segurança Pública 2025, 7–8). The paradox of the increasingly high numbers of reported cases of gender-based killing of trans and nontrans women in Brazil suggests that despite having a considerable legal framework in place, the implementation and enforcement of laws to address gender-based murders may be inadequate to produce a significant shift in systemic practices and cultural norms toward gender violence.

In the summer of 2023, I had the privilege to teach a one-week seminar to doctoral human rights students at Universidade Tiradentes (UNIT). Our conversations resulted in naming the affects that to them defined Brazil's relationship to the murders of trans and nontrans women and that give a name to this chapter: determination and tension. In this chapter, I trace how in Brazil mechanisms such as the Inter-American Commission on Human Rights and mobilizations by survivors, families, activists, and NGOs helped exert pressure to legislate against gender violence (including feminicide). I also examine the social media campaigns that were in the public sphere at specific moments of the legislative process. I then proceed to focus on the state-sponsored murder of politician and activist Marielle Franco in 2018 and the postmortem politics that ensued with the on-the-ground and hashtag activism after her death. That made evident the determination of feminist activists and the cultural and political tension fostered by Brazil's political shift to the extreme right with the election of President Jair Bolsonaro. I conclude by highlighting the inherently transfeminist and intersectional work of ANTRA's advocacy efforts to illustrate the potentiality of transmortem politics in the struggle for political recognition of the rights of trans and nonbinary people in Brazil.

Gender-Violence Legislation and Public Indignation on Social Media in Brazil

Brazil's efforts to modify social and cultural patterns concerning gender are deeply grounded in its democratic transition following the end of the civil–military regime (1964–1985), and reflect a broader national commitment to addressing social issues that were previously suppressed or neglected under the authoritarian military regime. Moving away from the authoritarian disregard toward women's rights was achieved through initiatives involving international human rights law, specifically those derived from the 1979 UN Convention on the Elimination of All Forms of Discrimination Against Women (CEDAW). In 1983 the Partido do Movimiento Democratico Brasileiro[4] (PMDB) established the Conselho Estadual da Condição Femenina in São Paulo[5] (Alvarez 1990). In 1984 Brazil's Decree n. 89.460 made it become one of CEDAW's member states, committing to promote women's rights to achieve gender equity and eliminate any discrimination against women ("Cronologia Dos Direitos Das Mulheres" 2016).

By 1985 the democratically elected PMDB government officially took federal power and set up Delegacias Especializadas no Atendimento a Mulher, women's police stations, a first in Latin America and the Caribbean, and the Conselho Nacional dos Direitos da Mulher (CDNM), the National Council for Women's Rights (Macaulay 2021, 37). Primarily staffed by feminists, the CDNM served as an advisory body to the Ministry of Justice and "was key in galvanizing women around the drafting of the new constitution" (Macaulay 2021, 14). In the 1988 constitution, Article 226, section 8, the Brazilian state committed to "ensuring assistance to the family, as represented by each member that makes up the family, by creating mechanisms to prevent violence within the scope of the relationships between family members."[6] By including this language in its constitution, Brazil signaled a strong commitment to addressing domestic violence and positioned itself as taking the issue seriously on the international stage.

At the behest of feminist federal deputies, Brazil's Chamber of Deputies supported a Parliamentary Committee Inquiry into gender-based violence in Brazil in 1991–1992. The report, based on 205,218 surveys, revealed that:

> 26.2 per cent of the crimes against women were based on physical injury; 16.4 per cent were criminal threats against the women; 3 per cent were "crimes of honour"; 1.9 per cent were crimes of seduction; 1.8 per cent were rape and 0.5 per cent were homicides. Other crimes, such as violence and indecent

---

4. *t.* Democratic Movement Brazilian Party

5. *t.* State Council for the Status of Women in São Paulo

6. ART 226 8º, O Estado assegurará a assistência à família na pessoa de cada um dos que a integram, criando mecanismos para coibir a violência no âmbito de suas relações.

> assault, kidnapping, private incarceration, racial discrimination and discrimination in the workplace constituted 51 per cent of the total. The Commission further found that of the women victims of physical violence, 88.8 per cent were housewives. Data also indicate that the majority of assaults against women take place at home, especially those against married women between 18 and 29 years of age. (Coomaraswamy 1997, 6)

However, neither the results of this inquiry, the hosting of the Belém do Pará Convention in 1994 (formally known as the Inter-American Convention on the Prevention, Punishment, and Eradication of Violence Against Women), nor the Decree n. 1.973 in 1996, which undertook to enact the convention's mission to prevent, punish, and eradicate violence against women, compelled the Brazilian government to pass legislation on domestic violence. Instead, the government launched Juiziados Especias Criminais, criminal-misdemeanor courts, to handle nonlethal domestic-violence cases (Macaulay 2005) that "were inappropriate for such a task because they effectively downplayed the seriousness of domestic violence and stressed inter-personal mediation over protection for the victim" (Macaulay 2021, 15).

By 1996 Brazil's failure to develop and implement policies to protect women caught the attention of the United Nations Special Rapporteur on Violence Against Women (UNSR), Radhika Coomaraswamy, who noted the choosing of "Brazil as a case-study for the issue of domestic violence because available data indicate a high prevalence of such violence in the country but also because of the many existing programmes and activities, both governmental and non-governmental, to combat and prevent such violence" (Coomaraswamy 1997, 3). The report, titled "Report on the Mission of the Special Rapporteur to Brazil on the Issue of Domestic Violence" (1997), took a rather intersectional approach by examining the role of race, class, and gender in how the Brazilian criminal justice system and social programs addressed domestic violence. It also underscored the general systemic failure of the Brazilian criminal justice system to address domestic violence, including concerns from Black and Indigenous communities. Specifically, the representatives of the Black community "felt that racist attitudes and the perceived discrimination against black people by the criminal justice system frequently prevent black women from seeking assistance" (Coomaraswamy 1997, 8); and the "representatives of the Indigenous community of Brazil were concerned that violence against Indian women is not treated seriously by the criminal justice system" (Coomaraswamy 1997, 9). The findings of this report "led feminist activists to enlist the regional human rights system to put pressure on the Brazilian government" (Macaulay 2021, 15) to pass specific legislation to address domestic violence.

In 1998 feminists and women's rights activists convinced Maria da Penha to enlist the help of two NGOs to take her case to the Inter-American Commission on Human Rights.[7] Maria da Penha had been shot by her husband while she was sleeping in 1983. While she survived the murder attempt, the injuries sustained from the shot left her paraplegic. During her recovery, her husband tried to electrocute her. Despite being charged with attempted murder, he was still free fifteen years after the fact because his sentencing had not been finalized. Empowered by the findings of the "Report on the Mission of the Special Rapporteur to Brazil on the Issue of Domestic Violence," Maria da Penha's case argued that the failure to convict and sentence her violent husband was a violation of various principles outlined in human rights conventions that Brazil, as a state party, had chosen to adopt, including the Belém do Pará Convention and the American Convention on Human Rights. This was the first time the Inter-American Commission on Human Rights had heard a case related to domestic violence (Macaulay 2021). The Brazilian government did not respond to inquiries from the Inter-American Commission on Human Rights.

By 2001 the Inter-American Commission on Human Rights had issued a report that declared the Brazilian state in noncompliance with the Belém do Pará Convention because of its "violation of women's rights for its failure to act," asserting also that it "was guilty of negligence, omission, and tolerance of violence against women" (Macaulay 2021). Although the report didn't directly produce domestic-violence legislation in Brazil, it catalyzed several important changes: the 2002 revision of Brazil's Civil Code establishing gender equality; the mobilization of feminist lawyers,

---

7. The two NGOs that helped Maria da Penha were the Center for Justice and International Law and the Latin American and Caribbean Committee for the Defense of Women's Rights. The Center for Justice and International Law was established in 1991 at a meeting in Caracas held by prominent human rights defenders; their goal was "to form a regional organization that would use international human rights law and the bodies of the Inter-American Human Rights System (IAHRS) to promote justice, liberty and a dignified existence for the citizens of the hemisphere" (CEJIL 2021). The Latin American and Caribbean Committee for the Defense of Women's Rights was established in Costa Rica in 1987 after discussions at the 3rd World Conference on Women of the United Nations in Nairobi; it consists of a network of women's-rights organizations and activists.

NGOs, and activists who successfully removed domestic-violence cases from the Juizados Especiais Criminais, specialized courts in Brazil that focus on minor offenses (Campos 2011; Carone 2018; Macaulay 2021); and Brazil's submission of its first—albeit eighteen years late—report to CEDAW, which cited Maria da Penha's case. In 2003 CEDAW responded by clearly stating that Brazil needed to formulate and pass legislation to address domestic violence (UN Committee on the Elimination of Discrimination Against Women 2003, 96).

In 2002 President Lula da Silva of the Partido dos Trabalhadores[8] (PT) was elected. On his first day as president, Lula created the Secretaria Especial de Políticas para as Mulheres[9] (SPM), a special office dedicated to formulating and implementing policies for women. The head of that office reported directly to the president's office and had a seat in his cabinet, making her status equal to that of other ministers. This level of political participation shifted how the Brazilian government addressed gender-based violence: "During the nearly 14 years of PT government (2003–2016), Brazil moved from being a state reluctant to comply with its international obligations to one that actively developed policies on gender-based violence" (Macaulay 2021, 16) and also promoted campaigns to destigmatize and pass laws granting the LGBTQI+ community certain rights.[10]

In 2004 the Lula administration launched the first Plano Nacional de Políticas para as Mulheres (the first nationwide plan of policies for women), and two years later in 2006, the Brazilian government unanimously passed Lei n. 11.340/2006 to address domestic violence—popularly known as Lei

---

8. Workers' Party

9. Special Secretariat for Women's Policies

10. In 2004 the Lula administration launched the political campaign *Brasil Sem Homophobia* (Brazil Without Homophobia) to ensure that public policy did not discriminate against the LGBTQI+ community. In 2009 the *Superior Tribunal de Justiça* (Superior Court of Justice) ruled that gender assignment was legal, including a gender change on a birth certificate if the person has undergone sex-reassignment surgery. In 2010 the *Superior Tribunal de Justiça* gave homosexual couples the right to adopt children. In 2011 the *Supremo Tribunal Federal* (Supreme Court) redefined the concept of family. In 2013 Brazil's National Council for Justice ruled that same-sex marriage was legal nationwide (only the Federal District, the city of Santa Rita do Sapucaí, and thirteen out of the twenty-six states had allowed it until then). In 2018 the *Superior Tribunal de Justiça* ruled that a trans person has the right to change their official name and sex without the need for surgery or professional evaluation, and the *Corregedoria Nacional de Justiça* published rules to be followed by registry offices.

Maria da Penha. This law enabled the creation of a national monitoring group, the Observatório Nacional de Implementação e Aplicação da Lei Maria da Penha,[11] which was funded by the SPM and international funds and brought together activists and feminist academics working in universities around Brazil (Maciel 2011; Macaulay 2021). For example, in 2007 the SPM coordinated the Pacto Nacional de Enfrentamento á Violência contra as Mulheres (National Pact to Combat Violence), an agreement that brought together state and municipal governments to strengthen support networks for victims, improving access to justice by ensuring the proper application of Lei Maria da Penha.

In 2009 Lula's government set up the Procuradoria da Mulher, an office centered on women's advocacy at the legislative, executive, judicial, and civil society levels. This office monitored all government programs, reports on violence against women, and discrimination against nontrans women, and it cooperated with national and international organizations and legislative bodies to promote nontrans women's rights. Also, in that year the Brazilian Congress passed Lei n. 12.015/2009, which addresses sexual crimes and modifies the Criminal Code with Article 213, which defines rape as "coercing someone through violence or serious threat to have sexual intercourse or perform other lewd acts" and sets a sentence of six to thirty years in prison (Lei n.12.015/2009 Artigo 213 [2009]); "Cronologia Dos Direitos Das Mulheres" 2016). By 2010 Lula's efforts to reform nontrans women's rights mechanisms were mirrored in states and municipalities and contributed to the success of "directing sufficient attention and resources to gender-based violence and bringing together diverse public bodies" (Macaulay 2021, 18). Also in 2010, the toll-free number 180 was put into operation nationally through Decree no. 7393, which was established by the SPM in 2005 so that the Brazilian population, especially women, could receive guidance and report situations of discrimination and gender-based violence in its various forms.[12]

In an unprecedented election in 2011, Brazil elected President Dilma Rousseff, the first woman to hold the Brazilian presidency until her contentious impeachment and removal from office in 2016. Under her leadership, the Brazilian Congress passed Lei 12.845 in 2013, which

---

11. *t.* National Observatory for the Implementation and Enforcement of the Maria da Penha Law

12. In 2016 the Brazilian artist Elza Soares popularized the phrase *Ligue 180* in her song "Maria da Vilha Matilde."

mandates that survivors of sexual violence receive comprehensive care. This includes specialized psychosocial care; diagnosis and treatment of physical injuries, including those affecting the genital area; assistance with reporting the assault and referral for forensic examination; access to pregnancy and STD treatment; an HIV test; and preservation of material that could serve as legal evidence against the aggressor (under the responsibility of the doctor and the health unit). The passage of these decrees and laws and the dedicated services, such as women's police stations, domestic-violence patrols, special-investigation units, domestic-violence courts, special legal aid teams, and special prosecutors (Macaulay 2021) speaks to the level of commitment from the Brazilian state to address issues of domestic violence in the country. However, despite their determined implementation, these legislative efforts struggled against entrenched sociocultural norms, failing to transform fundamental understandings of gender, improve the treatment of trans and nontrans women, or eradicate other forms of gendered violence—revealing a profound contradiction and tension between legal progress and cultural resistance.[13]

In 2014 Dilma Rousseff took office for her second term, but the rise of far-right evangelical politicians shifted the congressional demographics and the receptive political environment that had been passing women's and LGBTQI+ rights legislation without hostilities (Brunke 2015; Jalalzai and Santos 2015; Moreira 2023). That year, the Instituto Economico de Pesquisa

---

13. The 2003 report of the UN Committee on the Elimination of Discrimination against Women emphasizes the dissemination of stereotypes against women in Brazilian culture:

> It is worth emphasizing that the issues involving stereotypes are linked to common sense and strongly disseminated in the Brazilian society. They give rise to two serious problems: 1) the marketing of the image of women as a commodity associated with products that have men as their target audience (beer, cars, etc.); 2) the reproduction in media entertainment shows (soap operas, live shows, etc.) of the same consumption patterns or the maintenance of myths related to sexual and domestic violence, prostitution, etc. The aggravating circumstance in these cases is the fact that in Brazil the means of communication are granted by the State and, therefore, subject to constitutional rules. However, they are not subjected to any regulations regarding the limits of programming. (86)

The inclusion of this in the report also suggests the need for a paradigm shift in the way Brazilian society valued women.

Aplicada[14](IPEA) published the results of a nationwide study "Tolerância social à violência contra as mulheres" in which, they claimed, 65% of the 3,810 survey participants agreed that women who wore clothing that showed off the body deserved to be raped (Castro 2014; IPEA 2014).[15] This finding enraged trans and nontrans women in Brazil. The journalist Nana Quiroz formed a Facebook group named "Não Mereço Ser Estuprada" (I don't deserve to be raped) and within three days, 35,700 people had used the hashtag #EuNãoMereçoSerEstuprada. This marked the beginning of a determined but tense fight in the public sphere, on behalf of feminists and LGBTQI+ activists and against conservative far-right groups, to counteract sexual abuse and misogyny.

Facing increased political unrest, on March 9, 2015, President Rousseff signed Lei 13.104/2015, popularly referred to as Lei do Feminicidio, which provided modifications to the Criminal Code. The proposed law followed what other Latin American countries had been legislating, classifying feminicide as an "extreme form of gender violence that results in the death of women" (De Oliveira et al. 2020, 33). However, the approved law in Brazil differed in that it defined feminicide as "a qualifier of homicide" (Perrone 2023, 152):

> Feminicide
> VI—Against women for reasons linked to the condition of the female sex:
> Paragraph 2(A)—It is considered that reasons are linked to the condition of the female sex when the crime involves:
> I—domestic and familial violence;
> II—contempt or discrimination against the condition of woman. (Lei 13.104/2015)[16]

The inclusion of the words "conditions of the female sex" was modified from "conditions of gender" because of pressures from the evangelical caucus, who were concerned with the perceived disruptions of gender categories

---

14. *t.* Economic Institute of Applied Research

15. The federal agency issued a public apology a few days later stating that they had reversed the spreadsheet columns and that the correct number was 26% (Martin 2014).

16. Feminicídio:
VI—contra a mulher por razões da condição de sexo feminino:
§ 2º -A Considera-se que há razões de condição de sexo feminino quando o crime envolve:
I—violência doméstica e familiar;
II—menosprezo ou discriminação à condição de mulher

as part of their broader anti-LGBTQI+ agenda and attacks on "gender ideology" (Cunha 2017; Fonseca et al. 2018; Machado 2018; Machado and Elias 2018; Perrone 2023). The use of this sex-based language "impacts trans and gender nonconforming population, making it so that prosecutors, judges, and others involved in the legal apparatus of the state have a more constricted ground to operate within when the victim is trans and/or gender non-conforming" (Perrone 2023, 153).

The other big difference between what the Brazilian National Congress approved and what other countries in Latin America included in their laws is a specific classification of feminicide as a crime in cases where there is sexual violence with disfiguration or mutilation. This omission "grants more independence to both police and the judicial system in determining whether a murder is a feminicide" (Perrone 2023, 153), which complicates the reach of the law when police encounter difficulty understanding what qualifies as "disdain or discrimination against the condition of woman" (De Oliveira et al. 2020, 34).

By October 2015, the level of open harassment and misogyny by Brazilian men was put in the spotlight when male-identifying Twitter users began tweeting unnerving sexual comments about a twelve-year-old contestant, Valentina, on the program *MasterChef Junior*.[17] The collective Think Olga responded with a Twitter campaign #primeiroassedio (my first harassment), which invited Brazilian women to share their experiences of when they were first sexually harassed. Five days after the first tweet, there were over eighty-two thousand tweets and retweets, which when compiled together indicated that the average age of nontrans women in Brazil when they experienced their first sexual harassment was at 9.7 years old (Levischi 2019). The hashtag was soon accompanied by two other hashtags, #meuamigosecreto (my secret friend) and #meuqueridoprofesor (my dear teacher), which called attention to those who should be "safe" people but instead took advantage of their positions and harassed women and girls.[18]

---

17. Some of these tweets include comments such as "About this Valentina: if it's consensual, is it pedophilia?"; "Let me keep quiet to not be jailed"; "If she wants it, it's not pedophilia, IT'S LOVE" (Phillips 2021; Martins 2017).

18. These Brazilian movements have reverberances and parallels to the US's #TimesUp, which started in October 2018 with denunciations of Harvey Weinstein, and later to Alyssa Milano's call to have women share their stories of harassment and/or sexual violence under the hashtag #Metoo—which trended in over 196 countries. The movement was launched by Tarana Burke in 2006 to give voice to girls and women who had experienced sexual violence and let them know they were not alone.

In 2016 Dilma Rousseff was impeached, bringing the women's policy networks to an end, and under her vice president, Michel Temer, the SPM and Conselho Nacional dos Direitos da Mulher [19](CNDM) were reabsorbed into the Ministry of Justice (Macaulay 2021). In the cultural sphere, the slow rise of the far right became more evident in public discourse with the 2018 elections. Throughout 2016, however, the hashtags #NiUnaMenos and #VivaslasQueremos, which had been trending in Argentina, also trended in Brazil under the Portuguese incarnations #NemUmaMenos (Not one woman less) and #Asqueremosvivas (We want the women alive) but did not have the same political power they had in other countries in Latin America, perhaps because Brazil already had codified feminicide into law in 2015.

Then, in March 2017, the actress Susllem Tonani, protagonist of the popular soap opera *A Lei do Amor* (The Law of Love), publicized how she had endured sexual harassment by the actor José Mayer Drumond under the blog post *Agora é que são elas* (Now It's Their Turn), a space in the national newspaper *Folha do São Paulo* created specifically to give women a journalistic venue in this mainstream publication. In her account, Tonani details how José Mayer Drumond touched her vagina publicly while the cast and studio crew laughed, and was called a cow when raising concerns. This caused a rage-filled response that consolidated under the hashtag #mexeucomumamexeucomtudas (mess with one, mess with all).[20]

In July 2017 I traveled to São Paolo, Rio de Janeiro, and Florianópolis. The last of these cities, in collaboration with the Federal University of Santa Catarina, hosted the 13th Women's Worlds congress and the 11th Doing Gender (Fazendo Genero) conference the same week. Their united theme was "Transformations, Connections, Displacements" ("13° Mundos D e Mulheres & Fazendo Gênero 11" 2017). On August 2, 2017, the same day that President Michel Temer was tried in the Chamber of Deputies for the crime of passive corruption, the women at the 13th Women's Worlds congress and the 11th Doing Gender conference organized a march. I remember arriving at the meeting point with my friends Carla Nacke

---

19. *t.* National Council on Women's Rights

20. These very public denunciations of sexual harassment and sexual violence in combination with several highly public and mediatized collective rape and hate-crime cases led to the passage of Law 13.718 in September 2018. The law modifies the Criminal Code to include crimes of sexual harassment and the sharing of rape scenes and scenes depicting sexual violence. It also makes alterations to the prosecution of crimes against sexual freedom and sexual crimes against vulnerable people, making those aggravating circumstances. It determines that practices such as collective rape or corrective rape are aggravating circumstances in sexual crimes.

Conradi, Ivonette Pereira, and Gregory Balthazar da Silva; the energy was electric as Indigenous and Black women lined up at the front to lead the march. There was a plethora of posters and banners denouncing the sexist norms that harass, control, and kill women of all races in rural and urban areas (figs. 3.1 and 3.2). There were also body outlines drawn in pink on the asphalt in different places of the march. The march made headlines

Figure 3.1. Beginning of Mundos Mulheres march in 2017, banner held by Indigenous women leaders, while one is interviewed. *Source:* Photo by the author.

Figure 3.2. End of march, banner that reads: "Against racism Black and Indigenous women at Mundos Mulheres march 2017." *Source:* Photo by the author.

as "the largest feminist march" the state of Santa Catarina had ever seen (Medeiros 2017). Marching through the streets of Florianópolis, I did take notice of onlookers jeering and shouting "*Putas*" (whores) and "*Bruxas*" (witches) at us (figs. 3.3 and 3.4). The tension in the air was palpable, yet so was the determination of those around me to scream louder than those verbally attacking us, and to keep marching together until we had all completed the route.

The tension in the public between feminists and human rights advocates and the far right continued to heighten throughout 2017, especially as Jair Bolsonaro, an authoritarian ex–military officer, garnered widespread public support and became the front-runner for the Brazilian presidential elections by openly using crude, misogynistic, homophobic, and transphobic language. By 2018 Brazil was in a moment of extreme tension as it seemed that the legislative gains for women and LGBTQI+ populations would be dismantled. This was especially the case as Bolsonaro, his party's representatives, and his followers (many of them neo-Pentecostals) launched

Figure 3.3. A Black woman playing a drum as part of the drum line that marched behind Indigenous women at the Mundos Mulheres march in 2017. *Source:* Photo by the author.

Figure 3.4. Signs from the Mundo Mulheres march; an in-focus sign reads: "We are the granddaughters of the witches you weren't able to kill" #mexeucomuma-mexeucomtodas. *Source:* Photo by the author.

consistent rhetorical attacks on what they called "gender ideology," creating a moral panic (Biroli and Caminotti 2020) toward LGBTQI+ populations that resulted in an increased public display of verbal violence and physical crimes of misogyny, homophobia, and transphobia (Da Silva et al. 2023).[21]

Luto é Luta: "Transforming our pain, our mourning, into struggle"

With the rise of the far right in Brazil after the 2014 election, politicians who advocated for human rights, feminism, LGBTQI+ rights, and antiracism

---

21. Since 2007 the term *gender ideology* has operated as a potent rhetorical construct throughout Latin America, which Bolsonaro (and now in the United States under the second Trump administration) strategically deployed to mobilize conservative opposition to gender expansiveness—any identity outside the traditional men–women binary, particularly trans and nonbinary identities. Unlike critiques centered on feminism or patriarchy (both arguably ideological frameworks historically rooted in gender binaries), Bolsonaro's invocation of "gender ideology" deliberately reframed gender diversity not as a lived reality but as a dangerous, foreign "ideology" requiring active resistance—a framing that resonated with his base and legitimized policies restricting women's and LGBTQI+ rights.

were often met with increased resistance and discrediting mediatic campaigns. Marielle Franco, a bisexual Afro-Brazilian woman raised in the favela Maré and a member of the Partido Socialismo e Liberdade[22] (PSOL), was elected to serve in Rio de Janeiro's city council in 2016 with the fifth highest vote of all the fifty-one council members.[23] Her election marked a powerful moment of political representation for marginalized communities, particularly Black, LGBTQI+, and favela residents. Notably, her rise to office also coincided with President Temer's increased investment in militarized policing in Rio de Janeiro, which disproportionally targeted the very communities Franco was elected to represent. This juxtaposition underscored the growing tension between state-led securitization and emergent forms of political representation. She served in this position for a year and a half, consistently and very vocally advocating for Black, queer, and poor populations, abortion rights, and criticizing increased police violence and militia presence in the favelas of Rio de Janeiro (Medeiros and Flores 2021; Loureiro 2020; Hutta 2022; de Carvalho 2024). Specifically, "Marielle Franco presided over the Commission for the Defense of Women in the Rio de Janeiro chamber and brought the issue to legislative debates" (De Mattos Rocha 2019). She often faced challenges in getting laws she proposed approved; in fact, only seven out of the sixteen bills she proposed while serving as councilor were approved (De Mattos Rocha 2019).[24] Her tenure as a city-council member was truncated on the evening of March 14, 2018, when she was shot three

---

22. *t.* Socialism and Freedom Party

23. PSOL's (or the Socialist and Liberty Party) platform embraces socialism, anticapitalism, and anti-imperialist elements.

24. Five of these were approved after her death. The bills that were approved include:

> the regulation of the work of "motorcycle taxi drivers," very common in favelas; fiscal instruments ensuring the control of contracts made by the mayor's office; night-time nurseries for children of families that work or study during the night; the creation of the Day of the Black Woman and Tereza Benguela on the 25th of July; a campaign against the violence and harassment of women, particularly in schools; the Dossier Women's report that contained official information on violence against women; and a program centered on social reintegration of young people in conflict with the law. Voted on, although not approved, was a bill that would create a technical assistance department for housing construction in favelas and another for the creation of a Day against Homophobia, Biphobia and Transphobia. (De Mattos Rocha 2019)

times in the head and once in the neck.[25] Marielle was thirty-eight years old. Her driver Anderson Gomes was also fatally shot, but her assistant, Fernanda Chaves, survived.

Within hours after her murder, "Marielle" became a trending topic on Twitter worldwide with over 289,000 tweets (Conteúdo 2018). Most tweets had one question—"Quem mandou matar Marielle?" (Who ordered Marielle's killing?). All the following hashtags began or ended the tweets: #MariellePresente (Marielle is present), #Nãofoiassalto (It wasn't a robbery), #MarielleVive (Marielle lives).[26] The tweets also shared information about sites to gather and publicly mourn Marielle in major cities throughout Brazil. In Rio de Janeiro, thousands gathered on Thursday, March 15, one day after her assassination, outside the city's council chamber, transforming the site of her political work into a space of collective, embodied grief and resistance. In its coverage of the immediate public response, *The Guardian* reported that "the spontaneous demonstration brought together union members, feminists, leftists and residents of the city's poorer communities" (Phillips 2018). The report also referred to one of Marielle's tweets in which she called attention to police violence and also included statements from people at the demonstration who believed her assassination was politically motivated. It quoted former President Dilma Rousseff, who condemned the killing as a national tragedy: "Sad day for a country where a human rights defender is brutally murdered" (Phillips 2018). Streets were plastered with graffiti of her name, her face, quotes attributed to her such as "I am because we are," signs stating "Stop killing us" and "End to military police," and the question "Who ordered Marielle's killing?" (Reuters 2018).[27] Images of her face and poetry created by Brazilian women writers also permeated virtual spaces (fig. 3.5). Within thirteen days of her death, the magazine *Vida Secreta* published an anthology of twenty-two poems, illustrations, and

---

25. Earlier that evening Marielle had taken part in the event "Young Black Women Moving the Structures" at Casa das Pretas (Black Women's House) in the Lapa neighborhood. Marielle is seen in photographs from the event with Aline Lourena, coordinator of the activist collective AzPretaz, writer Ana Paula Lisboa from Black and Indigenous Women in Communication and Technology, rapper Hellen N'Zinga, and publicist Moara Valley. Throughout the event, they had a conversation about the participation of Black women in politics, ancestral knowledges, and life (Mesquita 2018).

26. Similarly to Mexico, Argentina, Colombia, and other parts of Latin America, the use of Marielle's name is a postmortem political strategy to keep her alive in public discourse.

27. Pictures from these demonstrations from across Brazil can be found at: https://www.reuters.com/news/picture/idUSRTS1NZP6/.

notes about Marielle's work called *Marielle, Presente!* (Marielle is present).[28] Writers in the anthology, such as Viviane Freitas, asserted that mourning Marielle was also an invitation to fight:

> porque a voz é coletiva
> voz de um, de todos, de
> mil
> voz do pobre, do negro, do brasil
> voz da mulher, da criança, do oprimido
> voz da igualdade
> e da disputa
> voz que se levanta e vai à luta (De Freitas 2018, 19)[29]

Freitas's poem embodies Marielle's voice calling on people to keep her voice from being silenced by confronting the Brazilian state (Marques and Da Silva 2024). The anthology *Marielle, Presente!* embodied the spirit of "Luto é Luta" (Mourning is fighting),[30] reminding Brazilians of their interconnectedness and calling on them to confront the Brazilian state.

These protests and online posts were also produced as a way to counter the spread of disinformation and misinformation about Marielle on WhatsApp, Twitter, and Facebook by right-wing politicians and their supporters that devalued her life by connecting her to organized crime, calling her a *cadaver comum* (common corpse) and exculpating police involvement by implying that she had been murdered because of her wrongdoings with members of organized crime (Bergamo 2018; Medeiros and Flores 2022). The emphatic campaign to discredit Marielle's life and work was because she "became a symbol of what is perceived in contemporary Brazilian culture as leftist values and causes, such as human rights, feminism, and anti-racism. The political scenario turned her into a metonymy of the left itself. When she died, in March 2018, Franco became the part for the whole. To attack her image was, therefore, to attack the left itself" (Medeiros and Flores 2022, 191).

---

28. A copy of the book can be found at: https://archive.org/details/marielle2cpresente21antologia/Marielle2C-presente21-Antologia.

29. *t.* because the voice is collective / voice of one, of all, of thousands / voice of the poor, of black people, of Brazil / voice of women, children, the oppressed / voice of equality and the dispute / voice that rises and goes to fight

30. *t. To mourn is to fight.* This is a phrase Marielle's family, friends, and activists can be heard saying in interviews, as well as in speeches in protests.

Figure 3.5. Restored staircase (after vandalism) in 2023, while visiting São Paulo on May 17, 2023. *Source:* Photo by the author.

The attacks on the left through postmortem attacks on Marielle's life and memory became inextricable from devaluing the lives of trans and nontrans women, specifically Black women, thus openly and unabashedly rematerializing the historical, racial, and gendered violence toward black women's bodies in Brazil (Gonzales 1984; Carneiro and Camargo 2016). This violence is reflected in the Anuário Brasileiro De Segurança Pública reports issued by the Fórum Brasileiro de Segurança Pública (Brazilian Public Security Forum). According to the 2023 report, Brazil recorded 1,463 feminicides in 2022, an increase of 1.6% from 2021. The 2024 report recorded 1,467 feminicides in 2023, marking the highest number since the passing of the 2015 Lei do Femnicidio. Notably, 63.6% of these victims in 2023 were Black women, up from 61.1% reported in 2022 (Fórum Brasileiro de Segurança Pública 2023, 142; 2024, 141).

Similarly, ANTRA in 2023 reported that of the 145 trans murders, 72% were of Black trans women. ANTRA made the comparison that between 2017 and 2023, the average of murdered Black trans women was 78.7% compared to 21.1% of white trans women (Benevides 2023).[31]

---

31. ANTRA's report is purposefully intersectional and also takes note of the one Indigenous trans woman who was murdered, thus highlighting the colonial legacy of

Marielle's family, friends, activists, and supporters in their postmortem politics became a unifying force to bring dignity to her life and resist attacks by the political class trying to exonerate themselves of their involvement. For example, in September 2018 the largest protest led by women in Brazil, throughout 114 cities, was unified by the hashtag #elenao (not him) denouncing then-candidate Jair Bolsonaro. Thousands of tweets and protest signs alluded to Marielle's feminicide by referencing the question "Who ordered Marielle's killing?" (BBC News Brasil 2018; G1 2018). Public mourning for Marielle continued throughout the year and garnered international attention as the campaign Justice for Marielle grew. By June 2018, the general belief was that she was executed by a paramilitary militia for denouncing police involvement in the deaths of young Black men. In 2019 De Mattos Rocha wrote on *openDemocracy*: "Everything indicates that Marielle was executed in order to silence her and bring to a halt her struggle in defense of the rights of favela inhabitants, women, black people, and the LGBT+ community; that is, of the exploited and debased working class." Her speculation echoed a widely shared suspicion among progressive activists and human rights groups, particularly those critical of right-wing narratives surrounding her death, especially after it was discovered that the ammunition used to kill Marielle and Anderson had a connection to the Federal Police in Brasilia (from a quantity sold to the Federal Police in Brasília in 2006) and had been used in a prior massacre in São Paulo in 2015 (G1 2018).

In 2020 Marielle's family founded the Instituto Marielle Franco (Marielle Franco Institute), a nonprofit that "was born to fight for justice, defend her memory, spread the legacy and water Marielle's seeds."[32] This institute has been instrumental in holding the Brazilian state accountable for Marielle's death. For example, their website has a counter indicating the time that they have spent waiting for answers about her murder. The institute also serves as a site of counterhegemonic discourse, especially during Bolsonaro's tenure as president. In October 2020 at the height of the COVID-19 pandemic, Marielle's sister, Anielle Franco, did a TEDx talk called *Do luto a luta: o legado de Marielle Franco* (From mourning to fighting: Marielle

---

violence toward Black and Indigenous bodies that continue to be abused in Brazil. At the same time, it offers a broader, interconnected analysis that reveals how trans people of all races and ethnicities continue to be targets of violence and murder.

32. The naming of the institute after Marielle is similar to the postmortem strategy of the Argentinian Observatorio de Femicidios en Argentina "Adriana Marisel Zambrano."

Franco's legacy).[33] There, Anielle discusses Marielle's fight for a more equal society where the voices of Black women are not silenced, and she refers to this society as the seeds of the legacy left by Marielle Franco that are being watered. The video posted on YouTube had over 1,013 views within days of its release on November 6, 2020.

Media-studies scholar Raiana de Carvalho (2024), based on a critical rhetorical analysis of the Marielle Franco Institute's YouTube videos and Instagram posts, argues that Marielle's online presence or "haunting" served as a "counter-hegemonic agent of memory in Brazil" (2). In her analysis of the widely used and circulated "Quem mandou matar Marielle?," Carvalho explains that it is "also a question about Brazil's haunting past: evoking the memory of Marielle also evokes ghostly memories . . . of racial, gender, and class violence that continue to inform Brazil's social relations" (3). During the four years of Bolsonaro's tenure (2019–2022), Marielle's memory and the postmortem politics of her family and supporters haunted his administration by demanding justice for her assassination with yearly protests commemorating her death, and filling public discourse with demands to know who killed her. For example, journalist Eliane Brum was one of many who consecutively tweeted since Marielle's death:

Eliane Brum
@brumelianebrum·Mar 24
  2.202 dias. 6 anos+ Quem mandou matar Marielle? E por quê?[34]

These strategies are examples of postmortem politics that shaped the counternarratives surrounding Marielle's death. The pressure on Bolsonaro's administration was constant. In 2019 there were persistent stories in the national and international press that linked President Bolsonaro to her murder (McCoy et al. 2019). This haunting is how Marielle continues to speak to the living and inform postmortem politics of those actively carrying on her agenda.

In 2023, after Lula was reelected, the new minister of justice and public security, Flávio Dino, committed to solving her murder, which five years after her death had remained unresolved. He told Marielle's mother and her sister, Anielle, whom Lula named head of the Ministry of Racial

---

33. The TEDx talk can be seen at: https://www.youtube.com/watch?v=ilNz9y6S7_Y.

34. *t.* 2,202 days. 6 years+ Who ordered Marielle's murder? And why?

Equity, that it was "uma questão de honra do Estado brasileiro empreender todos os esforços possíveis e cabíveis, e a Polícia Federal assim atuará, para que esse crime seja desvendado definitivamente e nós saibamos quem matou Marielle e quem mandou matar Marielle Franco naquele dia no Rio de Janeiro" (Barifouse 2023).[35] The commitment to solve Marielle's internationally renowned feminicide could also be understood as a way to comply with recommendations from the Inter-American Court of Human Rights two years earlier in 2021, which found the Brazilian state responsible for abusing parliamentary power in the case of the feminicide *Barbosa de Souza et al. v. Brazil.* In 1998, the same year Maria da Penha took her case to the Inter-American Commission on Human Rights, Márcia Barbosa de Souza was killed by asphyxiation. She was a twenty-year-old Black student from the state of Paraíba who had moved to the city of João Pessoa. On June 17, 1998, she went out on a date with Congressman Aércio Pereira and used his cell phone to make a couple of calls to her friends, who reported that she sounded distressed throughout the calls. The next day, a witness on the outskirts of João Pessoa saw her body being dumped from the congressman's car in a vacant lot. While investigations of her murder pointed to the congressman, his position granted him parliamentary immunity and the Legislative Assembly of the State of Paraíba did not grant permission to prosecute him for over five years. By the time they had authorized the process of a criminal inquiry, he was dead. On July 11, 2019, the case was taken to the Inter-American Court of Human Rights to address the defective procedural tactics of the case hearing in Brazil. It was noteworthy because the court addresses the power of government officials from the standpoint of legal accountability (both are relevant in Marielle's case), and it shed light on the Brazilian government's handling of feminicide.

On September 7, 2021, the Inter-American Court of Human Rights issued its judgment, drawing from previous feminicide cases including *González et al. ("Cotton Field") v. Mexico* and *Vicky Hernández et al. v. Honduras.*[36] The ruling was historic (CEJIL 2021). It held the Brazilian state

---

35. *t.* a matter of honor for the Brazilian state to make all possible and appropriate efforts, and the Federal Police will do so, so that this crime is definitively unraveled and so that we know who killed Marielle and who ordered Marielle Franco's death that day in Rio de Janeiro

36. From *González et al. ("Cotton Field") v. Mexico,* this judgment references the preliminary objection, merits, reparations, and costs of the judgment on November 16, 2009. Series C No. 205, para. 258. Then, from the case *Vicky Hernández et al. v. Honduras,* it references the merits, reparations, and costs of the judgment on March 26, 2021. Series C No. 422, para. 134.

responsible for the improper use of parliamentary immunity and recognized that "women in Brazil, especially Afrodescendant and poor women, continue to be immersed in a context of discrimination and structural violence" (Inter-American Court of Human Rights 2021, 52). The ruling made recommendations for the creation of a centralized system for the collection of data disaggregated by demographics to allow for quantitative and qualitative analysis of data specific to feminicide, training to give a gendered perspective to crimes against women, and indemnification for Maria's family of $150,000 (Inter-American Court of Human Rights 2021, 57). *Barbosa de Souza et al v. Brazil* has implications for how Marielle's case is handled on the national stage with special attention to whether and how Brazil implements the recommendations of the Inter-American Court of Human Rights within the given time frames for each recommendation (showcasing that affective dialectic between determination and tension), especially given that the court stated it "will consider this case closed when the State has fully complied with all its provisions" (Inter-American Court of Human Rights 2021, 60–61).

Whereas the Bolsonaro administration broadly ignored the recommendations and judgment issued by the Inter-American Court of Human Rights, cutting the budget for fighting violence against women by 90% from $19 million in 2020 to $1.7 million in 2021 (Resende 2022), under Lula, in March 2024, the reinstated Ministry of Women launched the National Pact to Prevent Feminicides Action Plan with a planned budget of about $5.2 billion. The plan was developed based on two axes: "structuring" and "transversal." The "structuring" framework comprises three forms of preventing violence against women: primary, secondary, and tertiary. The "transversal" is divided into data production, knowledge, and documents/norms (Ministério das Mulheres 2024). The ministry also launched a social media and educational campaign with the hashtag #Brasilporelas (Brazil with women) to confront misogyny and promote equality in Brazilian culture.

On March 24, 2024, Brazil's Federal Police arrested three men allegedly responsible for Marielle's assassination. A news headline described the case as a "nexus of politicians, police and paramilitaries" (Phillips 2024), accusing Rio's former Chief of Police Rivaldo Barbosa and prominent brothers and politicians, Chiquinho and Domingos Brazão, of authoring the crime. By October 31, 2024, two former police officers, Ronnie Lessa (who confessed to shooting Marielle) and Élcio de Queiroz (who confessed to being the driver), were convicted of having killed Marielle, giving a response to the question "Quem mandou matar Marielle?" (G1 2024; Nicas and Milhorance 2024). As of May 2025, the Brazilian Attorney General's Office had submitted final arguments to the Supreme Federal Court requesting the most severe form of incarceration allowed under Brazilian law for brothers Domingos and Chiquinho Brazão, former Chief of Police Rivaldo Barbosa, Military Police officer Ronald Paulo de Alves, and former Military Police officer Robson Calixto for their alleged roles in planning and facilitating Marielle's murder ("Fiscalía Solicita Condena De Acusados Por Asesinar a Marielle Franco" 2025). However, as the process unfolds it will undoubtedly expose more problematic procedural tactics of case hearings, as well as bring into question how the Brazilian state under Bolsonaro will be held accountable for the insolence and impunity involved in Marielle's assassination. Marielle's family may take her case to the Inter-American Court of Human Rights, but for now, what seems to be keeping the Brazilian state accountable (in addition to their obligations to the Inter-American Court of Human Rights) is that Marielle lives on in the postmortem politics of Luto é Luta.

The Potentiality of Transmortem Politics

The website Remembering Our Dead provides details of trans people who have been killed. It collates reports, based on data from publicly available sources, by trans activists and the Trans Murder Monitoring Project. According to the site, between January 1, 2024, and December 31, 2024, there were ninety-seven reports of trans women who were killed in Brazil (Remembering Our Dead, n.d.); they exist because they are named.[37] In Brazil, ANTRA has been an active advocate of trans rights since 1995.[38] In 1993 the organization Associação de Travestis and Liberaos[39] (ASTRAL) organized the first national meeting of Encontro Nacional de Travestis e Liberados que Atuam na Prevenção do AIDS[40] (ENTLAID) in light of the AIDS crisis in Brazil, a growing wave of violence against trans people, and a

---

37. See appendix, table 4: "2024 Deaths of Trans Women in Brazil" to honor the ninety-seven lives and learn where they were from, their age, and cause of death.

38. The name from 1993 to 2000 was Rede Nacional de Travestis e Liberados—RENTRAL (Network of Transvestites and Liberated People); it changed in 2000 to Articulação Nacional de Transgêneros (National Transgender Alliance), and in 2002 to Associação Nacional de Travestis e Transexuais (National Association of Transvestites and Transexuals) to better articulate the identities and goals of the organization.

39. *t.* Association of Transvestites and Liberated Persons

40. *t.* National Meeting of Transvestites and Liberated People Working to Prevent AIDS

decrease in access to health services (Kulick 1998; Benevides 2024; Tenaglia and De Oliveira 2025). By the third ENTLAID meeting, the participants realized they needed to create a national network to address trans issues across Brazil. According to Jovanna Cadoso, a leader in the organization, their agenda was to "organizar um sindicato nacional de travestis, mas sei que a palavra 'sindicato' poderia não ser adequada. Cheira a governo. Talvez 'rede' seja uma palavra melhor. O que estamos pedindo é que sejamos respeitadas" ("História" 2018).[41]

Since then, ANTRA's main work has consisted of producing reports and demanding solutions to the murders of trans people in Brazil, underscoring their determination to achieve recognition for transgender rights. They also promote education and present proposals to guarantee the rights for *trasvestis* and *transexuais* in Brazil; collaborate with other human rights organizations to develop joint platforms; report on all cases where prejudice or discrimination, or both, based on gender identity is detected; support all efforts to prevent HIV/AIDS, viral hepatitis, and other STDs; engage directly in political advocacy and in pushing for favorable policy; and continue organizing annual meetings to "potencializar as bandeiras de lutas e encaminhar as demandas de suas afiliadas" ("História" 2018).[42] Throughout its twenty-nine years of advocacy, ANTRA has generally embraced the ethos *Resistir pra Existir* (Resist to Exist) and has worked in coalition with over 127 institutions including the Coletivo Nacional de Transexuais (CNT),[43] Fórum Nacional de Travestis e Transexuais Negras e Negros (FONATRANS),[44] Casa1 (House 1), LGBT Institute, the Brazilian Lesbian, Gay, Bisexual, "Travesti," Transgender, and Intersex Association (ABGLT),[45] Support for AIDS Prevention of Bahia (GAPA-BA), Instituto Mais Diversidade,[46] and

---

41. *t.* organize a national transvestite union, but I know that the word "union" might not be appropriate. It smells like government. Maybe "network" is a better word. What we are asking is that we be respected.

42. *t.* to further strengthen the fight against hardships faced by the trans community and disseminate the demands.

43. *t.* National Transexual Collective

44. *t.* National Forum of Black Transvestites and Transexuals

45. *t.* The Brazilian Lesbian, Gay, Bisexual, Transvestite, Transgender, and Intersex Association

46. *t.* More Diversity Institute

Somos (We Are).[47] In 2004, when Black trans women Fernanda Benvenutty and Keyla Sympson served on the National Health Council (SUS), they launched the campaign "Travesti e Respeito" (Trans and Respect) (Brasil de Fato 2022) funded by the Ministry of Health, which also established January 29 as Trans Visibility Day in Brazil (Carvalho and Carrara 2013, 2015; Coacci 2014; De Souza Nascimento and Brito 2022)).

In 2013 Jair Bolsonaro proclaimed, "Yes, I am homophobic—and very proud of it" (Sullivan 2018). In his years as a congressman, he made that very clear by giving speeches about his hatred toward the LGBTQI+ community. His influence on the far right became notable after 2014, when lawmakers who were more conservative were elected to Congress and promulgated an antitrans platform making verbal and physical violence toward trans people increasingly visible and politically legitimized. In 2018, after the Superior Tribunal de Justiça ruled that trans people have the right to change their official name and sex without the need for surgery or professional evaluation, the far right concentrated on spreading misinformation and moral panic about trans people, framing the community in opposition to "Brazilian values" (Pedro et al. 2022; Marques and Da Silva 2024). Bolsonaro's commitment to fight "gender ideology" emerged more clearly in his hate-filled speeches toward the LGBTQI+ community as his presidential candidacy made him more visible.[48] His supporters justified violence toward trans populations in his name. For example, they would scream at trans bodies, "You are all going to die now" (Sullivan 2018) and there were three cases where trans women, Pricila, Laysa Fortuna, and

---

47. These are just a few organizations, but there are many more. These can be found on the ANTRA'S website; the website Portal de Impacto; or on MOPS, an open-access portal of services, public facilities, and social programs (Map of Community Networks and Services for LGBTQI+ Refugees and Migrants).

48. In the United States, the Trump administration has adopted parallel strategies, such as restricting the recognition of gender identity in federal programs, redefining "sex" under Title IX to refer strictly to biological sex assigned at birth, and limiting access to gender-affirming care. These executive actions mirror Bolsonaro's approach by casting protections for transgender and nonbinary people as extreme ideological impositions rather than civil rights, thus mobilizing conservative fears and reinforcing a binary, biologically determined concept of gender at the policy level. Both leaders leveraged the "gender ideology" narrative to frame gender diversity as a threat to national values and women, while endorsing legislation that actively threatens women's lives by dismantling reproductive care and endangering women, justifying regulatory rollbacks, and emboldening broader anti-LGBTQI+ movements.

Kharoline, were stabbed to death while the perpetrators shouted, "Bolsonaro presidente" (Sudré 2018). In all three cases the murderers were either set free for lack of evidence or were on the run, pointing to shortcomings in police investigations and in the criminal justice process. Keila Simpson, president of ANTRA, responded to these attacks by tracing Bolsonaro's history of hatred toward trans populations. She explained, "Essas pessoas que estão violentando, matando, esfaqueando, machucando as pessoas, estão alimentados por esse discurso que o candidato tem e teve durante toda sua carreira política de 27 anos sem fazer absolutamente nenhum projeto interessante. Isso resulta exatamente na naturalização da violência que vemos no Brasil polarizado" (Sullivan 2018).[49] Simpson thus articulated how vulnerable trans populations are, especially considering that no laws guarantee trans people's rights to hold people who commit or incite violence against them accountable.

In 2018 ANTRA issued its first report, "Assassinatos e da violência contra pessoas Trans em 2017,"[50] calling attention to the human rights violations of transvestites and transsexual women in Brazil (a total of 179 murders with only 10% of the cases resulting in arrests of the suspects). The report also detailed how 94% of the 179 murders (169 cases) were of trans women, 70% were of sex workers, and 80% of the victims were identified as Black. These statistics underscored the importance of either including these crimes as part of Lei do Feminicídio or passing a separate law that would criminalize the systematic killing of trans people. Bento argues for classifying transfeminicide as a crime because:

> O assassinato é motivado pelo gênero e não pela sexualidade da vítima. Conforme sabemos, as práticas sexuais estão invisibilizadas, ocorrem na intimidade, na alcova. O gênero, contudo, não existe sem o reconhecimento social. Não basta eu dizer "eu sou mulher," é necessário que o outro reconheça este meu desejo de reconhecimento como legítimo. O transfeminicídio seria a expressão mais potente e trágica do caráter político das identidades de gênero. A pessoa é assassinada porque além de

---

49. *t.* These people who are raping, killing, stabbing, and hurting people are fed by this discourse that the candidate has and has had throughout his 27-year political career without doing any interesting projects. This results exactly in the naturalization of violence that we see in polarized Brazil.

50. *t.* Murders and Violence Against Trans People in 2017

> romper com os destinos naturais do seu corpo-generificado, faz
> isso publicamente. (Bento 2014)[51]

ANTRA used Bento's scholarship in their report to frame the problem with the sex-based definition of feminicide in the Lei do Feminicido and to present trans people's existence as a matter of human rights worthy of including transfeminicide as part of Brazil's Criminal Code.

In its recommendations at the end of this report, ANTRA suggests that those involved in formulating public policy commit themselves to changing their behavior toward trans populations so that they can guarantee their human rights. ANTRA saw that defining transgender rights as human rights offered a strategic, political pathway forward. With the support of the broader LGBTQI+ community, they worked to establish public policies that would address transphobia through the Ministries of Education, Health, and Public Safety (Associação Nacional de Travestis e Transexuais 2018, 113). Since 2018 ANTRA has released seven yearly reports each January 29, Brazil's Day of Trans Visibility. Although the reports vary by year, ANTRA works methodologically with publicly accessible information and stories covered in the press. Their researchers' teams include researchers and experts from various disciplines in Brazilian and international institutions.

In 2019 the news portal *LGBTQI+ Athos* produced and released a video as part of a trans-awareness campaign. The production company FAUNA implemented a transinclusive methodology to design the campaign and invited producer and screenwriter Luh Maza, one of Brazil's main trans screenwriters, and the scholar Uni Corrêa to develop a story specific to the trans experience and its nuances in Brazil. The resulting video *Forever Young* (Athos 2019) tells the story of Guto and Onika, a real-life trans couple, with the song "Forever Young," interpreted by the Black trans artist Liniker and performed by the band Alphaville. The video features statistics from ANTRA's 2019 report and underscores the data point that the life expectancy of a trans person in Brazil is thirty-five. In an interview with *Marie Claire* (2019), Luh Maza explains:

---

51. *t.* Murder is motivated by the victim's gender and not their sexuality. As we know, sexual practices are invisible, they occur in private, in the bedroom. Gender, however, does not exist without social recognition. It is not enough for me to say "I am a woman," it is necessary for the other person to recognize my desire for recognition as legitimate. Transfeminicide would be the most powerful and tragic expression of the political character of gender identities. The person is murdered because, in addition to breaking with the natural destinies of their gendered body, they do so publicly.

Esta música um hino popular, acessa a memória afetiva de muitas pessoas, e resignificamos seus versos para transmitir esse dado tão alarmante que é a mortalidade jovem das pessoas trans no Brasil. Curiosamente a música completa 35 anos em 2019—e segue viva, assim como esperamos seguir vivos enquanto trans para muito além da estatística. A escolha da Liniker para gravar a música era inevitável, não existia voz melhor para essa campanha que uma das maiores cantoras da atualidade que sente todo impacto de ser trans e negra no Brasil. A interpretação soul dela mistura amor e protesto, o que sintetiza perfeitamente nossa mensagem. (Redação Marie Claire 2019)[52]

Forever Young (Athos 2019) has over fifty thousand views on Luh Maza's YouTube account and over six hundred views on Vimeo. While these numbers may not be so significant in a saturated media ecosphere, they do point to viewer engagement with the video. The incorporation of ANTRA's work in media that center trans lives in Brazil not only reflects the importance and reach of their research but also emphasizes how their work fosters content creators' and production companies' emergent awareness of trans lives and their representation.

Through these reports, its social media presence on Twitter, Instagram, and Facebook, and its public campaigns, ANTRA informs the potentiality of transmortem politics. Since its very first report, ANTRA has centered on trans lives and deaths by specifically dedicating the reports to:

àquelas que deram suas vidas por um mundo melhor e tantas outras pessoas que seguem na luta contra as violações e a violência, uma velha conhecida, sempre presente nas vidas de todas as Travestis, Mulheres Transexuais, Homens Trans e demais pessoas Trans no Brasil. Aos amigos e parceiros que sempre estiveram do nosso lado, apoiando e incentivando a seguir em frente. Especialmente a todos que aceitaram o convite para contribuir com

---

52. *t.* This song, a popular anthem, accesses the emotional memory of many people, and we reframe its verses to convey this alarming fact, which is the young mortality of trans people in Brazil. Interestingly, the song turns 35 years old in 2019—and is still alive, just as we hope to live on as trans people far beyond statistics. Choosing Liniker to record the song was inevitable, there was no better voice for this campaign than one of today's greatest singers who feels the full impact of being trans and Black in Brazil. Her soulful interpretation mixes love and protest, which perfectly summarizes our message.

> este relatório. Que essas mortes não sejam ignoradas, preteridas
> ou que as histórias dessas moças e rapazes não sejam esquecidas.
> Que a indignação nos motive a seguir em frente. E que nossa voz
> nunca seja silenciada. É nosso dever gritar por elas, por eles, por
> nós! (Associação Nacional de Travestis e Transexuais 2018, 4)[53]

By explicitly dedicating the report to the victims of violence in the form of transfeminicide and transphobia, ANTRA aimed to impart dignity to the stories of the deaths of trans people by keeping their memory alive.[54]

The reports also present some cases of trans deaths between 2007 and 2023 that best illustrate the issues described in ANTRA's report. Every year these stories are different, but they broadly draw attention to the intersectional and antiracist nature of the trans struggle in Brazil, and what ANTRA calls *patrulha de cisgeneridade* (the cisgender patrol/gender police) and their attacks on *trasgenderidad* (transgenderism). The reports recognize that violence toward the trans community has been on the rise since 2000 even throughout the tenure of Partido dos Trabalhadores (PT). Gaining certain rights without laws that guarantee trans people's right to a life free of violence has resulted in social backlash in the form of transphobia and transfeminicide.

Furthermore, in its last four reports (2021–2024) ANTRA has stressed two paradoxical trends in Brazil affecting trans communities: an increase in consumption of trans bodies in porn and an increase in transexclusionary feminism. The reports document a paradox and to some degree, tension: While far-right hate speech and antitransgender policies have intensified violence against trans people in Brazil, there has been a simultaneous exponential increase in the consumption of the searches for trans bodies on websites such as PornHub and RedTube, enabled by the perceived anonymity these platforms provide (Benevides 2024, 112; Benevides 2023a; Nacimento and Brito 2022). This trend makes evident another contradiction in Brazilian culture: living between desire and hatred

---

53. *t.* to those who gave their lives for a better world and so many other people who continue in the fight against rape and violence, to that old acquaintance, always present in the lives of all transvestites, transsexual women, trans men, and other trans people in Brazil. To friends and partners who have always been by our side, supporting and encouraging us to move forward. Especially to everyone who accepted the invitation to contribute to this report. May these deaths not be ignored, overlooked, or the stories of these girls and boys forgotten. May indignation motivate us to move forward. And may our voices never be silenced. It is our duty to shout for them, for them, for us!

54. The video can be seen at: https://www.youtube.com/watch?v=5KHta5xSdys.

toward the trans community. Similarly, the reports also point to another contradiction—the coalition between transexclusionary radical feminists (TERFs), the far right, and religious-fundamentalist groups—especially given that they differ on the issue of abortion but seem united in their conviction that they are protecting women and insistence on understanding womanhood as a "natural" sex-based occurrence. It is this alliance that makes TERF participation in spreading trans panic especially concerning, because they contribute feminist and human-rights-based language to disinformation campaigns embraced by the religious fundamentalists and antitrans groups invested in the "protection of women," which in turn dehumanize, ridicule, and deny trans people access to spaces and rights, contributing to their criminalization.

In its 2023 and 2024 reports, ANTRA also details the political gains in representation and legislative efforts for trans people in Brazil.[55] Specifically, these reports highlight the work of Erika Santos Silva and Duda Salabert to legislate the elimination of the harmful and unscientific practice of conversion therapies by referencing Brazil's commitments to international rights agreements and citing other countries that have banned them (Benevides 2024, 105). ANTRA's 2024 report documents the political, gender-based, and transphobic violence experienced by both Erika and Duda from fundamentalist groups within the Câmara Federal (Chamber of Deputies) (Benevides 2024, 22).

ANTRA's work, partnerships, website, social media content, campaigns, and reports are transurority in praxis and part of a political project. They are transmortem politics that not only document trans lives but also bring dignity to those whose deaths leave a genealogy of experiences of violence, conferring political potential on their lives. Moreover, ANTRA's transmortem politics invite people to use their affective responses (their indignation, their pain, their mourning, their rage) toward political action. ANTRA's work highlights the determination and tension that can lead people to embody their resistance and make it political by engaging in the public sphere, thus harnessing the potential of transmortem politics or, as their philosophy states: "Resistir pra existir, existir pra reagir."[56]

---

55. In 2020 Erika Santos Silva was elected councilor in the Municipal Chamber of São Paulo (affiliated with PSOL), becoming the first openly transgender councilor in Brazil. In 2022 Erika and Duda Salabert became the first openly trans people elected to the National Congress of Brazil. Similarly, Linda Brasil made history for being the first trans woman in the Chamber of Aracaju, Sergipe, and the most-voted-for parliamentarian in the city.

56. *t.* Resist to exist, exist to react

Chapter 4

Indignation and Persistence

Lessons from Indigenous Activism in Canada and the United States

The Indigenous paradigm of Respect, Reciprocity, Responsibility, and Relationship to others, and to the Earth—and for others and for the Earth—encompasses more than maintaining the integrity of our own lives, it includes the air, plants, water, and animals as much as our ancestors and those yet to be born. This framework for assuring a restored world in which all life is nurtured, flourishes and participates in its respective place within the cycle, lays an unwavering foundation for sustainable livelihoods and balanced world order and is a harmony based, holistic paradigm. It is completely distinct from Western or mainstream/settler thought. In its very collectivist nature—it is relationship-based, it's about sharing and achieving balance, it differs significantly from the individual-oriented, acquisition-based, oppositional nature of Euro-centric thinking and being. A paradigm of taking.

—Tia Oros Peters[1]

---

1. Tia Oros Peters (Zuni) is chief executive officer of the Seventh Generation Fund for Indigenous Peoples. This excerpt is from her essay "To Be a Good Ancestor: Resisting Colonial Violence & Uplifting Native Women & Girls," which she contributed to *MMIWG2 & MMIP Organizing Tool Kit*, published by the Sovereign Bodies Institute in partnership with MMIWG2 families, Indigenous survivors of violence, and their allies in 2021.

Twenty-two-year-old Savanna Lafontaine-Greywind was eight months pregnant. She lived in a basement apartment with her mother Norberta, father Joe, twenty-year-old brother Joe Jr., eighteen-year-old sister Kayla, and sixteen-year-old brother Casey at 2825 9th Street North, Fargo, North Dakota. Norberta is a member of the Turtle Mountain tribe, while Savanna, her father, and her siblings belong to the Spirit Lake Tribe. Around midafternoon on August 19, 2017, Savanna had ordered pizza and texted her mother and boyfriend that she was going to her neighbor's apartment to model a dress.[2] Afterward, Savanna was supposed to take her brother Casey to work and when she didn't show up, Norberta sent her brother to the neighbor's apartment, but no one answered the door. Then Savanna's father, Joe, went upstairs to talk to the same neighbor, and the neighbor told him they had not finished working on the dress. Concerned, but needing to tend to the ride needed by her son, Norberta hoped that Savanna would be back when she returned from taking her son to work. When she came back, she panicked because Savanna was still not home. Norberta went upstairs to the same neighbor's apartment to inquire about Savanna's whereabouts. The neighbor told her that Savanna had left earlier. Norberta told reporters: "I immediately knew something was wrong because her car is here. . . . She's eight months pregnant. Her feet were swollen, so she wouldn't have taken up walking like that. There was pizza here that she hadn't eaten. She would not just leave that lady's apartment and go somewhere" (Gumprecht 2017). That same day, Norberta called the Fargo Police Department (Fargo PD) and reported Savanna missing. The police arrived and after talking with Norberta, made their way to the apartment upstairs, as that was the last place Savanna had been seen (Gable 2023). Fargo PD searched the apartment twice, once that day and a second time the following day, August 20. Both times the searches did not achieve any result. According to the *Duluth News Tribune,* "Fargo police conducted two K-9 searches. U.S. Customs and Border Protection did an aerial search. The Fargo Fire Department searched the Red River, and Savanna's uncle did the same with a personal watercraft" (2019). Savanna's family and boyfriend put up "Missing" flyers around Fargo; her sister posted on her Facebook page: "Has anyone seen my sister??? She's been missing since around 2:00 today in the FARGO MOORHEAD AREA! This is not like her. PLEASE SHARE AND GET THE WORD OUT. BINRG MY SISTER HOME"

---

2. I have chosen not to include any of the names associated with the neighbor so as not to give them more notoriety.

(Savanna LaFontaine-Greywind Official 2017). Norberta kept insisting she felt her daughter was in danger and that something was wrong (*Duluth News Tribune* 2019).

On Sunday, August 20, 2017, the deputy police chief stated publicly that there was "nothing to suggest criminal activity" (Swenson 2021). According to several news outlets, the family felt that the police initially took the case seriously, but subsequently "they just had no care" (Swenson 2021; *Duluth News Tribune* 2019; Gumprecht 2017; Gable 2023). On August 23 the family held a candlelight vigil at the main entrance of Sanford Medical Center in Fargo and invited the public to attend. That same day, Fargo PD learned that the boyfriend of the Lafontain-Greywind neighbor had been telling coworkers that he had a new baby at home. This was enough evidence for a search warrant of the neighbor's apartment for the fourth time. On Thursday, August 24, Fargo PD found the neighbor and a healthy newborn baby girl inside the apartment. A DNA test confirmed the baby, Haisley Jo, was Savanna's and her boyfriend's. Both the neighbor and her boyfriend were arrested.[3] The police were not able to explain how this newborn came into the world or where she was the other three times they searched the apartment, while both the neighbor and her boyfriend were present. On the afternoon of August 27, 2017, two kayakers on the Red River near Moorhead, Minnesota, found the body of Savanna LaFontaine-Greywind wrapped in plastic and duct tape; it had been caught on a log.[4]

Savanna's murder is one of 146 documented murders of Indigenous women in North and South Dakota from 1900 until today, according to figures reported by the Sovereign Bodies Institute (2020).[5] According to

---

3. The details of Savanna's murder by her neighbor and the neighbor's boyfriend are viscerally heinous and can be easily found online; there is no need to reproduce them here.

4. There is also a book by Mona Gable, *Searching for Savanna: The Murder of One Native American Woman and the Violence Against the Many.*

5. As with data on feminicide in Mexico, Argentina, and other parts of the Americas, nonprofit organizations have taken on the task of documenting murders of Indigenous women, girls, and two-spirit relatives given that official data appears to severely underrepresent on-the-ground experiences. The Sovereign Bodies Institute (SBI) (https://www.sovereign-bodies.org/mmiw-database) and the Urban Indian Health Institute (UIHI) (https://www.uihi.org/) are two of these nonprofits documenting missing and murdered Indigenous people including women, girls, and two-spirit people. In Canada, the Royal Canadian Mounted Police (RCMP) maintains a national missing-persons database, available at https://canadasmissing.ca. However, the lead investigator for each case has discretionary authority to decide what case will go on the database. In the United States, the Federal Bureau of Investigation's National Crime Information Center tracks missing persons. In

Sharon Day, leader of Nibi Walk, a two-week-long and 550-mile walk following the Red River north was organized to honor missing and murdered Indigenous women along US Highway 75. She explains that "from 1979 until today there are over 134 Indigenous bodies that have been pulled from the river" (Bolin 2019). Savanna's body is also part of those statistics. Her murder exemplifies the colonial logic implicit in seeing Indigenous women as "extracted and exploited as women" (Oros Peters 2020, 9). In Savanna's case, a white woman "ripped open" (9) Savanna's body and extracted her baby. Savanna's body was the land that provided the precious resource of a child that would be the child her neighbor desired. Savanna's body was "desecrated" (9) and was then discarded by the neighbor's white boyfriend in the Red River, like trash.

The high number of murders and disappearances of Indigenous women, girls, and two-spirit people is inseparable from colonial practices and historical processes specific to the treatment of Indigenous populations in the United States and Canada. The affects of indignation and persistence repeatedly emerged in the research by Indigenous scholars, in conversations with Indigenous women, and on social media posts. Naming is a decolonizing methodology. Although it mainly involves renaming the landscape, when building on the notion of naming I understood that by naming these affects, indignation and persistence, Indigenous activists were also naming "realities which can only be found, as self-evident concepts" (Smith1999, 159), and I chose these affects to name this chapter. These affects are particularly evident in Indigenous activism, which continues to challenge colonial logics and structures through both naming practices and direct action. To examine the indignation of Indigenous activists over the Canadian and US governments' lack of reaction to increasing numbers of missing and murdered Indigenous women, I employ a mixed-methods approach that primarily draws from Indigenous decolonizing methodologies, material rhetoric, and quantitative data collected by Indigenous activists. Concomitantly, I interrogate how this indignation has resulted in persistent efforts to take matters into their own hands by training communities to do searches, setting up listening circles,

---

2016 they reported 5,712 missing Native American and Alaska Native women and girls. Of these reports, only 116 were logged into the Department of Justice's federal missing-persons database (a database that allows law-enforcement agencies to share information). The National Missing and Unidentified Persons System (NamUs) (https://namus.nij.ojp.gov/) was created in 2007 to help solve missing- and unidentified-missing-person cases; however, it only includes cases verified by responding law-enforcement officers, who also underreport cases based on their discretionary understanding of the case.

producing reports, and collaborating with senators to legislate protections for Indigenous communities.

MMIWG2 as Colonial Practice
in the United States and Canada

To investigate the inextricable relationship between the colonial logics of conquest, extractive industries, and the rising numbers of MMIWG2 on the one hand, and the affects of indignation and persistence on the other, I draw on the Indigenous critique of history as being "assembled around a set of interconnected ideas" (Smith1999, 31) that are patriarchal and totalizing. I trace how settler-colonial violence legally allowed gender violence toward Indigenous communities as an extension of the ideology of conquest, Manifest Destiny, displacement, extraction, and capitalism. Building on Smith's (1999) methodologies of reframing and claiming histories—which "establish the legitimacy of the claims being asserted . . . because they have been written to support claims to territories and resources, or about past injustices" (144)—I center the claiming histories of Indigenous scholars to document how violence toward Indigenous women parallels and extends from violence toward the earth.

To discuss MMIWG2 is also to name the process and practices in the ongoing colonializing efforts by the United States and Canada on sovereign Indigenous lands, because the colonization of land and of Indigenous people are inextricable from each other (Harry 2006; Lugones 2008; Quijano 2007; Deer 2015; Glenn 2015; Johnston 2022; Gobby and Everett 2022; García Del-Moral et al. 2023; Monárrez Fragoso 2023; Aujla et al. 2023; Bejarano 2023; Segato and Vitenti 2023; Messing et al. 2023).[6] The United States' and Canada's (and all of the Americas') process of colonization began based on the "Doctrine of Discovery," whereby European kingdoms acquired titles to lands they "discovered" per the authority granted by a series of papal bulls in the late fifteenth century (Reid 2010; Dunbar-Ortiz 2015a, 2015b).

---

6. I specifically refer to the ongoing colonizing efforts by the United States and Canada to allow space for the "unrelenting pressure that incursion and occupation continue to have on the health and well-being and futurity of Indigenous Peoples" (Oros Peters 2020, 7), the condition of Puerto Rico as a territory-colony of the United States, and the nexus between Canadian and US extractive industries and their lobbying of their respective governments for land in these countries as well as across the Americas.

Pope Nicholas V authorized the conquest and enslavement of Indigenous people to claim and extract, and profit from the land. According to the Indigenous legal scholar Robert A. Williams (Lumbee), this Doctrine of Discovery marked "the West's first tentative steps towards this noble vision of a Law of Nations that contained a mandate for Europe's subjugation of all peoples whose radical divergence from European-derived norms of right conduct signified their need for conquest and remediation" (1990, 59). This doctrine starkly contradicts Indigenous peoples' understanding of land, where "Indigenous peoples don't share a Western capitalist understanding of private property and land ownership; instead, land is understood as being a relative we live in harmony with, and this reciprocal relationship represents . . . claims to lands" (Bourgeois 2023, 467). The Doctrine of Discovery meant that Indigenous inhabitants were not considered to have rights to the land they inhabited when Europeans arrived and claimed the land as theirs, and that they also had to be subjected to a process of domination defined by: occupation and control, exploitation of local economic resources, destruction of Indigenous political, economic, cultural, and spiritual systems, and the development and imposition of new systems in the image of the colonizing powers. For example, in Canada this domination is codified in the federal Indian Act, which has been in place since 1876 and "attempts to control all aspects of Indigeneity in Canada, including who officially counts as Indigenous" (Bourgeois 2023, 467). Similarly, American history is marked by numerous laws, negotiations, broken treaties, and forced displacement and resettlement of Indigenous peoples. In both countries, the codification of colonial domination into laws has facilitated claims to Indigenous lands.

The domination of the Indigenous people of Turtle Island or *Abya Yala* (the Americas) required "brutal access to people's bodies through unimaginable exploitation, violent sexual violation, control of reproduction, and systematic terror" (Lugones 2010, 744). This process was and continues to be (through racism, norms, stigmas, sexual abuse, and generational trauma) especially violent for trans and nontrans women and girls. When Europeans saw the Americas as *terra nullius* (a Latin expression for land belonging to no one), they also saw women's bodies as commodifiable and conquerable. In Canada, the legal doctrine of terra nullius allowed for the British monarchy to grant land to the Hudson Bay Company, which at one point owned 70%–80% of Canada's land mass (Reid 2010). According to the *Violence on the Land, Violence on Our Bodies* (2017) report, "this legal concept has also been used as justification that Indigenous bodies are empty and open for conquering" (81). The Indigenous scholar and survivor Robyn Bourgeois (2023) explains that the roots of the violence and femicide experienced by Indigenous women and girls in Canada is colonialism, achieved through white supremacy, heteropatriarchy, and other dominant interlocking social systems of oppression. Colonialism involves the illegal theft and occupation of Indigenous lands by white settler societies through genocide directed at Indigenous peoples. Colonialism is enabled through racism that establishes white supremacy and the right to claim and occupy Indigenous lands through the dehumanisation and elimination of Indigeneity and Indigenous peoples. Simultaneously, colonialism and racism are explicitly gendered and directed at securing heteropatriarchy. All of these are reinforced through other social systems of oppression, including economic exploitation and exclusion, ableism, ageism, and religious discrimination. (467)

This can be seen best when referencing Canada's Indian Act of 1876, whereby the law enshrines a mechanism for eliminating Indigenous people through sex-discriminatory provisions. These were specific to Indigenous women and their children to exclude them from being officially recognized as "Indian," in the case that they married or procreated with someone who was not Indigenous (National Inquiry into Missing and Murdered Indigenous Women and Girls 2019, 249–52). Furthermore, Bourgeois maintains that Indigenous femicide "is indispensable to the colonial order of things in Canada," which secures its existence by "annihilating the original occupants with legitimate claims to their land base" and "reduces the number of Indigenous peoples that the government is legally and financially accountable to through existing treaty obligations . . . which is why the nation's social systems and institutions enable, perpetuate, and normalize violence against Indigenous women and girls" (2023, 473). Bourgeois underscores the inextricable and insidious ways that colonialism and its practices actively threaten Indigenous women in Canada.

Similarly, in the United States the Doctrine of Discovery shape-shifted into the myth of Manifest Destiny, which is "embedded in the minds of nearly everyone in the United States" (Dunbar-Ortiz 2015c, 2). The myth materialized in the legal and documented practices of "forced removal, displacement, and destruction" (Deer 2015, 12) affecting Indigenous, Black, Latine, and Asian populations, which unfortunately are "not over . . . it is continuing, and like a shapeshifter takes on different forms" (Oros Peters 2020, 7). In 1801 President Thomas Jefferson wrote to James Monroe stating his intentions of expansion for the United States "beyond those limits [referring to the geographical and political boundaries of the newly formed US territory and envisioning a continent-wide unification] and cover[ing] the whole northern, if not southern continent, with a people speaking the same language, governed in similar form by similar laws" (Thomas Jefferson to James Monroe 1801, 2). The historian Roxanne Dunbar-Ortiz argues that Jefferson's "version of manifest destiny found form a few years later in the Monroe Doctrine, signaling the intention of annexing or dominating former Spanish colonial territories in the Americas and the Pacific" (2015, 12), which materialized through treaties, laws, and policies throughout the nineteenth, twentieth, and twenty-first centuries.

In the case of Indigenous populations, the US Supreme Court cases known as the Marshall Trilogy (*Johnson v. McIntosh*, 1823; *Cherokee Nation v. Georgia*, 1831; *Worcester v. Georgia*, 1832) took Indigenous lands using the Doctrine of Discovery to rationalize and justify the invasion; established that tribes could only sell or cede land to the federal government; established tribes' relationship to the United States as "a ward to his guardian" and characterized them as "domestic dependent nations" (*Cherokee Nation v. Georgia*, para. 18); and recognized Indigenous peoples as having limited but persistent sovereignty over tribal lands. In 1886, however, the Supreme Court decided that Congress could suspend tribal sovereignty at any time (*United States v. Kagama*, 1886). The Indian Removal Act of 1830 forced thousands of Indigenous peoples from their homelands, and the 1887 Dawes Act deliberately broke up reservation land and sold it to non-Indigenous peoples. The 1934 Indian Reorganization Act encouraged tribal governments to develop similar court systems to those of the United States. Other laws like the Major Crimes Act (1885), the Indian Civil Rights Act (1968), and the Supreme Court case *Oliphant v. Suquamish* (1978) took away power from tribal courts by giving the federal government jurisdiction over sexual-assault and homicide cases, thus limiting tribal governments' ability to prosecute them.

In her lecture "Sovereignty of the Soul: Confronting Sexual Violence in Native America," Sara Deer explained to Amherst College students: "When you have a system that cannot hold people accountable, what is the message? The message to perpetrators is 'I can get away with it,' and the message to survivors is 'no one will do anything to help me.' And . . . I think that this perfect storm of legal problems explains why Native people suffer from such high rates of violence" (Park 2018). The colonial–ward relationship that the US federal government has established with Indigenous communities not only limits their ability to prosecute certain crimes, but also their ability to support their criminal justice systems and have the resources to help both the victims and their families.

At present, Manifest Destiny continues to shape-shift "through Genocide, Terracide, and Aquacide and identifies the compulsion to consume Mother Earth—and for the purposes of this discussion, the devouring of Indigenous women and girls' lives through our bodies" (Oros Peters 2021, 7). These forms of domination and materialization of Manifest Destiny through the law and cultural ethos are pertinent to this discussion on MMIWG2 because they are part of "a history of forced removal, displacement, and destruction" (Deer 2015, 12). These laws shape cultural norms in the United States, promoting state-sanctioned, enforced assimilation through a "melting pot" ethos that eradicates difference at all costs. These laws also rationalize the separation of Indigenous women from their children, a practice that has shaped the lives of Black, Latina, and Asian women and children, in turn creating mothers who have lost their children through boarding schools, the child-welfare system, or both. Their children, in turn, often struggle with mental health issues and addictions that can make them particularly vulnerable to various types of violence that can increase the risk of going missing or being murdered.

In the case of sexual violence against Indigenous women, girls, and two-spirit people, Deer argues that "sexual assault mimics the worst traits of colonization in its attack on the body, invasion of physical boundaries, and disregard for humanity" (2009, 150). Deer goes on to explain that "it is irrefutable that, based on available data violent crime is experienced by Native women at per capita higher rates than almost all other groups in the United States" (2015, 1). Deborah Miranda (2010) notes that "Indian bodies do not belong to Indians, but to those who lay claim to them by violence" (96). Lee Ann Littlewolf (Leech Band of Ojibwe) explains the ripple effects of rape as trauma, saying that "being raped disconnects everything . . . the violation cannot be explained and it makes it impossible to reconcile . . . it changes the very reality of life" (Deer 2015, 11).

According to data collected in the 1998 National Violence Against Women Survey, one in three Native women will be raped during her life.[7] Deer (2015) explains that "Native women know that there is a high likelihood

---

7. The 1998 report highlights this number as being 34.1% of Indigenous women compared to 24% of mixed-race women, 18.8% of African American women, 17.7% of white women, and 6.8% of Asian/Pacific Islander women.

of experiencing rape at some point in their lives, and preparing for this violence resembles a full-time job" (5). More recent studies do not signal a change in that statistic. A 2017 study by the Urban Indian Health Institute (UIHI), a tribal epidemiology center, found that 5,712 cases of MMIWG were reported in 2016, but only 116 were logged in the Department of Justice Database. They also found 506 MMIWG cases across 71 selected urban cities, of which 66 were tied to domestic and sexual violence, 128 were cases of missing Indigenous women, and 280 were cases of murdered Indigenous women with the youngest victim being a baby less than one year old and the oldest a woman of eighty-three. The report documents the difficulty in collecting data from law-enforcement agencies due to institutional racism and poor recordkeeping protocols.

For two-spirit individuals, the violence inflicted upon them is profoundly shaped by colonization and produces a shift in how they are treated by their communities (Driskill et al. 2011; Hayes 2020; Hayes et al. 2023). Before being colonized and indoctrinated by religious institutions, Indigenous communities viewed two-spirit individuals as "healers, parents to orphaned children, nurses, conveyors of oral traditions and songs (Yuki), foretellers of the future (Winnebago, Ogala Lakota), name-givers of children and adults (Ogala Lakota, Tohono, O'odham), nurses during war expeditions, potters (Zuni, Diné, Tohono O'odham), matchmakers (Cheyenne, Omaha, Oglala Lakota), makers of feather regalia for dances (Maidu) and special role players in the Sun Dance (Crow, Hidasta, Oglala Lakota)" (Hayes 2020, 45). In addition to these two-spirit roles being lost in some Indigenous communities, languages with specific words that described these individuals were also lost through assimilationist interventions and boarding schools. For example, in Diné, the term *Nádleehí* describes a gender that is both male and female. In the essay "Including and Caring for Two Spirit Relatives in the MMIWG2 Movement," Lenny Hayes (Sisseton Wahpeton Oyate) documents the explanation of the elder Hmuya Mani (Richard Two Dogs):

> The "Wapetokeca" were men who lived in a woman's body or women who lived in a man's body. They were highly respected. . . . The modern world has changed that view amongst many contemporary Lakota and the beliefs about the "Winkte" or "Wapetokeca." Modern society had made the LGBTQ community out to be bad and the stigma passed down to the younger. I believe this came from Indians who served in the military and learned that to be "Winkte" was to be ostracized, ridiculed, and

eventually discharged from the military with a dishonorable or a medical discharge. They brought this brainwashing back to the reservations. (2020, 45–46)

As part of the effects of colonial processes and their influence on Indigenous peoples, two-spirit people went from being understood as "spiritual beings" to "sexual beings," which in turn resulted in them being "ostracized within" (Hayes 2020, 43) tribal communities, making them especially vulnerable to rejection, discrimination, transphobia, sexual assault, sex and human trafficking, or being reported missing or murdered or both. Similar to the case of Indigenous women and girls, there is a lack of research and data. Although there are a "few tribes in the country that have specific laws to protect individuals who may identify as Two-Spirit/Native LGBTQ" (Hayes 2020, 47), a severe lack of policies prevails. These dynamics "can also be the cause as to why individuals who identify as Two-Spirit/Native LGBTQ and their families don't come forward to report" (47). This colonial form of domination legally allowed gender violence toward Indigenous communities as an extension of the ideology of conquest, Manifest Destiny, displacement, extraction, and capitalism.

There is an intertwined relationship between, on the one hand, the colonial understanding of the land and the codification of *terra nullius*, the Doctrine of Discovery, and Manifest Destiny, and, on the other, the crafting of contemporary laws. It is these policies that are then implemented through various forms of violence, including but not limited to sexual assault, family separations, displacement, forced sterilization, genocide, and supporting policies that benefit extractive industries. These, in turn, contribute to the increasing numbers of MMIWG2 in both the United States and Canada.

The Birth of MMIWG2 and the Resulting Policy in Canada

In this section I build on material-rhetoric approaches that view physical reality and language as creating each other (Barad 2003, 2007; Mauthner 2016; Hesford 2021; Hill 2024) to show how Indigenous Canadian activists built the MMIWG2 movement. This methodological approach allows me to document how Indigenous activists' talk about MMIW2G co-constitutively shapes how the killing of Indigenous women and two-spirit relatives is perceived and responded to by the public and governmental entities—meaning that how activists organized and communicated also physically materialized into governmental responses.

The movement for Missing and Murdered Indigenous Women and Girls (MMIWG) can be traced back to two movements founded by mourning family members: the Missing Women's Memorial March in Vancouver, British Columbia, and the memorial walks on Yellowhead Highway 16, or the Highway of Tears (as it is commonly known), which connects communities across the northern part of British Columbia. The murder of Cheryl Ann Joe, an Indigenous woman found on Powell Street in Vancouver's Downtown Eastside (DTES), cemented the annual Women's Memorial March for her mother Linda Joe and other women who lived in DTES (Oppal 2012).

The Missing Women's Memorial March in DTES was founded by women who lived there on February 14, 1991 (Oppal 2012; Winton 2014; Dean 2015; Bourgeois 2023, 469). The memorial walk has been held every year since 1992. The march was the result of postmortem politics originally organized as a healing walk for family members to honor the murder of loved ones. These primarily Indigenous family members had been noticing that within DTES, Indigenous women had been disappearing since 1970 (Martin et al. 2019). It is estimated that "between 1970 and 2002, at least 68 women disappeared from the DTES, a neighborhood dominantly defined by abject poverty and criminality" (Bourgeois 2023, 469). When attempting to report the disappearances of these women, their family members were met with indifference, dismissiveness, and condemnation by police and community leaders (Oppal 2012; Bourgeois 2014, 2023; Aujla et al. 2023).

In 2002 a white pig farmer, Robert Pickton, was arrested. While the "remains or DNA of 33 women, many picked up from Vancouver's Downtown Eastside, were found on Pickton's farm [. . .] he once bragged to an undercover police officer that he killed a total of 49 women [. . .] Pickton's confirmed victims were six: Sereena Abotsway, Mona Wilson, Andrea Joesbury, Brenda Ann Wolfe, Papin and Marnie Frey" (Associated Press 2024), and he was only convicted for killing these six women in 2007. This conviction and the injustice in the process pointed to the complicity of law enforcement, producing a sense of indignation. The conviction mobilized organizers of the walk to take over public space, demand action and justice from the police, and advocate for inquiries into MMIWG2. Finally, their persistence resulted in the provincial government of British Colombia launching the Wally Oppal Inquiry into the neglect and complicity of law enforcement in cases related to Indigenous women in DTES. The British Columbia

Commission of Missing Women Inquiry found that systemic bias within law enforcement toward women who were Indigenous, unhoused, involved in sex work, or using substances contributed to a broader institutional failure to hold Pickton accountable sooner and prevent additional deaths (Oppal 2012). The February 14 Missing Women's Memorial March is still being held today, "to remember, heal, and demand justice for MMIWG" (Bourgeois 2023, 469), and has held solidarity events in other cities across Canada.

The memorial walks on the Highway of Tears began in 1994 after sixteen-year-old Ramona Wilson was murdered. Her mother and her sister, Matilda and Brenda, organized the memorial walk and have continued to do so annually since that year. Indigenous groups suggest over forty women have disappeared or been murdered since the 1970s (McDiarmid 2020). These disappearances and the mourning of the families who have lost family members became visible and relevant to law enforcement in 2005 when a white woman disappeared along the highway, "leading many Indigenous people to conclude that racism played a role in this delayed response" (Bourgeois 2023, 470). In 2006 the Indian Chiefs in British Columbia organized a Highway of Tears symposium. The event brought Indigenous community members, police, and government officials together to address the violence against the missing and murdered Indigenous women and girls by crafting thirty-three recommendations (Lheidli T'enneh First Nation et al. 2006). However, of these recommendations "almost none . . . have been implemented" (Bourgeois 2023, 470). That same year, Gladys Radek and Bernie Williams—who also had family members disappear along the Highway of Tears—organized another walk to seek justice for these women and formed the group Walk4Justice, which traversed 722 kilometers (449 miles) along the highway between Prince George and Prince Rupert in British Columbia to request an inquiry into MMIWG2. In 2008 they walked 4,125 kilometers (2,563 miles) from Prince George to Ottawa to demand that the federal government form an inquiry into MMIWG2, this time with more supporters. In 2009 and 2010, they walked 2,025 kilometers (1,258 miles) from Kamloops and Winnipeg, gaining supporters along the way. In 2011 they walked 4,847 kilometers (3012 miles) from Prince Rupert to Ottawa to demand that the Canadian government conduct a national inquiry into MMIWG.

Their persistence, in tandem with the findings and recommendations of the Truth and Reconciliation Commission (TRC), held the Canadian government accountable. For example, recommendation 41 of the 94 included in the TRC's report states:

41. We call upon the federal government, in consultation with Aboriginal organizations, to appoint a public inquiry into the causes of, and remedies for, the disproportionate victimization of Aboriginal women and girls. The inquiry's mandate would include:

i. Investigation into missing and murdered Aboriginal women and girls.

ii. Links to the intergenerational legacy of residential schools.

Canadian Prime Minister Justin Trudeau accepted the TRC's final report, and as a result the Canadian government launched the National Inquiry into Missing and Murdered Indigenous Women on December 8, 2015 (Bourgeois 2023).[8] It is important to note that this national inquiry was also in part due to the three-decade-long fight by MMIWG2 families and activists. Similarly to the Wally Oppal Inquiry, the National Inquiry into Missing and Murdered Indigenous Women provided an official process for uncovering the truth and examining the systemic disregard of cases involving missing and murdered Indigenous women, girls, and two-spirit people, as well as the broader patterns of violence by law enforcement in enabling or

---

8. The Indian Residential Schools Settlement Agreement is the largest class-action settlement in Canada. One of its provisions was the establishment of the Truth and Reconciliation Commission of Canada (TRC) to "facilitate reconciliation between students, their families, their communities and all Canadians" (Government of Canada 2024). The Canadian government provided $72 million to support the work of the TRC. Part of its work involved traveling to all parts of Canada, hearing from over 6,500 witnesses, hosting seven national events across the country, and engaging the Canadian public so as to educate people about the history and legacy of the residential-schools system while at the same time honoring the experiences of former students and their families. The TRC also created a historical record of the residential-schools system, now housed at the University of Manitoba. In June 2015, the TRC presented its executive summary of what is now a multivolume report and ninety-four recommendations for further reconciliation between Canada and Indigenous people. Volume 4 of the TRC reports specifically focuses on missing Indigenous children and unmarked graves, framing these losses as earlier forms of the MMIWG2 crisis. The violence and trauma inflicted through the residential-schools system laid the groundwork for ongoing violence across generations, contributing to continued patterns of disappearance, physical violence, and death. The TRC reports can also be found at the National Center for Truth and Reconciliation's website: https://nctr.ca/records/reports/.

failing to prevent this form of gender-based violence across Canada (2019). In addition to following the legal process involving lawyers and methods of legal examination, receiving written submissions, and examining existing research, policy, and legislation pertinent to MMIWG2, the commission was tasked with putting MMIWG2 families first, as "the process was intended to be trauma-informed and decolonising, including being organised around Indigenous ways of knowing and being" (Bourgeois 2023, 472). The National Inquiry, which led an inquiry similar to the TRC, held that

> more than 2,380 people participated in the [inquiry], some in more ways than one. Four hundred and sixty-eight family members and survivors of violence shared their experiences and recommendations at 15 Community Hearings. Over 270 family members and survivors shared their stories with us in 147 private, or in-camera, sessions. Almost 750 people shared through statement gathering, and 819 people created artistic expressions to become part of the National Inquiry's Legacy Archive. Another 84 Expert Witnesses, Elders and Knowledge Keepers, front-line workers, and officials provided testimony in nine Institutional and Expert and Knowledge Keeper Hearings." (National Inquiry Into Missing and Murdered Indigenous Women and Girls 2019, 49)

The National Inquiry released its final two-volume report titled *Reclaiming Power and Place* on June 3, 2019. In it they found that the MMIWG2 crisis involved race- and gender-based genocide committed by Canada, and made 231 calls for justice that addressed governments, institutions, industries, social service providers, and all Canadians (National Inquiry into Missing and Murdered Indigenous Women and Girls 2019). It took the Canadian government more than two years to respond to the inquiry; on June 10, 2021, the government released a national action plan to address MMIWG2 that was heavily influenced and informed by a National Family and Survivors Circle representing First Nations, input from both urban Indigenous peoples and LGBTQIA2S+ populations, and a report from Les Femme Michif Otipemisiwak, a group representing Métis women. The action plan includes short-term priorities to address the violence against Indigenous women, which entail addressing educational opportunities, housing disparities, and changes to the health, justice, and child-welfare systems (Bourgeois 2023, 473). While the Canadian government has rhetorically embraced this plan, it has yet to legislatively and materially support it, including the creation of oversight bodies to track the developments of the priorities.[9] This lack of implementation has left survivors and advocates disappointed and frustrated (Deer 2022). However, Indigenous mourning family members and activists have shifted their postmortem politics from simply raising awareness of MMIWG2 to advocating to decolonize and shift governmental structures and programs that contribute to violence toward Indigenous women, girls, and two-spirit people.

Legislating MMIWG2 in the United States

Extending the material-rhetoric framework from the previous section and conducting a legislative genealogy, in this section I trace how Indigenous activists' postmortem politics in the United States materialized into legislation, with a specific focus on the development and passage of Savanna's Act. The US government manifests a complicated and often contradictory relationship between the freedoms it claims to protect and who is guaranteed these protections. Historically, those excluded from the freedoms safeguarded by the US Constitution have comprised marginalized groups including but not limited to Indigenous, Black, Asian, and Latino people, women, girls, and LGBTQI+ people. Throughout the 1970s and 1980s, inspired by the power movements of the late 1960s and 1970s including the women's movement, several attempts were made at passing the Equal Rights Amendment (all failed) and codifying marital rape as a crime in all fifty states. In 1993 all fifty states finally criminalized marital rape.

The following year, 1994, Congress passed the Violence Against Women Act (VAWA), introduced by then-Senator Joe Biden as part of that year's

---

9. This situation illustrates a key feature of the United States and Canada: They follow common-law tradition, which differs significantly from the legal frameworks in Latin America and Caribbean countries. In the US and Canada (except for Quebec), both written laws and court decisions matter because court rulings set precedents that must be followed in future cases. Most Latin American and Caribbean countries use civil-law systems, where written laws are more important and court decisions don't usually set binding precedents. These differences mean that gender activists must use different strategies depending on which legal system they are working in. In the US and Canada, because of the common-law system activists need to focus on both changing laws and influencing court decisions, while in the rest of the Americas the focus is more on changing the written laws themselves.

Violent Crime Control and Law Enforcement Act "in recognition of the severity of the crimes associated with domestic violence, sexual assault, and stalking" (Office on Violence Against Women 2024). The act gained the bipartisan support of 226 sponsors in the House and 68 in the Senate.[10] The 1994 version of VAWA provided and enhanced sentencing of repeat federal sex offenders; mandated restitution to victims of specified federal sex offenses; and authorized grants to state, local, and tribal law-enforcement entities to investigate and prosecute violent crimes against women. In examining the effects of VAWA, Fregoso (2023) explains that this approach to gender violence "is inseparable from the unprecedented growth and privatizations of the prison industrial complex during the past three decades [and] although VAWA is not the sole reason for the rise in mass incarceration, it is part of a neoliberal capitalism's tendency to individualize and criminalize social problems" (41). Fregoso points to the paradox between protecting the rights of women while at the same time expanding the carceral industry instead of investing in other forms of prevention and rehabilitation such as restorative justice. VAWA is also impermanent, meaning it is a law that must be renewed, modified, and strengthened—and depending on the agenda of the president and Congress, it can fail to be reauthorized.[11] VAWA has been

---

10. This was the first time the US government had designated a legislative package to end violence against women; however, it took four years for the bill to pass because of strenuous opposition from Chief Justice William Rehnquist to a provision that allowed victims of gender-based violence to sue their attackers. Nevertheless, advocates of VAWA and congressional legislators were able to pass VAWA by arguing that domestic violence cost taxpayers between $5 and $10 billion a year in health care, criminal justice, and related costs, qualifying VAWA under the Commerce Clause and the Fourteenth Amendment of the Constitution. In 2000, however, Chief Justice Rehnquist wrote the 5-4 decision in *United States v. Morrison* (529 U.S. 598) that part of VAWA was unconstitutional because it exceeded the powers granted to Congress under the Commerce Clause and the Fourteenth Amendment's Equal Protection Clause. This forced Congress to reauthorize a different version of VAWA in 2000.

11. The reauthorization of VAWA lapsed between 2018, under the first Trump administration, and 2022, creating a significant gap in the federal protections for survivors of domestic violence and sexual assault. In a separate but related challenge to gender justice, the US Supreme Court decided in the 2022 case *Dobbs v. Jackson Women's Health Organization* to overrule the federal right to abortion established by *Roe v. Wade.* This ruling has affected nontrans women's and trans people's access to reproductive health care, with documented cases where physicians delayed necessary care for pregnancy complications due to legal concerns. Together, VAWA's lapse and the Dobbs decision highlight a gap in federal protections and significant challenges for gender-justice activists and advocates in the United States.

reauthorized four times: in 2000, 2005, 2013, and most recently 2022. I provide this background to contextualize the legislative efforts in the case of MMIWG2 in the United States.

The postmortem politics of mourning families of MMIWG2 in the United States has deep historical roots spanning almost five centuries. The history of activism is characterized by persistent Indigenous resistance to US-government and settler land appropriation—actions that directly contributed to the disappearance and murder of Indigenous women and girls, the eradication of multiple genders, and as a result, the persecution and murder of two-spirit individuals. Throughout this long struggle, Indigenous communities—especially those that have resisted assimilation—have opposed virtually every piece of legislation that facilitated these land seizures that brought with them ensuing violence. However, the terms MMIWG, MMIWG2, and MMIP began gaining significant attention early in 2010 through various advocacy efforts, marches, and campaigns highlighting how Indigenous women experienced significantly more violence than any other population in the United States. For example, in 2013 Hanna Harris was sexually assaulted and murdered in Lame Deer, Montana. Her mother Malinda Limberhand and sister Rose Harris were forced to seek justice for Hanna with little help from government authorities because of a lack of information sharing and jurisdictional issues between local law enforcement and the Bureau of Indian Affairs. Eventually Hanna's murderers, a couple, were arrested, found guilty, and each sent to prison for fifteen years (Johnson 2019). In the aftermath of the 2014 trial, Malinda and Rose organized annual memorial walks to raise awareness of MMIW2S, for the dignity of Hanna, and to speak on the issues that affected them as surviving family members. They also collaborated with Montana legislators to advocate for laws that would foster the development of policies and fund studies to promote cooperation between state and tribal governments.

Their indignation at the judicial process and their persistence led Senator Steve Daines (Rep., Montana) to introduce Resolutions 60 (2017), 401 (2018), and 144 (2019) to establish May 5, Hanna Harris's birthday, as the National Day of Awareness for Missing and Murdered Native Women and Girls. Resolution 144 was passed on May 2, 2019 (116th Congress 2019).[12]

---

12. It is important to note that in the 2018 midterm elections, a hundred Indigenous people ran for office in the United States. Fifty-two of these were women. Two states elected Indigenous women to Congress—Rep. Debra Haaland (D-NM) and Rep. Sharice Davis (D-KA)—while other states elected Indigenous people to offices in state legislatures.

That same year in Montana, State Representative Rae Peppers (Dem.), with the help of Malinda and Rose, introduced Hanna's Act (House Bill 21) to instate a missing-persons specialist employed by the Department of Justice to create and oversee a missing-and-murdered-person database, provide law-enforcement trainings on MMIWG2 and MMIP, support and provide resources to families of missing and murdered people, and help investigate cases. Although Rose Harris was scheduled to testify before the Montana Senate's Judiciary Committee at the first hearing for Hanna's Act in March 2019, she began crying before she testified and had to walk out of the hearing. She later stated that she "was planning on telling the committee about what it was like searching for her sister and the feeling of not being able to see her when she was found" (Johnson 2019). Hanna's Act was voted to a tie, tabled, voted down, and finally passed on April 21, 2019, giving Malinda's and Rose's postmortem politics the possibility of leading to structural change in Montana.

In 2019 several other bills relevant to addressing the MMIWG2 crisis in the United States were introduced. Senator Tom Udall (Dem., New Mexico) presented the Bridging Agency Data Gaps and Ensuring Safety (BADGES) for Native Communities Act (H.R. 4289 & S. 1853); Congresswoman Deb Haaland (Dem., New Mexico) led the Not Invisible Act (H.R. 2438 & S. 982); Senator Lisa Murkowski (Rep., Alaska) and Senator Catherine Cortez Masto (Dem., Nevada) reintroduced Savanna's Act (S. 227); while Congresswomen Norma Torres (Dem., California) and Deb Haaland (Dem., New Mexico) along with Congressman Dan Newhouse (Rep., Washington) introduced a companion bill (H.R. 2733).[13] In addition, Senator Jon Tester (Dem., Montana) introduced the Studying the Missing and Murdered Indian Crisis Act of 2019 (H.R. 2029 & S. 336); Senator Steve Daines (Rep.,

---

Montana, for example, elected eleven tribal candidates to office, five of whom were women. Then in 2020, Yvette Herrell (R-NM) and Kaiali'i Kahele (D-HI) were elected to Congress. Kaiali'i Kahele is the second Native Hawaiian lawmaker to represent Hawaii in Congress since it became a state in 1959. This change in demographics, while small, signals how some of these bills gained greater visibility.

13. Savanna's Act was previously introduced by Senator Heidi Heitkamp (D-ND) during the 115th Congress (2017–2018) in honor of Savanna LaFontaine-Greywind. This version of the bill directed the Department of Justice to review, revise, and develop law-enforcement and justice protocols to address missing and murdered Indigenous people and directed the FBI to include gender in its annual statistics on missing and unidentified persons published on its website (115th Congress 2018). Although the bill passed the Senate, it was held back in the House of Representatives.

Montana) introduced the Tribal Reporting and Accountability to Congress (TRAC) Act (S. 1982); and Congresswoman Karen Bass (Dem., California) presented the Violence Against Women Reauthorization Act (H.R. 1585 & S. 2843/S. 2920), which in Sec. 903 included key provisions that would restore tribal jurisdiction over non-Indians for certain crimes involving children, sexual violence, stalking, sex trafficking, obstruction of justice, and assaults against law enforcement and corrections personnel and provisions aimed at improving the response to cases of missing and murdered Native women in Sections 702 and 905 (H.R.1585-116 Congress [2019–2020]). These seven bills were all presented before Congress in the 116th legislative session from 2019 to 2020 and indicate the visibility of the crisis of missing and murdered Indigenous women in the United States. They also underscore the years of postmortem politics and advocacy carried out by surviving Indigenous family members who, in collaboration with other Indigenous activists, organizations, culture and content creators, and legislators, have been calling for firm action to address the missing and murdered Indigenous women, girls, two-spirit people—and more broadly all missing and murdered Indigenous people.

Of these seven bills, only two were signed into law on October 10, 2020: Savanna's Act and the Not Invisible Act. According to the Indian Law Resource Center, "these new laws represent an overdue first step by the United States in responding to the crisis of missing and murdered Indigenous women and fulfilling [what was promised in the 2005 VAWA reauthorization . . . its] federal trust responsibility to assist tribal governments in safeguarding the lives of Indian women" (Indian Law Resource Center 2020). This version of Savanna's Act (H.R. 2733 & S. 277), besides honoring Savanna LaFontaine-Greywind, whose story opened this chapter, directs the Department of Justice (DOJ) to review, revise, and develop law-enforcement and justice protocols to address missing or murdered Native Americans. It authorizes the DOJ to provide grants for the development of policies and protocols and for the compiling and annual reporting of data about cases of MMIP, and requires federal law-enforcement agencies to modify their guidelines to incorporate the guidelines developed by the DOJ; and requires the Federal Bureau of Investigation to include gender in its annual statistics on missing and unidentified persons (116th Congress 2019).[14]

---

14. While Savanna's Act aimed at addressing the crisis of missing and murdered Indigenous people through data collection and protocol development, it is important to note that naming laws after murdered women can sometimes be politicized and redirected toward

Complementarily, the Not Invisible Act (H.R. 2438 & S. 982) establishes an advisory committee (inclusive of tribal, local, and federal stakeholders) to the Department of the Interior and the Department of Justice. They will make recommendations and outline best practices to fill gaps in services for victims of violent crimes. The bill also improves the response to missing and murdered Indigenous people by directing the Department of the Interior to designate an official to enhance cross-agency coordination efforts to address missing, trafficked, and murdered Indigenous people and requires the secretary of the interior and the attorney general to respond to the advisory committee's recommendations.

On February 9, 2022, Senator Diane Feinstein (Dem., California) introduced the Violence Against Women Act Reauthorization Act of 2022 (S. 3623), which had lapsed in 2019. It was signed into law by President Biden on March 15, 2022. The 2022 VAWA reauthorizes all VAWA programs until 2027, but most importantly it specifically addresses the MMIWG2 crisis by:

> Expanding special Tribal criminal jurisdiction (STCJ) to cover non-Native perpetrators of sexual assault, child abuse, stalking, sex trafficking, and assaults on Tribal law enforcement officers on Tribal lands. It also authorized a pilot project to enhance access to safety for survivors in Alaska Native villages. The Department

---

agendas unrelated to gender-based violence. The case of Laken Riley illustrates this contrast. On February 22, 2024, Riley, a white nursing student at the University of Georgia, was murdered by a man who entered the United States without governmental authorization. Unlike in the case of Savanna's Act, which addressed the underlying crisis of violence against Indigenous women, Riley's murder was rapidly leveraged by both the Republican and Democratic parties to advance immigration-enforcement agendas during an election year. Her father publicly decried this politicization, stating, "I think it's being used politically to get those votes. . . . It makes me angry. I feel like, you know, they're just using my daughter's name for that. And she was much better than that, and she should be raised up for the person that she is" (Gabbatt 2024). Despite these concerns, the Laken Riley Act was introduced and passed by the 118th Congress, with President Trump signing it into law on January 29, 2025, as the first legislative act of his second term (Darnell 2025). Whereas Savanna's Act mandated data collection and protocol development specifically targeting violence against Native Americans, the Laken Riley Act focused exclusively on immigration enforcement, empowering the Department of Homeland Security to detain unauthorized immigrants and allowing states to sue DHS for perceived enforcement failures. This contrast highlights how legislation named after murdered women can either address the systemic causes of gender-based violence or be redirected toward unrelated political agendas.

> of Justice moved quickly to identify and deploy resources to support Tribal implementation of STCJ, including by issuing or announcing awards for new technical assistance and to establish an Alaska-specific Intertribal Technical Assistance Working Group. OVW also issued an interim final rule to reimburse Tribes for expenses incurred in exercising STCJ, which will permit OVW to administer the Tribal Reimbursement Program starting in 2024. (The White House 2023)

This expansion of tribal criminal jurisdiction addresses the issue of holding people accountable. Over the next couple of years, it will be necessary to analyze the impact of this jurisdictional shift, as well as the implementation and success of the pilot program for survivors in Alaskan villages and its impact on the MMIWG2 crisis.

While these legislative modifications in a sense address the aftermath of many of the causes of MMIWG2, the postmortem politics of family members also focus on advocating for preventive measures, such as eliminating "man camps" (camps of men working in extractive industries set up near tribal land) and protecting the land from extractive industries. They are also working to address misogynistic practices and decolonize institutions and social systems that currently enable, perpetuate, and normalize violence against Indigenous women, girls, and two-spirit people, which interconnectedly will also reduce violence toward women, girls, and members of the LGBTQI+ population belonging to other racial groups. For example, in the United States, movements have been organized that center on specific communities' experiences. One of these, Say Her Name (#sayhername), stemmed from Black Lives Matter (#Blacklivesmatter); the #translivesmatter and #genderliberation movements underscore the increasing number of trans women murdered in the United States—thirteen from January 1, 2025, to July 4, 2025 ("Remembering Our Dead" n.d.); and two other movements focus on the recent murders of military service members Vanessa Guillen and Katia Dueñas Aguilar as well as activism focused on immigrants, using the hashtag #familesbelongtogether. The postmortem politics of family members of MMIWG2 also extends beyond the borders of Canada and the United States. Indigenous groups throughout the Americas are also claiming a presence within the contra-feminicide movements and addressing practices that result in the murder of Indigenous women and are specific to their geopolitical contexts such as deforestation, normalization of violence toward Indigenous women, and their erasure from data. For example, in the early years of contra-feminicide movements across Latin America and the Caribbean, women categorized as mestizas, the data showed, were frequently of Indigenous heritage (as discussed in chapter 1) though this identity was obscured through classification. The recent assassinations of Indigenous-women activists in Latin America and the Caribbean highlight this pattern of targeted violence: Berta Cáceres (Lenca), Maria de Fátima Muniz (Pataxó Hã-Hã-Hãe), Nicolasa López and Victoria Méndez (both Xinca), Mary Cruz Pertro (Zenú), Libia Quiguanás (kiwe thë'j Nasa), Juana María Martínez (Pech), and Gertrudis Cruz de Jesús and Cliserina Cruz Merino (both Triqui) were killed for defending their communities and lands against extractive industries and environmental destruction.

This pattern of violence against Indigenous-women environmental defenders connects directly to the broader postmortem politics of MMIWG2 family members across the Americas. Just as these families advocate for preventive measures, Indigenous movements throughout the hemisphere are challenging similar threats. Their work extends beyond reactive legal reforms to address the root causes: They aim to decolonize institutions, transform misogynistic practices, and dismantle systems that normalize violence against Indigenous women. This transnational movement recognizes how environmental exploitation, data erasure of Indigenous people, and normalized violence toward Indigenous populations create similar patterns of Indigenous feminicide, regardless of national borders. By connecting these struggles across contexts, Indigenous activists demonstrate how protecting Indigenous women's lives requires addressing both immediate violence and its underlying colonial and extractive foundations.

Postmortem MMIWG2S Representations

While my material-rhetoric and legislative genealogy in the previous two sections highlights how Indigenous activism translated into policy, equally important is examining how MMIWG2 and its activists' postmortem politics came to be represented in various forms of media, why these representations matter, and for whom. For this task, I turn both to the Indigenous decolonizing methodologies of testimonies, storytelling, remembering, and representing (Smith1999) and to theories of representation advanced by Indigenous cultural-studies scholars—specifically, Vizenor's (2008) concept of "survivance," Raheja's (2011) idea of "visual sovereignty," and Simpson's (2014) "politics of refusal"—to investigate how the postmortem politics of

Indigenous activists are depicted in several key mainstream representations of MMIWG2 since the 2010s, as well as the reach and cultural impact of these portrayals. I trace how these representations have shifted from white-helmed projects infected with colonial representation systems to Indigenous-made projects that assert sovereign self-representation and showcase the protagonism and persistence of Indigenous advocacy for MMIWG2 justice as well as the protagonism of the dead themselves in the lives of the living.

In August 2017, Savanna Lafountaine-Greywind was murdered and Taylor Sheridan's film *Wind River* was released. The film grossed $33.8 million in the United States and Canada alone and another $11.2 million worldwide, demonstrating its wide reach and popularity with global audiences. The film, a thriller, follows a wildlife officer (played by Jeremy Renner) after he finds the body of an eighteen-year-old Indigenous woman on tribal land in Wyoming. When the autopsy report reveals the woman had been raped multiple times, an FBI agent arrives to investigate (Elizabeth Olsen). The film represents the jurisdictional issues of trying to resolve cases of missing and murdered Indigenous women, the presence of extractive-industry man camps, and echoes the real cases of other Indigenous women who have been killed. The film ends with a postscript: "While missing person statistics are compiled for every other demographic, none exists for Native American women. No one knows how many are missing" (Sheridan 2018). While the film is not based on a true story, it is rooted in the experiences of missing and murdered women and girls. In his congressional testimony in support of Savanna's Act, Sheridan explained:

> During my late 20s, I was welcomed into the Oglala Sioux Tribal community on the Pine Ridge Indian Reservation. While there, community members shared with me the story about a young Oglala Lakota woman, who I will refer to as "Natalie." Natalie was a basketball star with exceptional athletic ability and a student leader with an impressive academic record that would make her the first in her family to attend college. By all accounts, Natalie's path in life pointed towards her escaping the cycle of poverty endemic to Indian reservations, and the possibility of becoming a future leader in her community and elsewhere. In a tragic turn of events, after missing [*sic*] for days, Natalie's body was found in a remote part of the reservation. Very little is known about the circumstances surrounding Natalie's death, but stories like hers have become commonplace. Natalie's story—and countless

others like hers—was the inspiration for Wind River, which tells the story of a young woman's rape and murder on the Wind River Indian Reservation, as well as the heartache and difficulties endured in bringing her perpetrators to justice. (Sheridan 2018)

The representation of the complexities of jurisdictional authority over certain crimes on tribal land brought more visibility to the MMIWG2 movement in Canada and introduced mainstream US audiences to the issue and the growing MMIWG2 movement in the United States.

While the film does humanize missing and murdered Indigenous women and the challenges in seeking justice, it "perpetuates the myth that the FBI investigates MMIW cases" (Nagle 2023). Another divergence is the blatant absence of the persistent advocacy of MMIWG2 family members in seeking justice for their loved ones. Princella RedCorn (2018), communications officer for the National Indigenous Women's Resource Center, explains that what is missing from *Wind River* is "the heart and healing power of Native women's voice, the tireless, all-inclusive, and solution-driven work" (33).

Sheridan has continued to represent the MMIWG2 crisis and has made attempts to depict the labor of Indigenous women in his subsequent work. For example, in the sixth and eighth episodes of the third season of the Paramount Network's *Yellowstone* (2020), Sheridan depicts the story of Sila, an Indigenous girl. In episode 6, Sila's disappearance leads tribal Chief Rainwater to work with Kayce the land-stock commissioner, Monica who is a tribal member and married to Kayce, and community members volunteering with the National Indigenous Women's Resource Center to try to find the girl. They eventually find Sila's body in a ditch. In the aftermath, Monica expresses frustration at the lack of resources and the time it took for them to locate Sila. Kayce tells her not to make it her fault, to which she replies, "I'm not making it my fault, I'm making it my problem" (Sheridan 2020). This statement is a form of representing the postmortem politics of Indigenous women that is rooted in the interconnectedness between all beings. Monica represents Indigenous activists' and mourning family members' advocacy to change the systems that perpetuate issues in cases of MMIWG2.

Two episodes later Monica, in collaboration with Chief Rainwater and the local authorities, makes herself prey to catch Sila's murderer. Monica pretends her car has broken down, and when a man offers her a ride, he takes her to the part of the reservation where Sila's body was found. Once there the man begins choking her; Chief Rainwater and the authorities swarm the area and he gets shot. In the aftermath, Chief Rainwater tells

Monica, "People talk about making a difference, but they don't 'cause they don't risk. You risked everything. Today you made a difference" (Sheridan 2020). Although the scene satisfies the viewer's penchant for justice in ways that rarely (if ever) occur off-screen, this statement could be a nod to the activism of Indigenous women who have and are risking everything in the fight for awareness and systemic change to address the MMIWG2 crisis.

Sheridan has used his position as a white man with power in Hollywood to raise awareness for missing and murdered Indigenous women and to hire Indigenous actors in supporting roles, including Gil Birmingham (Comanche), Mo Brings Plenty (Oglala Lakota), and Julia Jones (Choctaw), both for *Yellowstone* and *Wind River*. In 2023, while discussing the fact that his movies and shows have not won awards, he told the *Hollywood Reporter* that "[*Wind River*] actually changed a law, where you can now be prosecuted if you're a U.S. citizen for committing rape on an Indian reservation, and there's now a database for missing murdered Indigenous women. . . . So keep your fucking award. Who's going to remember I won an award in 10 years? But that law had a profound impact. All social change begins with the artist, and that's the responsibility you have" (Hibberd 2023). The statement reflects Sheridan's perspective on the responsibility of the artist in social change; here he is specifically talking about the 2022 VAWA reauthorization. For Fregoso (2023), "the capacity of art and film to witness involves more than just the documentation of an event; it refers to the act of testifying and to art's 'responsibility for truth'" (101). Thus, Sheridan's statement in its lack of recognition of Indigenous-women activists and forebears before him emanates from a colonizing white-savior complex rooted in the ethos of Manifest Destiny that, in turn, mirrors the lack of presence of women activists in the film and series themselves. His responsibility for truth as an artist is problematic because the manifestation of this cultural norm through his statement underscores how insidiously rooted colonialism—and its counterpart, patriarchy—is in the culture of the United States, and the ways that even mainstream-media content addressing the issues erases and disappears the "power of Native women's voice" (RedCorn 2018, 33), including the years of postmortem politics, advocacy, and persistence of Indigenous women. In distinction to Sheridan's representations, these women have been "at the forefront, seeking justice through inclusive and healing ways such as engaging men, prayer circles, traditional healing practices and ceremonies, and relying on traditional Native culture for strength, healing, and resilience in the uphill battle for respect and treating women as sacred" (RedCorn 2018, 33).

After Sheridan's interview was published, Illuminative (2024), a Native-woman-led racial and social justice organization focused on challenging narratives about Native people and their visibility (Illuminative 2024), called in Taylor Sheridan on Instagram (fig. 4.1). Illuminative appealed to Sheridan to examine how his behaviors play a role in erasing Indigenous women's experiences, illustrating Vizenor's (1999, 2008) idea of survivance—countering representations of Indigenous peoples as vanishing or victims. Illuminative's "call in" models an Indigenous form of decolonization that involves a process of reflexivity regarding our impact on Indigenous communities' stories and representation. It also illustrates Simpson's (2014) politics of refusal as a sovereign act that rejects the terms of recognition and representation offered by the settler.

Figure 4.1. Screenshot of Illuminative's Instagram post. *Source:* Screenshot by the author.

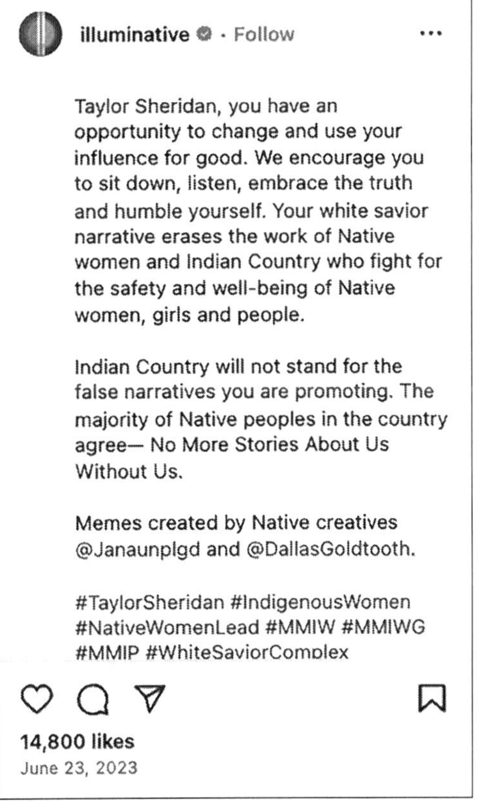

The call of "No More Stories About Us Without Us" has resulted in several television series that feature Indigenous characters and storylines, and that include Indigenous artists and content creators making use of visual sovereignty (Raheja 2011)—which subverts Hollywood's long history of misrepresentation. Perhaps the most prominent is *Reservation Dogs* (2021–2023) created by Sterlin Harjo and Taika Waititi. It follows the lives of four Indigenous teenagers in rural Oklahoma. The show addresses intergenerational trauma and its repercussions, all the while representing how ancestors speak to us and through us in the characters of Spirit and Deer Lady. Spirit, a warrior who died at the Battle of the Little Bighorn, appears to Bear Smallhill, one of the four main characters known as "reservation dogs." Throughout the series, Bear has a series of visons in which Spirit appears and has in-depth conversations with Bear, representing how the dead speak through us by providing guidance and opportunities for reflexivity. In season 2, episode 3, Spirit tells Bear:

> We cry for those that we lost. We mourn them. We cut our hair. We cut ourselves. We go through all the feels. We take our relatives—their bodies—and we make clothing out of it. This is my auntie right here. We airbrush their faces on T-shirts. We get their names tattooed on our bodies in Old English script. We tear ourselves to pieces so that we can build ourselves anew on the other side. You go through all of it so that they know that they can go. That we'll miss them, but that we'll be okay without them. (Harjo et al. 2022a)

Through this monologue, Spirit is teaching Bear how to grieve and mourn the loss of his friend Daniel, and why that is important. In a sense, Harjo and Waititi represent a different paradigm of death to that of Christian teachings, which is represented in non-Indigenous media content. Spirit embodies the normalization of ancestral wisdom without falling into the Western clichés of the "supernatural" or "magical realism"; rather, the show allows audiences to accept Spirit as a part of Bear's experience.

Reservation Dogs addresses the MMIWG2 crisis indirectly by weaving in the story of Deer Lady (Kaniehtiio Horn) throughout its three seasons.[15]

---

15. The story of Deer Woman or Deer Lady is popular among Indigenous peoples from the Eastern Woodlands and the Central Plains who were relocated to Oklahoma as well as the Pacific Northwest. The story as it was told to me is that she was a woman who

Audiences are first introduced to her in episode 5 of the first season through a shot of a beautiful Indigenous woman who is hitchhiking on the Muscogee Reservation. The scene ends with her getting into a car with a young man; then the camera moves downward to reveal her hooves, implying that she is Deer Lady. In this same episode, a flashback depicts how Deer Lady began to protect Big (Bodhi Okuma Linton) after his grandmother died. Deer Lady attends her funeral and tells Big: "You're gonna want to give up, but imagine your grandma is with you every single step of the way. Be good, fight evil, and you'll never have to see me again" (Harjo et al. 2021). This statement cements Deer Lady's protagonism in *Reservation Dogs* as a vigilante spirit that not only punishes bad people but also teaches them how to be better people.

Deer Lady makes two more appearances in *Reservation Dogs'* storyline. In episode 8 of season 2 (Harjo et al. 2022b), she appears to Big to guide him in achieving justice. Episode 3 of season 3 (Harjo et al. 2023) is aptly named "Deer Lady" and weaves the Deer Lady's story with the history of boarding schools in the United States. The episode follows Deer Lady and Bear. Through flashbacks, audiences learn that as a young girl, Deer Lady (Georgeanne Growingthunder) lived in a Christian-run Indian boarding school where her hair braids were chopped off, English was strictly enforced, and Christianity was drilled into her and the other Indigenous kids. Audiences witness how she is treated as less than human, how she runs away to the forest where she encounters a deer spirit who offers her a choice: Live a short and painful human life, or a longer life where she'll become something more than human. This form of witnessing "involves testifying to the events, observed historical facts, but also to the meaning of those events which goes beyond what the eye can see" (Fregoso 2023, 103). While this episode provides a backstory of Deer Lady's character, the writers of the episode, Sterlin Harjo, Chad Charlie, and Tika Wititi, and the director

---

was heinously raped, and her body was found in the woods next to a fawn who lay down next to her so she would not die alone. A deer spirit then grants her the gift of being reborn as half human and half deer. In this form, she lures her rapists to the woods where she tramples them to death. She is thought of as a protector of fertility, love, and beauty. However, her power lies in that she attracts men who usurp women's power and prey on or ignore women and children; once lured by Deer Lady, those men are never seen again. In some communities, artwork depicting Deer Lady has become an emblem of the localized MMIWG2 movements; however, a red handprint over a mouth is the most recognizable symbol of the movement as it stands for all missing and murdered whose voices are not heard.

Danis Goulet, steer away from representing her as a victim; instead, what her character manifests is the rage that fuels her life because of her history.

Other television series that address the MMIWG2 crisis have hired Indigenous writers to ensure accurate portrayals of Indigenous people and cultures. For example, in 2022 ABC released *Alaska Daily*, a crime series about the MMIWG2 in Alaska created by Tom McCarthy. The story follows Eileen Fitzgerald (Hillary Swank), an investigative reporter who is forced to work alongside Indigenous reporter Roz Friendly (Grace Dove-Secwepemc) to cover the cold case of an Indigenous woman's murder. Besides hiring Indigenous actress Grace Dove and other Indigenous actors, the producers hired Andrew Okpeaha MacLean, an Iñupiaq filmmaker, and Vera Starbard, a Tlingit playwright and TV writer who incorporated Native languages into the script and helped the show model the cultural competence needed for journalists looking to report on Indigenous issues. This series also includes a representation of postmortem politics through the story of a mother and her efforts to bring justice to her daughter's murder through the press, the criminal justice system, and legislation. The show was canceled after its first season due to high production costs and low ratings.

Two series addressing MMIWG2 premiered in 2024: *Under the Bridge* developed by Quinn Shepard and based on the book by Rebecca Godfrey, and season 4 of *True Detective: Night Country* created by Mexican director Issa López (2024). This indicates a shift in mainstream-media representations of Indigenous people and MMIWG2 that reflects a broader commitment by showrunners to the communities that they represent, in tandem with the capacity of social media users to call out and call in. These two series also center Indigenous women's activism and advocacy, and the porousness between the living and the dead in Indigenous thought rather than the Western approaches represented in Sheridan's work. Both shows include Indigenous content creators and actors, and they both represent postmortem politics by family members seeking justice for their missing relatives. *Under the Bridge*, created by Quinn Shepard (2024), focuses on the true story of Canadian-Punjabi teen Reena Virk, killed by her classmates, and the ways her parents and family members engaged with law enforcement and lobbyists to get antibullying legislation passed in Canada. Cam Bentland (Lily Galdstone), an Indigenous woman and law-enforcement officer, realizes that she is Indigenous and was taken from her Indigenous community as a child as her investigation of Reena's murder unfolds. This fact makes evident the colonial practice of taking Indigenous children from their communities and changes her choice to serve as a Canadian law-enforcement officer.

True Detective: Night Country, on the other hand, weaves the fictional story of eight scientists who disappear from a research station with the murder of Annie Kowtok (Nivi Pedersen), an Iñupiat woman. The show's plot, while fictional, is inspired by the real-life murder of Annie Le, a Yale student who worked at a research lab and was murdered by a real man named Raymond Clark, and by the unsolved mysteries of Dyatlov Pass and the *Mary Celeste* (Busis 2024). In the show, Kowtok is stabbed to death and her tongue cut out after protesting the construction of a local mine in the fictional town of Ennis, Alaska, and the show begins with her murder having been unsolved for six years. *True Detective: Night Country* represents both how the dead speak through us and postmortem politics by evoking audiences' biases toward Indigenous People. For example, in the first episode of the season when the scientists are found frozen out in the tundra, Alaska Native Trooper Evangeline Navarro (Kali Reis-Seaconke Wampanoag) questions Rose (Fiona Shaw), an older woman who lives in a remote area and claims to be able to see the dead. When Navarro asks how she found the scientists, Rose matter-of-factly responds that her dead husband showed them to her. This sets the tone for the rest of the season where the boundary between the living and the dead is consistently blurred and women's knowledge is dismissed.

Another example is the protagonism of Indigenous women activists, who are represented trying to seek justice for Annie and who continue to protest the Silver Sky mine in her honor. The show weaves in the story of Leah (Isabella Star LaBlanc-Sisseton, Wahpeton Dakota), the adoptive daughter of Police Chief Danvers (Jody Foster), to illustrate how this rage and activism are intergenerational. Throughout the season, the tension between Chief Danvers and Leah hinges on Leah's increased association with her Indigenous heritage through this activism and her being in spaces with other Indigenous women.

The final episode lays bare the audience's biases, which limit the subjectivities that are visible to them. The sixth episode of the fourth season of *True Detective: Night Country* (2024) reveals that Indigenous-women workers and the research lab's cleaning ladies attacked the researchers. When pressed, the women confess to Danvers and Navarro that they discovered the secret lab and evidence that Annie was killed there, so they avenged Annie's killing by forcing the researchers out into the cold, with Annie's spirit ultimately punishing them. As final acts of postmortem politics, Danvers and Navarro close the case by declaring that the researchers died of natural causes. This allows the experience of the Indigenous women to stand on its own with the understanding that the complicity of law enforcement and the mine led the women to take matters into their own hands. In the final scene, Chief Danvers leaks a video recording of one of the scientists, Raymond Clark, exposing the consequences of the Silver Sky mine's pollution to the Ennis and surrounding communities, leading to the closure of the mine. Through this action, Danvers begins to disrupt the entrenched alliances among law enforcement, political authorities, and representatives of extractive industries, signaling a shift in the power relations that sustain settler-colonial resource exploitation.

The representations of Indigenous storylines, including the postmortem politics and activism of Indigenous women and family members with their calls for decolonizing systems, engage with the politics of representation. Films like *Wind River* (2017) and *Killers of the Flower Moon* (2023) portray how the US federal government, law enforcement, and extractive industries relate to Indigenous communities. These box-office hits erase Indigenous presence while centering white characters as saviors (Vizenor 1999), illustrating the politics of representation. In contrast, *Fancy Dance* (2024), a film written, directed, and acted by US Indigenous actors, engages in visual sovereignty, which reclaims representational authority (Raheja 2011) and embodies the Indigenous decolonizing projects of storytelling, remembering, and representing (Smith1999). However, *Fancy Dance* (2024), while premiering at the 2023 Sundance Film Festival, received only a limited theatrical release before moving to Apple TV+, making it available exclusively to paid subscribers and limiting its cultural impact and reach.

While these films have raised visibility and awareness of the colonial historical processes that continue to affect Indigenous communities, more work needs to be done in the film industry to reconcile how these stories are told and by whom, and how they are distributed to achieve larger reach. Television series such as *Reservation Dogs* (2021–2023) and the film *Fancy Dance* (2024) set a model to follow where Indigenous perspectives are prioritized, grounding the narrative and centering Indigenous characters. These films offer another avenue, besides social media, to represent postmortem politics and affective agency that lives alongside (and in interrelation with) legal advocacy. Perhaps in the not so distant future, Indigenous-women writers and directors will materialize their voices and respective experiences in films and television series. This will contribute to the cultural shift needed to reclaim the sacredness of women and two-spirit people and to be reflexive of the audience's relationships with Indigenous communities off-screen.

Lessons in Persistence and
Indigenous MMIWG2 Activism in Nevada

Lastly, in this section I examine MMIWG2 Indigenous activism and postmortem politics by drawing on the decolonizing action-research methodologies of intervening, connecting, and sharing (Smith). By analyzing coalition-building strategies employed by Nevada's MMIWG2, I underscore and reflect on how their persistence has forged meaningful partnerships with key community and government entities to address MMIWG2 and MMIP, ultimately showing how the application of Indigenous decolonizing methodologies can transform Western advocacy practices.

In 2019, seven months after I had moved to Reno, I was invited by my colleague and friend Debra Harry to participate in an event called "No More Stolen Sisters: Demanding Justice for Missing and Murdered Indigenous Women and Girls." The event was organized by a planning group of all Indigenous women who had been working together on Standing Rock, the women's marches, and other Indigenous events in northern Nevada over the last few years. The event was held on February 13, 2019, and was emceed by environmental activist Autumn Harry (Pyramid Lake Paiute). The event included opening prayers; an honor song performed by the Mankillers All-Women Drum Group; panelist talks by April Carmelo (Maidu), Jolie Varela (Tule River Yokut and Paiute), and Lyla June Johnston (Diné [Navajo]) and Tsétsêhéstâhese [Cheyenne]); a Jingle Dress Dance choreographed by Teresa Melendez (Pokagon Band of Potawatami) and Tziavi Melendez (Paiute); a closing performance by Lyla June Johnston; and a silent auction to raise funds for a mural on MMIWG to be done in Reno.

During the performance, Lyla June Johnston, a scholar, musician, and community organizer, performed a song she had written called "Mamwlad." Johnston introduced the song by explaining that the title was Welsh and meant "motherland." She had chosen it because of her biracial ancestry, and because Welsh as an Indigenous European language was an example of how earth-based cultures were destroyed in Europe in a similar way to Native American cultures. She then explained how no woman should ever be killed because of her spiritual practice and began singing the words, "Six million women thrown to the flames / the library is burning / I'll remember their names / the first colonization of the human race didn't happen in America / it happened in the place of Mamwlad / mother country." As she sang, I noted how she was deliberately weaving the eradication of

Europe's earth-based healers (the witches)—who were burned, drowned, raped, beaten, and tortured—with the experiences of Native Americans in the United States. The crowd focused on every word Johnston sang. As I looked around the ballroom where the event was being held, I saw people nodding when she sang the lyrics "These were Europe's healers / we descend from healers" or "Remember the beauty of our people before the conquers came / I will not choose war, I will choose peace, and honor the ancestors alive inside of me." Perhaps the most affecting moment of the song came when Johnston sang, "Feeling is healing / and these tears are falling like rain / feeling is healing / and this is why we remember their names." I found myself tearing up and as I lifted my gaze, I saw others wiping away tears and smiling melancholily. While I was familiar with Johnston's earlier songs, I had not heard this one.

After the event, I went home and looked up the video on YouTube, which presently as of July 2025 has over 156,025 views. In the description of the video there, Johnston (2018) explains:

> Our elders have taught us that any assault on the women of a society is also an assault on the men who love them. Imagine having your wife, or daughter burned alive and being restrained from helping her. This is what so many of our grandfathers went through and it drove them purely mad. We must too pray for the soul of the masculine that was tricked into thinking it was insufficient, tricked into thinking it "failed to protect." These are all psychological tactics to make us hate ourselves across the board and have damaged us for too many generations. This is healed through self-love and the forgiveness of this unimaginable cruelty of others. It is time to throw off these chains and throw off these lies and affirm our sacredness and worth as men and women in the eyes of Creator.

The description says much more, linking the burning of witches in Europe to intergenerational trauma for both women and men and the impact this had on those descending from Europeans and Native Americans. This event and this song mark the beginning of my relationship with Indigenous-women activists in northern Nevada, collectively known as Indigenous Women Rising. Over the last five years, my interpersonal relationships with some of these women, especially—especially Autumn, her mother Beverly, Jolie, Teresa, and Debra—have helped me unlearn settler-colonial ideas about the land

and deepened my understanding of how women's experiences of violence are intimately connected to spiritual practice and to their relationship to the land.

Their persistence has informed their activism, especially after the deaths of Anna Scott and Amanda Davis. Since 2021 Beverly and Autumn Harry have collaborated with numerous Indigenous women across the Great Basin to organize the now yearly Red Dress Powwows and walks at the Pyramid Lake Reservation. These events honor the lives of Anna Scott, Amanda Davis, and other missing and murdered relatives in the Great Basin region. I have witnessed these women's efforts to build cross-movement solidarity by building coalitions with Black Lives Matter, Tu Casa Latina, the Nevada Women's March organizers, and environmental organizations in demonstrations and events.

In 2022 they successfully worked to get then-Governor Steve Sisolak to recognize and adopt the observance in Nevada of National Day of Awareness for Missing and Murdered Indigenous Women and Girls. They are also collaborating with legislators to introduce and advocate for state laws and policies that would address structural inequalities and jurisdictional limitations in the state. For example, in 2023 the Nevada Legislature passed AB125, which requires law-enforcement agencies to accept reports from tribes and colonies in the state, regardless of jurisdiction, and enter the reports on the National Crime Information Center and National Missing and Unidentified Persons databases. It also requires the Department of Public Safety to maintain a tribal liaison to communicate on missing or murdered Indigenous persons with tribes and law-enforcement agencies. In 2024 the activists successfully worked to get the City of Reno to sign a proclamation acknowledging May 5 as the Missing and Murdered Indigenous People Awareness Day, the same year that President Biden issued his Proclamation on Missing or Murdered Indigenous Persons Awareness Day.

Through their work and in my collaborations with Indigenous Women Rising and the Healing Waters Institute I have learned a great deal, both about the struggles faced by those fighting for justice and spreading awareness of MMIWG2 and about my relationship to Indigenous advocacy as an ally of Indigenous communities in Nevada and elsewhere. I have learned, for example, that it is essential to amplify the voices of families and survivors and to be mindful of the various acronyms used in events (MMIW, MMIWG, MMIWG2 and MMIWG2S, and MMIP) because some of these are not inclusive of two-spirit people. As someone who did not grow up in an Indigenous community and whose background whitewashed my connections with Indigenous ancestors, I had to ask myself if my motivations for participating in MMIWG2 spaces were tied to my personal experiences and how those experiences informed my participation in gatherings. I learned about trauma-informed organizing—and how everything from the language we use to the images we select to the spaces we build and choose to use matters. I also had to unpack my biases and communicative practices; I realized, rather quickly, that I was unconsciously reproducing colonial practices and needed to be willing and open to learning other ways of knowing. I learned and continue learning how to listen and be present with those I share space with. I have had to reflect on how my actions and thoughts affect the Indigenous women I share space with, my family members, those I interact with, and the land I live on and travel through because how we make decisions today is critical for future generations.

I have been able to learn because I had to be willing to listen to the Indigenous-women activists, advocates, colleagues, and friends willing to call me in, to reflect on their teachings, and to change my own deeply embodied colonial logics. Through our conversations and collaborations, I continue to witness the importance of the interrelatedness of their postmortem politics in legal and media spaces. Their persistence continues to alter representations of Indigenous people, knowledge, and MMIWG2 in films and television series and is driving legislative change; it has slowly started to drive the cultural shift needed to decolonize our unconscious and reconnect with Indigenous ways of knowing.

Conclusion

The Perseverance of Transmuting Grief

Tu yóosal ak láak'on, ku xíimbak Montejo
Tu yóosal xko'olelo'ob ku ba'atelo'ob Puerto
Tu yóosal x-ko'olel tu xámanil tak Nóojol
Tu yóosal na'tsilo'ob ku ba'atel Tahdziú

Ma' sáajko'on k'aayi', ki k'aatko'on jets'óolal
Kin wawato'on yóosal jujuntul ts'o'ok u sa'atal
Ka k'áamchajak u juum, in k'aat kuxanilo'on
Ka'luubuk yéetel muk', le kíinsaj ko'olel,
Ka'luubuk yéetel muk', le kíinsaj ko'olel
Y retiemblen sus centros la tierra
Al sororo rugir del amor
Yéetel yáabanak u chumuk lu'umil
Ti' u yáambal yaabilal ak kíik

—Vivir Quintana / version: Belle Delouisse[1]

In the spring of 2024, I was asked to teach a graduate-level class on
feminist theory. At the time I was writing the manuscript for this book, so
I decided to teach the class under the title "Global Theories of Feminicide,

---

1. *t.* For our friends protesting on Montejo / For all women battling in Puerto / For
the female commanders fighting for Nóojol / For the mothers who keep searching in
Tahdziú / We sing fearless, we ask for justice / We shout for every missing woman /
Let it be heard: We want us alive!/ Down with the feminicidal killer / Down with the
feminicidal killer! / And the center of the earth shall tremble / At the sisterly roar of
love / And the center of the earth shall tremble / at the sisterly roar of love/.

MMIWG2, and Transfeminicide."[2] The class had fifteen students from varied backgrounds and disciplines: two nontrans men, three nonbinary folks, and ten nontrans women from the fields of philosophy, anthropology, English, sociology, and gender, race, and identity. The syllabus focused on readings from activists, scholars, and public figures, and explored how scholarship, legislation, and culture all informed each other to address this form of extreme gender violence. My goal was to challenge students to think about how often we tend to blame this form of violence on the evil of one individual or one system—and ignore how in reality we experience, consume, and yes, even (unconsciously and consciously) daily reproduce forms of gender violence through our interpersonal relationships, our jobs, the media we choose to engage with, the laws, and so on. As part of guiding students through this challenge, one of the activities required them to lead a discussion about one of the readings with the flexibility to lead it in the manner they wanted—they could do a traditional Power Point or be creative in their exposition of the text. One of the students, Ren Frick, who also happens to be the cofounder of the Reno Community Closet, led a discussion about readings on social responses to feminicide during the eleventh week of the semester. As part of their discussion, they suggested the class create a zine that could capture everything they had learned so far in the class. The class agreed and by the fifteenth week, everyone had brought their page or pages to contribute to the zine, which they named *Rabia: Righteous Anger,* because while *rabia* means "rage" in Spanish, it also means "spring" and the beginning of life in Arabic.[3] The students' learning and praxis on these zine pages is a form of postmortem politics.

Another one of these assignments required them to engage weekly with and think about everyday representations of feminicide in culture in the United States and abroad and relate what they had observed to the readings. I started the assignment to give them an example. My post presented the songs "Hey Joe" (1966), interpreted by Jimi Hendrix, and "No Body, No Crime" by Taylor Swift and HAIM. I justified my choices by telling them that there was a fifty-four-year difference between the release dates of the two songs, yet they are both discussed in popular discourse as revenge songs grappling with the subject of the killing of women. I asked them to reflect on my initial post, relate these videos to both readings, analyze what

---

2. See appendix B for the syllabus.

3. With my students consent you can see the contents of *Rabia* in appendix C.

cultural context or narrative they represented, and write one critical-thinking question. These are some of the most relevant questions the students posed to each other:

> "How can femicide be portrayed in the media in a way that does not desensitize us to violence, but makes us aware of the problem at hand? In other words, is it possible to portray the reality of femicide within artistic media in a way that does not make us numb to its horror and consequences?"

> "When thinking about how women's bodies are disposed of and how men have the autonomy to flee undesirable circumstances (specifically, Joe to Mexico and Este's husband to another woman), how do we think about gendered bodies, movement, and the circumstances that dictate how they function and move under capitalism and patriarchy?"

> "What elements do you think are necessary to create an autonomous feminist aesthetics—meaning an aesthetic that is outside of the patriarchy's portrayal of women?"

> "What are the moral implications of capitalizing off of the death of women?"

These questions indicate that students began to see how nuanced the issue of femicide is, especially when considering the ethics in the representation of various forms of gender violence including feminicide.

Throughout the semester, students took this assignment seriously, posting about a plethora of social justice campaigns' street art, subcultures, and performances. One of these students, Elisha Harris, shared the African American Policy Forum (AAPF) and Center for Intersectionality and Social Policy Studies campaign #sayhername. While reading his post, I recalled how the Black Lives Matter movement also partook in postmortem politics through the practice of their call-and-response chant "Say His Name," whereby one person would name a person, for example, "Michael Brown, say his name, say his name, say his name," and then others would scream the name.

The #sayhername campaign was launched in 2014 "to bring "awareness to the often-invisible names and stories of Black women and girls who have been victimized by racist police violence and provides support to their families" (African American Policy Forum 2020). The AAPF website challenges the notion that a movement for Black lives must also include all lives. They explained in a previous version of the website of the African American Policy Forum, "If our collective outrage around cases of police violence is meant to serve as a warning to the state that its agents cannot kill without consequence, our silence around the cases of Black women and girls sends the message that certain deaths do not merit repercussions" (African American Policy Forum 2020; Winfrey-Harris 2020; Jonson 2024). As the movement gained traction, artists participated in postmortem artivism (art that is also activism) by creating content with the names of those who were murdered by police and racial violence. Although most of these solely focused on nontrans men, in 2015 Janelle Monáe released a song with her Wonderland artist collective called "Hell You Talmbout"[4] and introduced the names of Aiyana Jones, Sandra Bland, Miriam Carey, and Sharonda Singleton. This song is described as "less song and more of a chant, with some gospel overtones" (Breihan 2015). Monáe performed the song at the 2017 Women's March in Washington, DC, and focused the lyrics primarily on Black women and girls.

Wonderland and Monáe released a subsequent instrumental track of the song so that people could make their own versions. Vita Cleveland, a transgender-rights advocate, released "Hell Y'all Ain't Talmbout" in 2018, which focused on names of murdered Black trans women and called out the Black Lives Matter movement for not being inclusive of Black trans women. She sings:

> Ain't no time to pray, ain't no time to waste
> Y'all be acting like trans people don't be dying everyday
> But we don't show up in your songs
> We just show up in your bags
> We don't get tagged in your statutes
> But the status of bodies with tags . . . the sum of us or none
>   of us—flatout

---

4. In standard English, the phrase "Hell You Talmbout" would be "What the hell are you talking about?" In the song title "Hell You Talmbout," it becomes a more urgent and emotionally charged demand—one that calls attention to the erasure or distortion of Black lives and narratives, thus centering Black speech and cultural expression, signaling resistance to dominant linguistic and political norms, and emphasizing the Black musical and protest traditions of orality, rhythm, and repletion.

These demands to invoke trans women's names as well materialized when in 2021, Janelle Monáe released a seventeen-minute-long revamp of her 2015 song "Hell You Talmbout" and renamed it "Say Her Name (Hell You Talmbout)." This version of the song featured Professor Kimberlé Crenshaw, prominent Black trans and nontrans women, and nonbinary artists and activists, including Beyoncé, Alicia Keys, Brittany Howard, Chlöe x Halle, Tierra Whack, Isis V., Zoë Kravitz, Asiahn, MJ Rodriguez, Jovian Zayne, Angela Rye, Nikole Hannah-Jones, Brittany Packnett Cunningham, and Alicia Garza. The revamped song was also released along with a video that was inclusive of trans women's names and whose proceeds benefit the African American Policy Forum. On her Instagram account, Monáe wrote, "Please join us as we honor the 61 Black girls and women whose lives mattered and should be with us today. Black women and girls are often left out of the conversation when it comes to police brutality. Today we say their names. We tell their stories" (2021). In this case, Janelle Monáe's revamping brings dignity and honor to the lives of Black trans and nontrans women and girls whose lives had not been acknowledged. It is an act of postmortem politics through artivism that benefits a political organization focused on direct advocacy.

Another one of the students in my class, Itzel Perez, chose to introduce the class to the songs "Un violador en tu camino" (2019) by the feminist collective Las Tesis and "Canción sin miedo" (2020) by Mon Laferte and Vivir Quintana. Upon seeing their post, I remembered the global impact of both songs in feminist movements from the moment each was first performed. Because my argument throughout this book has been that grief and mourning mobilized by activists' responses to the killing of women in Ciudad Juárez opened an affective hemispheric dialectic with other responses by activists in the Americas, I will only focus on "Canción sin miedo" since it names the affect of fear, or rather, it names the absence of fear in the title.

"Canción sin miedo" (2020) was first performed by Mon Laferte, Vivir Quintana, and the Palomar choir in front of eighty thousand people on the evening of March 7, 2020, in Mexico City's Zócalo—the main public square that serves as a central gathering place for cultural events and demonstrations (De Cultura de la Ciudad de México 2020). [5] The Chilean Mexican artist Mon Laferte tells the audience that she sent Vivir Quintana a WhatsApp message asking her to write a song to be sung at

---

5. The video of the performance can be found here: https://www.youtube.com/watch?v=_J_V4WFPTzo. I recommend watching it before continuing to read this chapter. A video with English translations can be found here: https://www.youtube.com/watch?v=reMLhEj3hyE,

the Zócalo for the Tiempo de Mujeres Festival "para reflejar la situación por la que vive nuestro país México"[6] (Puntos Suspensivos Comunicación 2020). Vivir Quintana wrote the song in a couple of hours in the style of Mexican mariachi and sent it back to Mon Laferte, who was left speechless. In the performance at the Zócalo, Vivir Quintana dedicates the song to all women in Mexico and Latin America.

The song went viral and became the unofficial anthem of Latin American struggles for reproductive justice and against feminicide. It was embraced by feminist activists throughout the continent, inspiring localized adaptations in a similar fashion as the song "Un Violador en tu Camino" (2019) by the Chilean collective Las Tesis. As of March 2025 the song had over twenty million plays on Spotify, and the video on Vivir Quintana's YouTube channel had over twenty-five million views as of 2024 as well. Also, on YouTube, there are many videos of interpretations of the song from different places throughout Latin America, the Caribbean, and Europe, in corresponding languages that have anywhere from three thousand to over twenty-five million views.

Because of the reach and subsequent affective and translocal adaptations of "Canción sin miedo," I draw on what the ethnomusicologist Ruthie Meadows (2023) coins as the "efficacy of sound"—an embodied relational "core logic of engagement, potentiality and actionability" (43). For Meadows, the efficacy of sound opens possibilities to study the use and usefulness of music because it treats sound as "a capacious, transformative force intricately linked to embodied forms of relationality and the entanglements of language, materiality, and visuality" (34). "Canción sin miedo" (2020) became an efficacious, affective sonic template used by artists and activists across the Americas: The translation of its original lyrics across languages underscores its potentiality and actionability for artists and activists engaged in postmortem politics hemispherically. In numerous recorded versions, the core backing track of the song remains the same even as the instruments of specific regions are introduced in complementary and locally resonant textures (e.g., the saxophone, the flute, the Brazilian cuica and rebolo, the Puerto Rican barril de bomba).

The following original lines recount places where feminicidal violence made headlines in Mexico during 2019–2020:

---

6. *t.* to reflect on the situation experienced by our country Mexico

> Por todas las compas marchando en Reforma
> (For all the friends marching on Reforma)[7]
> Por todas las morras peleando en Sonora
> (For all the girls fighting in Sonora)
> Por las comandantas luchando por Chiapas
> (For the commanders fighting for Chiapas)
> Por todas las madres buscando en Tijuana
> (For all the mothers searching in Tijuana)

However, in other versions of the song these places are changed for places pertinent to the community that chose to adopt the manner in which the song calls out actionability. If we refer back to this chapter's epigraph, which is in the Yucatec Maya language, the places have been changed to: Montejo, Puerto, Nóojol, and Tahdziú. In this case the lyrics of "Canción sin miedo" (2020) were adapted by the Yucatec singer Belle Delouisse in 2021 because "Quería darle algo a las mujeres con lo que pudieran sentirse identificadas. Parte de la canción se enfoca en las mujeres indígenas, ya que muchas veces son las que menos voz tienen, es por ello que la adaptación tiene parte de la letra traducida en lengua maya"[8] (Soto 2021). Belle Delouisse's adaptation makes "Cancion sin miedo" (2020) actionable by translating it into a language that the Indigenous women of the Yucatán peninsula can relate to and feel sonically represented with. There are various adaptations of the song in Indigenous languages from across the Americas.[9] The song's

---

7. Reforma refers to Avenida Reforma or Paseo de la Reforma in Mexico City, which is a central site for demonstrations and marches (often feminist, labor, against state violence, and Indigenous movements). The avenue was originally commissioned by Maximilian I to connect the Chapultepec Castle to the city center, and it was lined with government buildings, corporate headquarters, embassies, banks, and iconic monuments such as the Angel of Independence, Diana the Huntress, and the Monument to the Revolution. Along this avenue one can also see antimonuments—public installations that challenge state-sanctioned monuments and demand accountability, often erected without authorization. Along Reforma there are antimonuments for the forty-three "disappeared students" from Ayotzinapa, feminicide victims, and political prisoners.

8. *t.* "I wanted to give women something they could relate to." Part of the song focuses on Indigenous women because they are often the ones who least have a voice. This is why some of the lyrics in the adaptation are translated into the Mayan language.

9. The videos can be found on YouTube by searching for "Canción Sin Miedo—Versión Yucatán—Belle"; "Canción sin miedo—Juntanza de mujeres indígenas colombianas"

capaciousness also allows for each adaptation to build on others. For example, the video of the Brazilian song titled "Georgia Brown—Canção sem Medo (Brasil)—Bloco Não é Não e Coró Mulher" includes statistics of the number of feminicides and transfeminicides, and it incorporates: Indigenous and trans women; the green bandannas from the Latin American reproductive-justice movement and the purple bandanna from the contra-feminicide movement; a clip from Mon Laferte and Vivir Quintana's performance of the song; and other stills of women marching in other areas of South America. The Puerto Rican version of the song "Canción sin Miedo: Barrileras del 8M, Puerto Rico" also includes the presence of the green and purple and localizes the song's message through the intersectional inclusions of Afro-Caribbean rhythms and ritual dancing, Indigenous women, a sign-language interpreter, and nonbinary and trans people.

The song's transnational adoption as the unofficial anthem of the contra-feminicide movement reenvisions the feminist struggle as an embodied ritual. The song sonically transmutes grief into a mobilizing force by invoking the names of disappeared and murdered trans and nontrans women and girls that become embodied in the lines "Soy Claudia, soy Esther y soy Teresa / Soy Ingrid, soy Fabiola y soy Valeria / Soy la niña que subiste por la fuerza."[10] These names also get changed according to the names of those relevant to other contexts, making this song actionable and transformative to other regions besides Mexico. Those of us who sing the song, who hear the song, who feel the song, become fearless in invoking these names. We channel their plea for justice. Our bodies bring these women to life through our voices, our movements, and our playing of instruments. By sonically embodying the spaces where we sing the song we engage others.

Furthermore, the song offers a form of postmortem politics that potentializes our lack of fear as transformative in a rather political way. The first stanza of the song reads:

> Que tiemble el Estado, los cielos, las calles
> (May the state, the heavens, the streets tremble)
> Que teman los jueces y los judiciales
> (May the judges and magistrates tremble)
> Hoy a las mujeres nos quitan la calma
> (Today they have taken away the calm of women)

---

10. *t.* I am Claudia, I am Esther, I am Teresa / I am Ingrid, I am Fabiola, I am Valeria / I am the girl you mounted by force.

Nos sembraron miedo, nos crecieron alas
(They sowed in us fear, we grew wings)

The stanza announces how that fear that was sown in women by the state, judges, magistrates, religion, and men in public spaces has been replaced by wings. The second stanza names how these political entities have contributed to feminicidal violence and disappearances and makes a plea for the president to not forget the names of those murdered:

A cada minuto de cada semana
(Every minute of every week)
Nos roban amigas, nos matan hermanas
(They steal our friends, they kill our sisters)
Destrozan sus cuerpos, las desaparecen
(They destroy their bodies, make them disappear)
No olviden sus nombres, por favor, señor president
(Don't forget their names, please, Mr. President)

Thus, by naming these political entities, the crimes that have caused these deaths, and pleading to the president to remember the names of those murdered, the song becomes a powerful force that kindles engagement with the political class.

The song as the unofficial anthem of Latin American feminist struggles also underscores the transformative power of postmortem politics through an alteration that echoes the Mexican anthem. However, instead of keeping the lyrics of the Mexican anthem, the song transmutes that sentiment into an interconnected call for change through love. It takes the highly patriarchal and violent line,

Y retiemble en sus centros la Tierra
(May the earth tremble to its core)
Al sonoro rugir del cañón
(To the resounding roar of the cannon)

And transmutes it into,

Y retiemblen sus centros la tierra
(May the earth tremble to its core)
Al sororo rugir del amor
(To the roaring sisterhood of love)

This last line remains in all the song's adaptations, regardless of how the lyrics change to be relevant to the translocal community that adopts them. The lyrics' alchemy of the masculine, violent, and patriarchal Mexican anthem into an affective call to action reenvisions what is possible when grief as an embodied affect connects our bodies to our communities as a felt compulsion with political power.

Persevering

Concluding this book would imply that feminicide, MMIWG2, and transfeminicide are issues that can be neatly put away; however, as I have detailed throughout this book, that is not the case. Visibility and awareness of these issues are essential, and the postmortem and transmortem politics of relatives and friends have led the way to bring this to our awareness and drive legislative change. I have detailed in chapters 1, 2, and 3 how Mexico, Brazil, Colombia, Argentina, and other parts of Latin America have moved toward laws to address gender violence and feminicide/femicide. Still, those laws' existence has not eradicated or diminished the rates of this violence.

In chapter 4 I focused on how the United States and Canada are slowly grappling with how the coloniality of their laws affects Indigenous people, and how women, girls, and two-spirit people are working to drive legislative change. However, neither country has specific laws to address feminicide/femicide nor transfeminicide, which suggests that the issue is so insidious in these countries that we still need to work at naming it. In the United States, we are obsessed with how many women are killed elsewhere in the world and even provide funding to protect their rights through VAWA. Yet, we fail to look at ourselves and connect the dots between the high rates of homicide of femme-identifying people and the gendered nature of their killing. We need to stop blaming singular systems or a specific person and realize that the criminal-justice system alone will not enact change.

On the other hand, culture alone is also not to blame. As Shahrzad et al. (2021) explain, "Culture is not the cause of violence per se; it is not the root of violence. At the center of the forms of imperialist violence against women is the intensification of the scale in which women's bodies and sexualities are treated as property, and that requires more explanation" (45). For example, twenty-two trans women were killed in the first six months of 2024 in the United States. According to the Violence Policy Center's (2023) report "When Men Murder Women: A Review of 25 Years of Female Homicide Victimization in the United States," 92% of females killed between 1996 and 2020 knew their killers, with the states of Alaska, Arkansas, Louisiana, Nevada, New Mexico, Oklahoma, South Carolina, and Tennessee having the highest rates of females killed by men. In most of these cases women were killed by guns, an issue recently addressed by the Supreme Court. On June 21, 2024, the court upheld a federal law that makes it a crime for people under domestic-violence restraining orders to have guns. While this ruling is a small step in the right direction, it does not address the broader issue: that the United States ranked thirty-fourth for intentional female homicides at a rate of 2.6 per 100,000 women (World Bank Group 2021), which is about three women killed by their intimate partners every day. These numbers should alarm us and lead us to question why we have yet to codify these female homicides as feminicides/femicides in our penal code or start naming these crimes as femicides in public discourse.

Perhaps the answer lies in the great need for a paradigm shift. We need to change the culture that creates, reproduces, and consumes gender violence. We need to reflect on how we continue perpetuating colonial paradigms and do the work of decolonizing ourselves so we might help transform the systems and industries that do not consider cis and trans women, girls, and two-spirit people as sacred or value their lives. Thus, I invite you to persevere and remember that change starts slowly. You must become an active participant in this change by thinking about your relationship to the place you live and the people you share space with. Ask yourself the following questions:

1. How do you contribute to the creation, reproduction, and consumption of gender violence and feminicide? What language do you use in your interpersonal relationships? In partnerships or romantic relationships, how do you work through conflict? Do you enjoy murder shows? Do you enjoy listening to, creating, and/or sharing lyrics that are discriminatory toward women or perpetuate colonial logics that justify violence toward women's bodies? Do you share videos with friends that represent and/or capture incidences of gender violence?

2. Are local conversations being held about feminicide, MMIWG2, and/or transfemicide? If so, who is having these conversations? Learn from them. Are there support groups? What work are they

doing? Ask how you can contribute. If not, consider starting the conversation with others who might also be interested.

3. Do you know of local organizations that provide confidential shelter and advocacy services to survivors of gender violence? If so, do you have the capacity to become a volunteer? If not, educate yourself and find out what resources are available.

4. Does the criminal-justice system in your community offer more than one option for victims and/or family members seeking justice?

5. Do the criminal-justice and welfare agencies reliably pursue and investigate reports by survivors and by family members of those who have disappeared or been murdered?

6. Are there perpetrators and/or predators in your organization, company, work environment, or school? Do they have power? Do they target women? Trans people? Young girls? Indigenous, Black, Asian, or Latino people? Does their behavior have a pattern? Is their behavior excused? If so, how? Take note of these things. And if possible, find people within these spaces to help you advocate for these institutions to hold them accountable; otherwise their violence will continue.

7. How does your awareness of practices that perpetuate gender violence affect those with whom you live, socialize, and share space?

I invite you to continue working toward a world where cis and trans women, girls, and LGBTQ2 people are no longer killed. I invite you to persevere by researching what the status of femicide is where you live and collaborating and organizing with those in your communities to address it, to decolonize yourself, to reflect on how you perpetuate, consume, and reproduce gender violence. Remember, it is a process.

Soy Isabel, Susana, soy Marielle y soy Savanna
(I am Isabel, Susana, I am Marielle, and I am Savanna)
Soy Rosa, soy Karla y soy Julia
(I am Rosa, I am Karla, and I am Julia)
Soy la niña que subiste por la fuerza
(I am the girl you mounted by force)

Soy la madre que ahora llora por sus muertas
(I am the mother who cries for her dead)
Y soy esta que te hará pagar las cuentas
(I am who will hold you accountable)
¡Justicia! ¡Justicia! ¡Justicia!
(Justice! Justice! Justice!)
Por todas las compas marchando en Latinoamerica y el Caribe
(For all the friends marching in Latin America and the Caribbean)
Por todas las personas peleando en Canada y Estados Unidos
(For all the people fighting in Canada and the United States)
Por las mujeres trans luchando por sus vidas
(For all the trans women fighting for their lives)
Por todas las madres buscando en el continente
(For all the mothers searching on the continent)

Appendix A

Table A.1. Sample Tweets Related to #niunamas in Mexico 2009–2010

adrián@chalalu Dec 11, 2009   En escueto comunicado, la SEGOB responde a sentencia de la CIDH, sobre caso de muertas del Campo Algodonero en Cd. Juárez #NiUnaMas
Jesús Robles Maloof@roblesmaloof Nov 20, 2009   #NiunaMas! Cruz que recuerda los feminicidios. Pte. Internacional Paso del Norte frontera México-EU http://pic.gd/cc7e9f
piojo eléctrico@fishoDec 9, 2009   RT @edhappy: Rihanna se hace tatuaje para recordar que fue agredida // las juarenses parecerían carceleras, ja #niunamas
Kristen Stewart@PelotasdeCarey·Jan 31, 2010   De #Juarez y sus masacres, hicieron a sus muertas un monumento a la impunidad, al repudio, al olvido y tambien a la esperanza… #niunamas
Lady Targaryen MX #DefiendoalINE@Muerdecabras·Mar 6, 2010   Unete a la Campaña #niunamas. Sube una foto de denuncie la violencia de género a tu profile de Twitter o Facebook http://bit.ly/cstDO6
Diego López@123pordiego·Apr 22, 2010   Replying to @mcristinaRT @mcristina Resulta que soy la clásica a la que le gusta que le peguen, ¿quién hubiera dicho? / creo q alguien no vio la campaña #niunamas
Tatiana S.@sotrois· Aug 19, 2010   Incrementan #femincidios en #Juárez #niunamás http://tinyurl.com/2d6zcf4
Lydiette Carrión@lydicar·Aug 24, 2010   RT @fandoeros¿Tanto escándalo por una María? #HIDALGO http://alturl.com/cqjnr #casoCuautepec RT #NIUNAMAS/ Caso terrible. Indignación

continued on next page

Table A.1. Continued.

Adriana R. Bautista@adrobattista·Aug 25, 2010 Replying to @FondoSemillasEs el colmo que crezca desaparicion de mujeres en Juarez ¿quien protege a los autores de esto? #niunamas
Víctor Esparza (coquette 🎀)@SoyElVick·Sep 18, 2010 #Noticias: Suman 79 mujeres asesinadas en Sinaloa en lo que va del año #NiUnaMas
Miss Protón@hellenistica·Sep 26, 2010 #niunamas basta de violencia, basta d sangre, basta d muerte! Xk las calles de #chih #cuu #juarez estan tenidas d rojo! Basta!
Juan Carlos Chávez B@JCChavezMX·Oct 29, 2010 #NiUnaMas la ofrenda del Instituto de las Mujeres de #Naucalpan cc @ sandymatac http://plixi.com/p/53695195
Liz@Lizita·Nov 11, 2010 RT @roblesmaloof: Contra la violencia #niunamas #niunomas estamos con #Juarez y con todo el país. http://plixi.com/p/56355278
Claudia Sosa Caustica@Ex_zorrita·Dec 8, 2010 Me uno a la condena en contra de un feminicidio más en #EdoMex la entidad con más feminicidios del país qepd @DarkaJim #Niunamas #PeñaNieto
Daptnhe Cuevas 💜 🦋@Daptnhe·Dec 17, 2010 Hoy a las 5pm en DF manifestación en Gobernación, repudio a asesinato de Marisela quien exigía castigo al asesino de su hija #niunamas
Misra. ™@Politiconsultor·Dec 18, 2010 En #Puebla tambien exigimos #NiUnAmAS #MaricelaEscobedo #ContingentePue http://plixi.com/p/63927798
Martha Tagle@MarthaTagle·Dec 25, 2010 9 días del asesinato de #MariselaEscobedo y ningún responsable en la cárcel #Justicia #niunamas

Table A.2. Legislative Efforts in Latin America and the Caribbean 2007–2014 and 2015–2024

Country	Year	Classification	Law
Bolivia	2013	feminicide	Art 154/252/256
Chile	2010	femicide	Law 20.480 reforms Law 20.066 Art. 390
Colombia	2008	femicide	Law 1257
Costa Rica	2007	femicide	Ley n8.589 25 2007
Dominican Republic	2011	femicide	Ley que facilita el acceso a la Justicia de las mujeres víctimas de violencia
Ecuador	2014	femicide	Art 141/142 Criminal Code
El Salvador	2012	feminicide	Special Comprehensive Law for a Life Free From Violence for Women Art 45/46/47/48
Guatemala	2008	femicide	Law Against Femicide and Other Forms of Violence Against Women
Honduras	2013	femicide	Article 118-A
Mexico	2012	feminicide	General Law on Women's Access to a Life Free of Violence reform Art 325 Criminal Code
Nicaragua	2012	femicide	Law Against Violence Towards Women and Reform to Law no. 641 in Criminal Code
Peru	2011	feminicide	Law 29.819/Art 108B/Art 377
Panama	2013	femicide	Art 41 Law Adopting Measures of Prevention Against Violence Against Women and Reforming Code N 82
Venezuela	2014	femicide	Organic Law On the Right of Women to a Life Free from Violence

continued on next page

Table A.2. Continued.

Country	Year	Classification	Law
Argentina	2021	Femicide/ tranvesticide/ transfemicide	Decreto 123/2021
Brazil	2015	feminicide	Law No13.104
Colombia	2015	femicide	Law 1791/Art 104A/104B
Paraguay	2016	feminicide	No. 5777
Uruguay	2017	femicide	Articles 310/ 312 of Criminal Code

Table A.3. Sample Tweets from Across the Americas using #niunamas 2010–2024

Coalición de Jóvenes@COJESSmx Nov. 7, 2010 RT @ENF2010 Respeto y garantía de Edo. Mex. a #vidalibredviolencia p/tod@s #Niunamás,#Niunomás Jue 11 Nov. 5pm Mnto a la http://mtw.tl/llh3w9
Alicia Guevara@Alicia_Guevara Oct. 26, 2011 @feminicidio en Chile: "Gustavo Lillo fue formalizado esta mañana por el delito de femicidio frustrado" #NiUnaMás http://latercera.com/noticia/nacional/2011/10/680-401340-9-sujeto-que-lanzo-a-ex-pareja-desde-tercer-piso-de-un-centro-comercial-quedo-en.shtml
Luis E. Caicedo@Luise56 Jun. 5, 2012 'Pedimos por Carolina Garzón, joven desaparecida en Ecuador. Es un caso olvidado' #NiunaMás http://soundcloud.com/el-tiempo/pedimos-por-carolina-garz-n
Redes Colombia@RedesColombia May 31, 2013 RT Ángela María Robledo@angelamrobledo A propósito del repudiable caso de Rosa Cely: "Este cuerpo es mío. NO se toca. NO se viola. NO se mata." #NiUnaMás
Edrianny Sanchez@Edrianny_nany Jun. 3, 2012 #niunamas cm dice mi adorada @alejaoficial #ALaMujerNiConElPetaloDeUnaRosa.... Desde Venezuela apoyando esta causa !!
Sonia Herrera Sánchez 🌴 @sonia_herrera_s Jan. 16, 2013 En 2013 ya hubo un #feminicidio cada dos días http://t.co/6mjGO25V vía @ mdzonline #Argentina #niunamás #machismomata
Noticias RCN@NoticiasRCN Mar. 18, 2013 Al menos 1.118 mujeres fueron asesinadas en Honduras entre 2011 y 2012, denunciaron organizaciones del país centroamericano. #NiunaMás
MARIPOSAS@OYENTAS Jun. 07, 2013 @RDfineMx: Muere joven que se hizo #aborto en clínica clandestina #RepublicaDominicana/ #niunamas http://t.co/1cVNp2udf0
Yanely GarcíaPA@yanelygarcia16 Oct. 3, 2013 POR FAVOR QUE ALGUIEN LE DIGA AL MOVIMIENTO #PANAMAAVANZA QUE CON SUS CUÑAS LO UNICO QUE AVANZA ES EL ASCO DE MILES DE PANAMEÑ@S #NIUNAMAS
Aireana Paraguay@aireanapy Nov. 25, 2013 RT @sentimosdiverso: Buenas noches para todas, que ninguna vuelva a ser víctima de violencia #25N, #25NTodosLosDías #NiUnaMás

continued on next page

Table A.3. Continued.

tatiana cepeda paez@tatacepe Feb. 18, 2014 RT @NOmaltratoalamu: En Peru ya empezaron con un granito de arena! Contagiemonos! #NIUNAMAS Tu tambien puedes hacer la diferencia, denuncia
NOmaltratoalamujer@NOmaltratoalamu Feb. 27, 2014 Alertan en Nicaragua por elevado índice de feminicidios!! No podemos seguir permitiendo esto. #NIUNAMAS
Damaris@DamarisCld Nov. 29, 2014 RT @SenadoraOruro: 25 DE NOVIEMBRE: DIA CONTRA VIOLENCIA DE GENERON!BASTA YA!#Bolivia #BastaDeViolencia #NiUnaMas #NoTeCallesDenuncia
Zuleima Castro@ZulyCas Nov. 25, 2014 Contra la violencia #PorLasMujeres #NiConElPetaloDeUnaRosa #NiUnaMas 25 de noviembre. @ Rio de Janeiro... http://instagram.com/p/v1N1sRQ0Ew/
ÐεNιυgυnísιмαΜαиεяα @KoalaSuspicaz Mar. 9, 2018 Séptima víctima de femicidio en Uruguay. Asesinada por su ex pareja JUSTO ayer, 8 de marzo. #VivasNosQueremos #NiUnaMenos #NiunaMuerteIndiferente #NiUnaMás #harta BASTAAAAA!!!!
Alianza por la Solidaridad@AxSolidaridad Dec. 18, 2018 Violencia contra las mujeres, juntos decimos NO: junto a otras organizaciones,@AxSolidaridadparticipa en un día de concienciación contra la violencia de género en #Haiti.#ViolenciadeGénero #NiUnaMas #NingunaMenos #NOEsNO #PorEllas #AxSolidaridad http://bit.ly/2EBtgK3
Betza @BetzaArauz Sep. 4, 2020 ¡Paren ya! Las mujeres queremos vivir sin miedo. Costa Rica de luto, nos estan matando 😞 🖤 NiUnaMenos #NiUnaMas #costarica #Feminicidio #Femicidio #Feministas #NoMasViolencia
Festivales Solidarios@festivalesgt Jan. 24, 2021 Acción colectiva de mujeres en Guatemala, organizaciones, colectivos y civiles, dejan ropas para conmemorar las vidas de mujeres y niñas asesinada como protesta simbólica, los asesinatos registrados durante el 2021 son alarmantes #NiUnaMenos #NiUnaMas
Asamblea feminista SV@AsambleaFemSV Nov. 25, 2022 #25N | Nos tomamos las calles, las pasarelas, los espacios públicos para exigir una vida libre de violencia para las mujeres y niñas en El Salvador Por las que ya no están, por nuestro derecho a vivir libres y sin miedo, Alza tu voz este #25N#NosotrasNoLasOlvidamos #NiUnaMás

Mujeres Al Sur@MujeresAlSur Feb. 16, 2023
En Canadá y Estados Unidos, unas 10.000 #MujeresNativas permanecen #Desaparecidas o sus muertes violentas siguen sin esclarecerse. #NiUnaMas #NiUnaMenos #NosQueremosVivas https://resumenlatinoamericano.org/2023/02/15/feminismos-eeuu-como-no-pudieron-matarnos-en-la-batalla-decidieron-hacerlo-lentamente/

Marta María Ramírez@Martamar77 Jul. 6, 2023
Otro feminicidio, esta vez en la comunidad trans cubana, que no puede ser debidamente cerrado, por necesidad de acceso a investigación y más, de que se revisen externamente dictámenes médicos sobre su muerte.
Vuela libre, Flavia!!! #NiUnaMás #NiUnaMenos #Cuba   @YoSiTeCreoCuba

Reporte Mx Noticias@ReporteMxNotic1 Jun. 22, 2024
Continúa la exigencia de justicia por el feminicidio de Elizabeth Elena Laguna Salgado, joven mexicana asesina en Utah, Estados Unidos
#NiUnaMás #NiUnaMenos @FGR_Chis@FGRMexico@SSPCMexico@SRE_mx
https://youtube.com/watch?v=fAeVB5oEth0

Table A.4. 2024 Deaths of Trans Women In Brazil (1/01/24–12/31/24).

Date	Name	Age	Location	Category	Cause
29 Dec. 2024	Jota Nogueira Oliveira	30	Manaus, Amazonas	violence	strangled
29 Dec. 2024	Rafaela de Sousa Oliveira	N/A	Teresina, Piauí	violence	shot
25 Dec. 2024	Mirella Albuquerque	21	Cabo de Santo Agostinho, Pernambuco	violence	stabbed
23 Dec. 2024	Thayla Aylla	24	Várzea Grande, Mato Grosso	violence	strangled
19 Dec. 2024	Bianca Castyel ("Bia")	20	Água Boa, Mato Grosso	violence	stabbed
17 Dec. 2024	Rafaela Lorena Soares da Rocha	N/A	Brasilia, Distrito Federal	custodial	not reported
16 Dec. 2024	Mayla Gomes	N/A	Novo Progresso, Pará	violence	murdered
14 Dec. 2024	Neuritânia Pacheco	48	Sobradinho, Bahia	violence	stoned
11 Dec. 2024	Monalisa	N/A	Fortaleza, Ceará	violence	shot
10 Dec. 2024	Berinjela	N/A	Jequié, Bahia	violence	shot
7 Dec. 2024	Preta Gil	N/A	Boca da Mata, Alagoas	violence	shot
7 Dec. 2024	Name unknown	38	Canoas, Rio Grande do Sul	violence	shot
4. Dec. 2024	Alana de Jesus ("Alana do Uber," "Lanna Alana")	27	Matozinhos, Minas Gerais	violence	shot
4 Dec. 2024	Name unknown	N/A	Ribeirão Preto, São Paulo	violence	beaten
4 Dec. 2024	Name unknown	N/A	Rio Verde, Goiás	violence	shot
2 Dec. 2024	E. Nascimento de Lima	34	Jataí, Goiás	violence	stabbed

Date	Name	Age	Location	Category	Cause
2 Dec. 2024	Pétala Espírito Santo Monteiro	20	Castanhal, Pará	violence	shot
30 Nov. 2024	Jhessyka Loren Loran Bezerra de Lima	43	Maceió, Alagoas	violence	shot
25 Nov. 2024	Name unknown	49	Santos, São Paulo	violence	murdered
10 Nov. 2024	Santrosa	27	Sinop, Mato Grosso	violence	tortured and decapitated
31 Oct. 2024	Isabela dos Santos	26	Peixoto de Azevedo, Mato Grosso	violence	shot
25 Oct. 2024	Débora Myrante Silva	42	Cruzeiro, São Paulo	violence	stabbed
24 Oct. 2024	Evellyn Marcelly ("Evinha")	about 30	Recife, Pernambuco	violence	suffocated
23 Oct. 2024	Luane Costa da Silva	27	Santos, São Paulo	violence	strangled
21 Oct. 2024	Amanda Eduarda Rios	28	São Carlos, São Paulo	violence	asphyxiated
20 Oct. 2024	Naira Victória Neris	27	São Paulo	violence	tortured and stabbed
19 Oct. 2024	Priscila	N/A	Coaraci, Bahia	violence	shot
29 Sep. 2024	Bárbara Vergetti Martins de Souza	34	Cachambi, Rio de Janeiro	violence	strangled
27 Sep. 2024	Letícia Antonella Maryon	22	Piracicaba, São Paulo	suicide	suicide
24 Sep. 2024	Bruninha	31	Itaúna, Minas Gerais	violence	shot
23 Sep. 2024	Aquilla	N/A	Itumbiara, Goiás	uncategorized	run over

continued on next page

Table A.4. Continued.

Date	Name	Age	Location	Category	Cause
9 Sep. 2024	Name unknown	41	Belo Horizonte, Minas Gerais	uncategorized	not reported
3 Sep. 2024	Beidy Gonçalves	27	Guaçuí, Espírito Santo	violence	burnt alive
29 Aug. 2024	Jullyane Fernandes	20	Bagé, Rio Grande do Sul	violence	stabbed and dismembered
23 Aug. 2024	Maria Eduarda Souza Lima	34	Campo Grande, Mato Grosso do Sul	violence	stabbed
21 Aug. 2024	Larissa da Silva	N/A	São Félix do Xingu, Pará	violence	stabbed
11 Aug. 2024	Safira Meneghel	39	Fortaleza, Ceará	violence	beaten and stoned
10 Aug. 2024	Daniela Henrique ("Dani")	26	Jequié, Bahia	violence	shot
10 Aug. 2024	Gabriely Lorrany ("Gaby Lima")	N/A	Santa Maria do Cambucá, Pernambuco	violence	beaten
3 Aug. 2024	Name unknown	28	Fortaleza, Ceará	violence	shot
2 Aug. 2024	Indianara Pereira de Souza	32	Várzea Grande, Mato Grosso	violence	run over
25 Jul. 2024	Gabriela Varconti ("Gabi")	37	Várzea Grande, Mato Grosso	custodial	beaten
24 Jul. 2024	Valéria Ferrugini	57	Nova Venécia, Espírito Santo	violence	murdered
22 Jul. 2024	Aryadina Montenegro	23	Teresina, Piauí	violence	stoned
21 Jul. 2024	Daniele da Silva	21	Juazeiro do Norte, Ceará	violence	stabbed
21 Jul. 2024	Luna Martins	N/A	Salvador, Bahia	violence	shot
2 Jul. 2024	Ketilly	27	Itabaiana, Sergipe	violence	shot
30 Jun. 2024	Cacau	41	Patos de Minas, Minas Gerais	violence	beaten and asphyxiated

Date	Name	Age	Location	Category	Cause
26 Jun. 2024	Gabriella da Silva Borges ("Gabi Campbell")	50	Belo Horizonte, Minas Gerais	violence	hanged
16 Jun. 2024	Oziel Branques dos Santos	40	Curitiba, Paraná	violence	stabbed
3 Jun. 2024	Duda Gaucha	N/A	Curitiba, Paraná	medical	cosmetic filler complications
20 May 2024	Name unknown	N/A	Ji-Paraná, Rondônia	violence	stabbed
11 May 2024	Paloma Mendes de Sousa	34	Timon, Maranhão	violence	stabbed
5 May 2024	Name unknown	N/A	Sobral, Ceará	violence	shot
5 May 2024	Cássia Vieira	45	Uberlândia, Minas Gerais	violence	stabbed
5 May 2024	Natasha Almeida da Silva	47	Timon, Maranhão	violence	shot
2 May 2024	Ramona Félix	44	Itapira, São Paulo	violence	shot
1 May 2024	Luma Ferrari	N/A	Mogi Guaçu, São Paulo	violence	stabbed
25 Apr. 2024	Marcinha Ribeiro	27	Ribeirão das Neves, Minas Gerais	violence	shot
19 Apr. 2024	Name unknown	30	Belo Horizonte, Minas Gerais	violence	shot
17 Apr. 2024	Samira Santos	36	Ribeira do Pombal, Bahia	violence	stabbed
13 Apr. 2024	Shayene	22	João Pessoa, Pariaba	violence	stabbed
13 Apr. 2024	Daniele Miranda Alves	21	São Paulo	violence	shot
12 Apr. 2024	Dadá	N/A	João Pessoa, Pariaba	violence	shot
11 Apr. 2024	João Fernandes Rodrigues	44	Palmas, Tocantins	violence	shot

continued on next page

Table A.4. Continued.

Date	Name	Age	Location	Category	Cause
8 Apr. 2024	Jorrana Patrícia da Silva	32	Macapá, Amapá	violence	shot
7 Apr. 2024	Gisa Ribeiro Lima	55	Cuiabá, Mato Grosso	violence	beaten
29 Mar. 2024	Name unknown	50	Vila Velha, Espírito Santo	violence	shot
23 Mar. 2024	Bianca	28	Rio Largo, Alagoas	violence	shot
21 Mar. 2024	Patrícia	26	Piracicaba, São Paulo	violence	strangled
21 Mar. 2024	Flávia Alves	30	Rio de Janeiro	violence	shot
20 Mar. 2024	Barbie Mucilon	65	Maceió, Alagoas	violence	strangled
19 Mar. 2024	Riana da Conceição dos Santos	21	Barra do Coda, Maranhão	violence	stoned
19 Mar. 2024	Joelma	N/A	Maceió, Alagoas	violence	beaten
16 Mar. 2024	Jhenifer Luíza	26	Guaíra, São Paulo	violence	strangled
15 Mar. 2024	Name unknown	40–50	Santa Luzia, Minas Gerais	violence	beaten
2 Mar. 2024	Noel Rodrigues Santos	20	São Cristóvão, Sergipe	custodial	suicide
25 Feb. 2024	Pâmela Andressa	40	Quaraí, Rio Grande do Sul	violence	shot
24 Feb. 2024	Haila Vitória	15	Santaluz, Bahia	violence	stabbed
21 Feb. 2024	G. Ferreira Gomes	23	Nanuque, Minas Gerais	violence	shot
17 Feb. 2024	Hellen de Roma	37	Porto Velho, Rondônia	violence	stabbed
4 Feb. 2024	Luma Barcelos	17	Salvador, Bahia	violence	murdered

Date	Name	Age	Location	Category	Cause
1 Feb. 2024	Ná	24	Recife, Pernambuco	uncategorized	not reported
31 Jan. 2024	Amanda Soares ("Mandy Gin Drag")	31	São Gonçalo, Rio de Janeiro	violence	stabbed
31 Jan. 2024	D. Gomes da Silva	N/A	Timon, Maranhão	violence	shot
29 Jan. 2024	Kal	N/A	Fortaleza, Ceará	violence	decapitated
23 Jan. 2024	Rafaelyyy Costa	N/A	Itaguaí, Rio de Janeiro	violence	stabbed
22 Jan. 2024	Kelly Sousa	N/A	Teresina, Piauí	violence	burned
16 Jan. 2024	Mayla Rafaela Martins	22	Lucas do Rio Verde, Matto Grosso	violence	stabbed
13 Jan. 2024	Bunitinha	57	Ribeirão Preto, São Paulo	violence	beaten and suffocated
12 Jan. 2024	Bruna Trindade/Bruna Andrade	39	Caraguatatuba, São Paulo	violence	beaten
10 Jan. 2024	Name unknown	55	Itajaí, Santa Catarina	violence	stabbed
10 Jan. 2024	Giovana Souza	28	São José do Rio Preto, São Paulo	violence	stabbed
9 Jan. 2024	Sofía Oliveira	21	Altamira, Pará	violence	shot
6 Jan. 2024	Estrela Souza ("Telinha")	25	Surubim, Pernambuco	uncategorized	drowned
5 Jan. 2024	Eduarda Dutra Silva	23	Goianésia do Pará	violence	shot
3 Jan. 2024	Laila Ketellen	23	Fortaleza, Ceará	violence	beaten

Appendix B

Syllabus

GRI 710: FEMINIST THEORIES

GLOBAL THEORIES OF FEMINICIDE, MMIWG2S, AND TRANSFEMINICIDE

SPRING 2024 | T 4:30–7:15PM | FH107
Lydia Huerta Moreno, PhD
Assistant Professor of Gender, Race, and Identity
Gender pronouns: she / ella
Office hours: Tuesdays 2–3 p.m. and by appointment

> *Lxs academicxs del norte no leen las invesitgaciones locales, y la cosa es que hay una carencia de perespecitva—y luego se convierte en imperialismo academico.* // Scholars of the north do not read the local scholarship, and the thing is that there is a lack of perspective—and then it becomes a practice of academic imperialism.
>
> —Estefanía Bonilla Hernandez

Course Description

In this graduate seminar, we will study diverse feminist theories from across the globe that address the killing of women (including trans women), through a focus on institutional, legal, social, criminological, statistical, and environmental realms. We will draw on theoretical frameworks from a range of disciplinary and interdisciplinary perspectives, including gender studies and feminist theory, critical race theory, materialist analysis, decolonial and indigenous studies, and queer and cuir studies. Working with scholarship, we will examine how theories and studies of femicide/feminicide, MMIWG2S, and transfeminicide are epistemologically situated within transnational feminisms and are situated within specific social, economic, and political contexts and often materialize and are in conversation with both philosophical questions and transnational processes. Throughout the course, students will complete writing assignments and projects that examine how feminist scholars understand gendered violence and how to engage in transnational transinclusive feminist research.

Course Requirements

15% Participation/Attendance (CO 1, CO 3)

- This class is HIGHLY participative! Your attendance and participation are part of learning how to discuss issues around gender violence and feminist transnational theory.

15% Critical Reading Notes (CRN) (CO 1, CO 3, CO 6, CO 10, CO 11, CO 13)

- The note is due by 5 p.m. the day before class and must be submitted via Canvas. You are required to complete the discussion "Critical Reading Notes" for one of the assigned readings for that week.

20% Leading Discussion (CO 1, CO 3, CO 6, CO 10, CO 11, CO 13)

- As a discussion leader, in class, you will summarize and synthesize central arguments from the selected readings, critically analyze the work to identify its contributions and limitations, and—most importantly—pose questions to guide our conversations about diverse theories. Please upload the discussion questions for the class on Web Campus "Discussion leader questions." Students will sign up to lead a discussion on the first day of the semester.

15% Cultural Artifact Discussion Moderation and Participation (CO 1, CO 3, CO 6, CO 10, CO 11, CO 13)

- You will be assigned to moderate an online discussion about a local, national, or global cultural artifact (this can be a film, show, song, performance, website, news article, podcast, painting, photograph, app, etc.) to extend the concepts we are learning in class beyond the classroom. This means you will create a discussion in which you assign students to engage with feminicide, MMIW2S, or transfeminicide via the cultural artifact of your choosing and create a discussion question that relates the artifact to the readings for the upcoming week. These discussions must be posted by Wednesday at 5 p.m. before the upcoming week. The rest of the class will respond by 4:30 on the Tuesday we have class.

35% The Interview and Reflection (CO 1, CO 3, CO 6, CO 10, CO 11, CO 13)

- For this nontraditional final project, you will interview a scholar, activist, or public intellectual on their work to address gender violence and feminicide; what other epistemologies and/or processes inform their work; what work still needs to be done in their geopolitical context; and if/how they engage with others transnationally. The assignment will require you to record, transcribe, write a five-page analytical reflection about the experience, and do a five-minute presentation about your interview. You will have opportunities to discuss your ideas with me individually.

PROJECT DEADLINES:

5% PART 1: 2/18 Identify interviewee and justification. (Weeks 5–12: Conduct interview)
15% PART 2: 4/21 Interview transcription and analysis.
15% PART 3: 5/7 Presentation of takeaways to class and turn in a five-page reflection.

Class Schedule

(This schedule is subject to change with fair notice. I will announce any changes in class.)

Week 1: Class Introduction
    Date: 1/23
    No readings: First class.

Discussion Lead: _______________ *CAD Moderator:* _______________

Week 2: Witch Hunts, Colonialism, and Femicide
    Date: 1/30   Due: CRN
    Global lens: Europe
    Readings:
    Excerpts from Federici, Silvia. *Caliban and the Witch*. 1st ed. New York: Autonomedia, 2004.
    Excerpts from Russell, Diana E. H., and Nicole Van de Ven, eds. 1990. *Crimes Against Women: Proceedings of the International Tribunal*. 3rd. ed. Berkeley, CA: Russell. https://www.dianarussell.com/f/Crimes_Against_Women_Tribunal.pdf.
    Excerpts from Radford, Jill, and Diana E. H. Russell. *Femicide: The Politics of Woman Killing*. New York: Twayne, 1992.

    Discussion Lead: _______________ *CAD Moderator:* _______________

Week 3: On Naming
    Date: 2/6   Due: CRN
    Global lens: Australia
    Readings:
    Excerpt from Lara, Maria Pia. *Narrating Evil: A Post-Metaphysical Theory of Reflective Judgment*. New York: Columbia University Press, 2007.
    Lagarde y de los Ríos, Marcela. "Feminist Keys for Understanding Feminicide." In Fregoso, Rosa Linda, and Cynthia L. Bejarano, eds. *Terrorizing Women : Feminicide in the Americas*. Durham, NC: Duke University Press, 2010.
    Russell, Diana. "Introductory speech presented to the United Nations Symposium on Femicide 11/26/2012."
    García del Moral, Paulina et al. "Femicide/Feminicide and Colonialism." In Vega, Saide Mobayed, and Myrna Dawson, eds. *The Routledge International Handbook on Femicide and Feminicide*. Abingdon, Oxon, UK: Routledge, 2023. https://doi.org/10.4324/9781003202332
    Valencia, Sayak, and Liliana Falcón. "Continuities and Discontinuities Between the Concept of Feminicide and Transfeminicide in Mexico." In Vega, Saide Mobayed, and Myrna Dawson, eds. *The Routledge International Handbook on Femicide and Feminicide*. Abingdon, Oxon, UK: Routledge, 2023. https://doi.org/10.4324/9781003202332

    Discussion Lead: _______________ *CAD Moderator:* _______________

Week 4: Theoretical Understandings and Perspectives

Date: 2/13   Due: CRN, ** 2/18 Part 1: Identify interviewee and justification**

Global lens: Afghanistan

Readings:

Excerpts from Wright, Melissa W. *Disposable Women and Other Myths of Global Capitalism*. New York: Routledge, 2006.

Brysk, Alison, and Vitória Moreira. "Femicide and the Global Political Economy." In Vega, Saide Mobayed, and Myrna Dawson, eds. *The Routledge International Handbook on Femicide and Feminicide*. Abingdon, Oxon, UK: Routledge, 2023. https://doi.org/10.4324/9781003202332

Mobayed Vega, Saide. "Femi(ni)cide: A Global Archeology of Knowledge." In Vega, Saide Mobayed, and Myrna Dawson, eds. *The Routledge International Handbook on Femicide and Feminicide*. Abingdon, Oxon, UK: Routledge, 2023. https://doi.org/10.4324/9781003202332

Discussion Lead: _______________ *CAD Moderator:* _______________

Week 5: Data and Methodological Considerations

Date: 2/20   Due: CRN

Global lens: Brazil

Readings:

Deer, Sarah. "Knowing Through Numbers? The Benefits and Drawbacks of Data." In *The Beginning and End of Rape: Confronting Sexual Violence in Native America*. Minneapolis: University of Minnesota Press, 2015.

Excerpts from Vega, Saide Mobayed, and Myrna Dawson, eds. *The Routledge International Handbook on Femicide and Feminicide*. Abingdon, Oxon, UK: Routledge, 2023. https://doi.org/10.4324/9781003202332

Zecha, Angelika et al. "Data Sources and Challenges." In Vega, Saide Mobayed, and Myrna Dawson, eds. *The Routledge International Handbook on Femicide and Feminicide*. Abingdon, Oxon, UK: Routledge, 2023. https://doi.org/10.4324/9781003202332

Illesinghe, Vathsala et al. "Femicide/Feminicide Observatories and Watches: Perspectives from Argentina, Colombia, Israel, Spain,

Panama, and Poland." In Vega, Saide Mobayed, and Myrna Dawson, eds. *The Routledge International Handbook on Femicide and Feminicide.* Abingdon, Oxon, UK: Routledge, 2023. https://doi.org/10.4324/9781003202332

Discussion Lead: _______________ *CAD Moderator:* _______________

Week 6: Understanding Subtypes and Contexts
Date: 2/27   Due: CRN
Global lens: India
Readings:
Monárrez Fragoso, Julia. "Systemic Sexual Feminicide: Colonial Scars in Bodies and Territories." In Vega, Saide Mobayed, and Myrna Dawson, eds. *The Routledge International Handbook on Femicide and Feminicide.* Abingdon, Oxon, UK: Routledge, 2023. https://doi.org/10.4324/9781003202332

Bourgeois, Robyn. "Colonial Femicide: Missing and Murdered Indigenous Women and Girls In Canada." In Vega, Saide Mobayed, and Myrna Dawson, eds. *The Routledge International Handbook on Femicide and Feminicide.* Abingdon, Oxon, UK: Routledge, 2023. https://doi.org/10.4324/9781003202332

Kisbui Mbasalaki, Phoebe. "Sex Work Femicide and the Making of #SayHerName Campaign by SWEAT." In Vega, Saide Mobayed, and Myrna Dawson, eds. *The Routledge International Handbook on Femicide and Feminicide.* Abingdon, Oxon, UK: Routledge, 2023. https://doi.org/10.4324/9781003202332

Segato, Rita. "Femigenocide." In Vega, Saide Mobayed, and Myrna Dawson, eds. *The Routledge International Handbook on Femicide and Feminicide.* Abingdon, Oxon, UK: Routledge, 2023. https://doi.org/10.4324/9781003202332

Purewal, Navtej, and Lisa Eklund. "Population Control and Sex-Selective Abortion in China and India: A Feminist Critique of Criminalization." In Vega, Saide Mobayed, and Myrna Dawson, eds. *The Routledge International Handbook on Femicide and Feminicide.* Abingdon, Oxon, UK: Routledge, 2023. https://doi.org/10.4324/9781003202332

Discussion Lead: _______________ *CAD Moderator:* _______________

Week 7: Governmental Responses

Date: 3/5   Due: CRN

Global lens: United States

Readings:

Dominguez Ruvalcaba, Héctor, and Patricia Ravelo Blancas. "Obedience and Compliance: The Role of Government, Organized Crime, and NGOs in the System of Impunity That Murders the Women of Ciudad Juárez." In Fregoso, Rosa Linda, and Cynthia L. Bejarano, eds. *Terrorizing Women: Feminicide in the Americas*. Durham, NC: Duke University Press, 2010.

Staudt, Kathleen. "Government Responses to Violence Against Women." In *Violence and Activism at the Border: Gender, Fear, and Everyday Life in Ciudad Juárez*. Austin: University of Texas Press, 2008.

Discussion Lead: _______________ *CAD Moderator:* _______________

Menjívar, Cecilia, and Shannon Drysdale Walsh. "The Architecture of Feminicide: The State, Inequalities, and Everyday Gender Violence in Honduras." *Latin American Research Review* 52, no. 2 (2017): 221–40. https://doi.org/10.25222/larr.73

Threadcraft, Shatena. "North American Necropolitics and Gender: On Black Lives Matter and Black Femicide." In Vega, Saide Mobayed, and Myrna Dawson, eds. *The Routledge International Handbook on Femicide and Feminicide*. Abingdon, Oxon, UK: Routledge, 2023. https://doi.org/10.4324/9781003202332

Discussion Lead: _______________ *CAD Moderator:* _______________

Week 8: Legal Responses

Date: 3/12   Due: CRN

Global lens: Latin America

Readings:

López Padilla Tostado, Adriana Isabel, and Helene Saadoun. "Femicide and Transnational Law." In Vega, Saide Mobayed, and Myrna Dawson, eds. *The Routledge International Handbook on Femicide and Feminicide*. Abingdon, Oxon, UK: Routledge, 2023. https://doi.org/10.4324/9781003202332

Dayan, Hava. "Femicide and the 'Heat of Passion' Criminal Doctrine." In Vega, Saide Mobayed, and Myrna Dawson, eds. *The Routledge*

International Handbook on Femicide and Feminicide. Abingdon, Oxon, UK: Routledge, 2023. https://doi.org/10.4324/9781003202332

Roth, Françoise et al. "The Latin American Model Protocol for the Investigation of Gender-Related Killings of Women (Femicide/Feminicide): A Partially Achieved Success Story." In Vega, Saide Mobayed, and Myrna Dawson, eds. *The Routledge International Handbook on Femicide and Feminicide.* Abingdon, Oxon, UK: Routledge, 2023. https://doi.org/10.4324/9781003202332

Unmasking the Hidden Crisis of Murdered and Missing Indigenous Women (MMIW): Exploring Solutions to End the Cycle of Violence: Oversight Hearing Before the Subcommittee on Indigenous Peoples of the United States of the Committee on Natural Resources, n.d.

Discussion Lead: _______________ *CAD Moderator:* _______________

Week 9: Cultural Representations
   Date: 3/19   Due: CRN
   Global lens: Mexico
   Readings:
   Excerpts from Driver, Alice. "Monuments, Memorials, Graffiti, and Street Art: Memory Creation in an Apocalyptic Landscape." In *More or Less Dead : Feminicide, Haunting, and the Ethics of Representation in Mexico.* Tucson: University of Arizona Press, 2015.
   Excerpts from Bolaño, Roberto. *2666.* New York: Vintage, 2009.
   Photo 3ssay: "Images from the Justice Movement in Chihuahua, Mexico." In Fregoso, Rosa Linda, and Cynthia L. Bejarano, eds. *Terrorizing Women : Feminicide in the Americas.* Durham, NC: Duke University Press, 2010.

Discussion Lead: _______________ *CAD Moderator:* _______________

López, Issa, creator. 2024. *True Detective: Night Country.* HBO Entertainment.

Szymanek, Angelique. "Elina Chauvet: Decolonizing Disappearance." *Latin American and Latinx Visual Culture* 4, no. 1 (2022): 58–74. https://doi.org/10.1525/lavc.2022.4.1.58

Discussion Lead: _______________ *CAD Moderator:* _______________

Week 10: SPRING BREAK: SELF-CARE IS A RADICAL ACT.

Week 11: Social Responses
     Date: 4/2   Due: CRN, 4/7 Paper draft
     Global lens: Canada
     Readings:
     Val, Helena Suarez, Catherine D'Ignazio, Jimena Acosta Romero,
          Melissa Q. Teng, and Silvana Fumega. "Data Artivism and Femini-
          cide." *Big Data & Society* 10, no. 2 (2023). https://doi.org/10.1177/
          20539517231215356.
     Belotti, Francesca et al. "Femicide, Digital Activism, and the
          #NiUnaMenos Movement in Argentina." In Vega, Saide Mobayed,
          and Myrna Dawson, eds. *The Routledge International Handbook on
          Femicide and Feminicide*. Abingdon, Oxon, UK: Routledge, 2023.
          https://doi.org/10.4324/9781003202332

     Discussion Lead: _______________ *CAD Moderator:* _______________

     Urban Indian Health Institute. 2017. Our Bodies, Our Stories: Sexual
          Violence Among Native Women in Seattle. Seattle, WA: Urban
          Indian Health Institute.
     Urban Indian Health Institute. 2018. *Missing and Murdered Indigenous
          Women and Girls: A Snapshot of Data from 71 Urban Cities in the
          United States*. Seattle: Urban Indian Health Institute.
     Bejarano, Cynthia. "Witnessing Across Borders: Truth-Telling About
          Feminicide in México and the MMIWG2S." In Vega, Saide Mobayed,
          and Myrna Dawson, eds. *The Routledge International Handbook on
          Femicide and Feminicide*. Abingdon, Oxon, UK: Routledge, 2023.
          https://doi.org/10.4324/9781003202332
     Valencia, Sayak, and Olga Arnaiz Zhuravleva. "Necropolitics, Post-
          mortem/Transmortem Politics, and Transfeminisms in the Sexual
          Economies of Death." *TSQ: Transgender Studies Quarterly* 6, no. 2
          (2019): 180–93. https://doi.org/10.1215/23289252-7348468

     Discussion Lead: _______________ *CAD Moderator:* _______________

Week 12: Feminicide and Global Accumulation
     Date: 4/9   Due: CRN
     Global lens: Sub-Saharan Africa

Readings:

Federici, Silvia, Liz Mason-Deese, Susana Draper, and Betty Ruth Lozano Lerma. 2021. *Feminicide and Global Accumulation: Frontline Struggles to Resist the Violence of Patriarchy and Capitalism.* Common Notions.

Discussion Lead: _______________ *CAD Moderator:* _______________

Week 13: WORK DAY (No class)

Date: 4/16   Due: ***4/21 Part 2: Transcript and analysis***

Week 14: Spheres of Insurrection

Date: 4/23   Due: CRN

Global lens: Turkey

Readings:

Rolnik, Suely, and Sergio Delgado Moya. *Spheres of Insurrection: Notes on Decolonizing the Unconscious.* Cambridge, UK: Polity Press, 2023.

Discussion Lead: _______________ *CAD Moderator:* _______________

Week 15: Force of Witness

Date: 4/30   Due: CRN

Global lens: Argentina

Readings:

Fregoso, Rosa-Linda. *The Force of Witness: Contra Feminicide.* Durham, NC: Duke University Press, 2023.

Discussion Lead: _______________________________________

Week 16: Papers

Date 5/7   Due: **Part 3: Presentation of takeaways to class and turn in a 5-page reflection** Student zine made by graduate students

Appendix C

Figure A.1. *Rabia*'s cover. *Source:* Photo by the author. Designed by students in the graduate class GRI 710 in spring 2024.

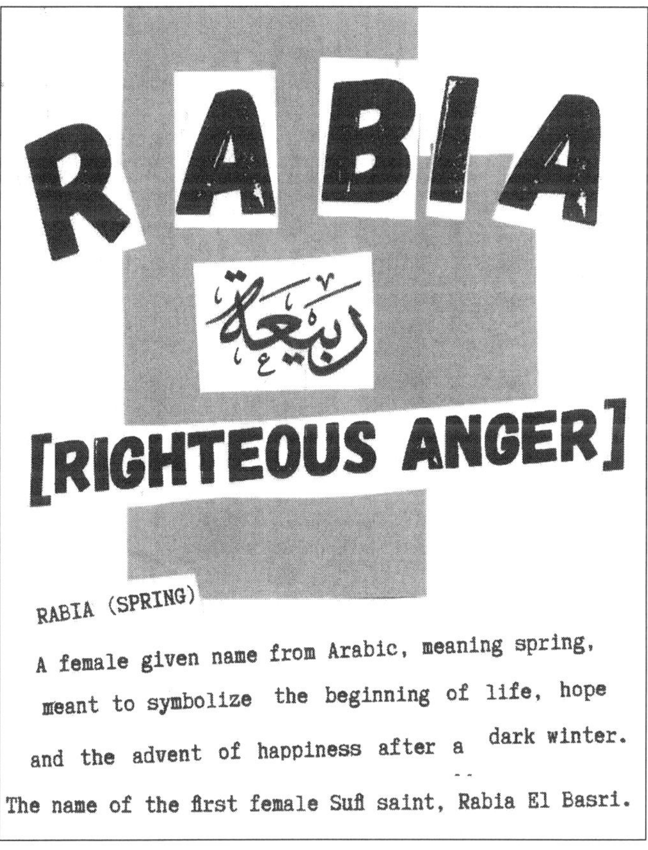

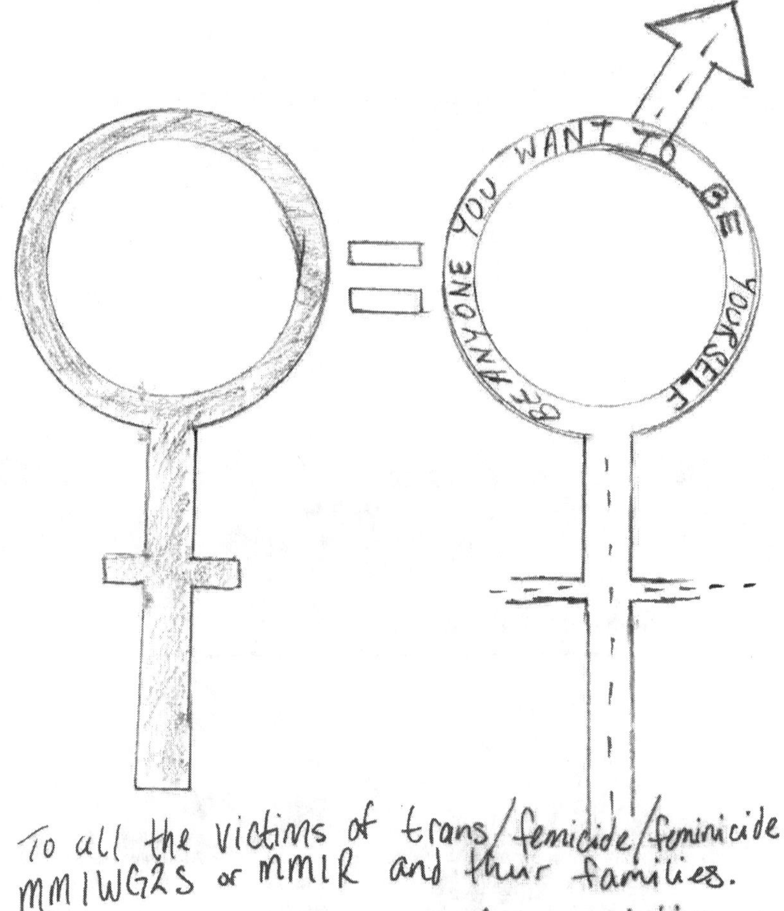

To all the victims of trans/femicide/feminicide
MMIWG2S or MMIR and their families.
Also to survivors, families, activists, relatives,
friends, scholars + educators doing the ground
work to keep their memories alive + bring
attention to this issue.   We stand with you

Figure A.3. *Rabia*, page 2: I don't know if justice exists. *Source:* Photo by the author. Designed by a student in the graduate class GRI 710 in spring 2024.

Figure A.4. *Rabia*, page 3: The fate of missing mothers and the tears they shed. *Source:* Photo by the author. Designed by a student in the graduate class GRI 710 in spring 2024.

Figure A.5. *Rabia*, page 4: The funeral. *Source:* Photo by the author. Designed by a student in the graduate class GRI 710 in spring 2024.

Figure A.6. *Rabia*, page 5: Mother Earth erasure. *Source:* Photo by the author. Designed by a student in the graduate class GRI 710 in spring 2024.

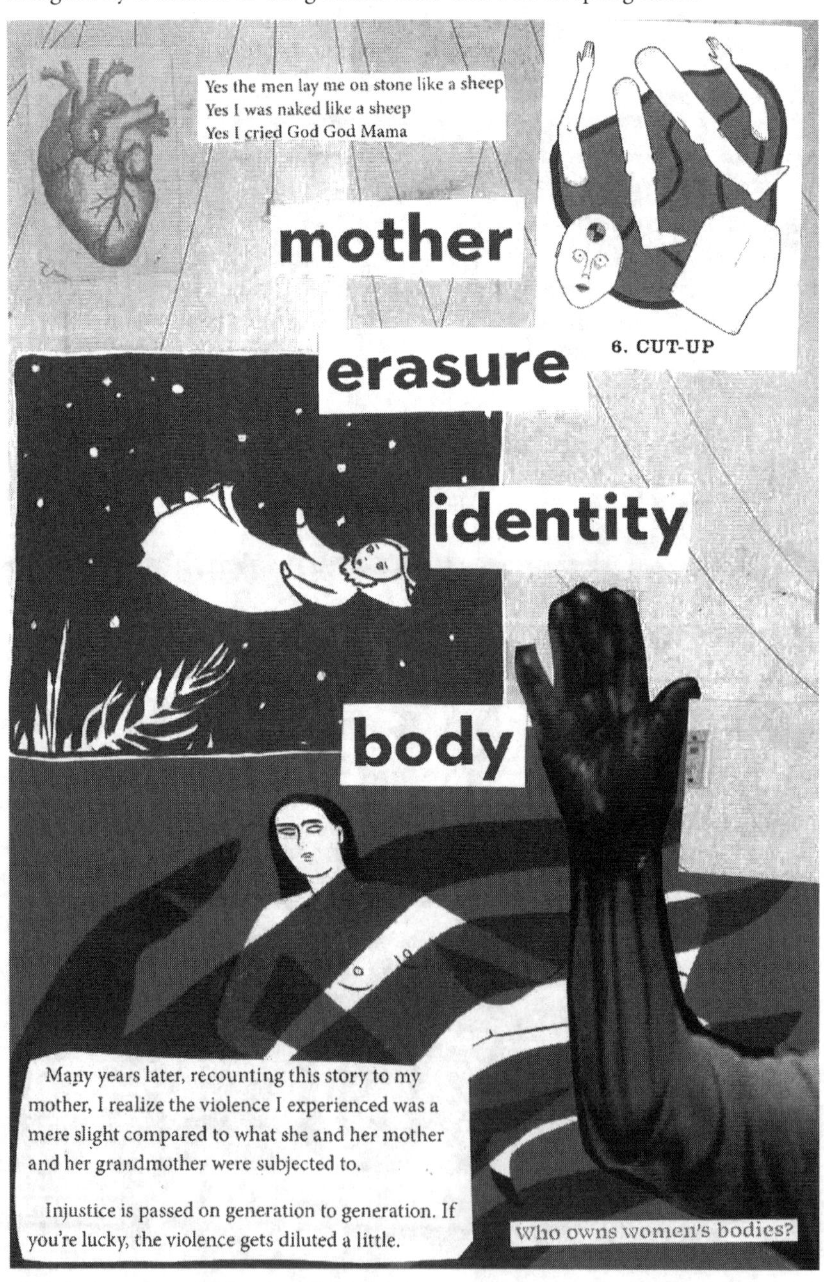

Figure A.7. *Rabia*, page 6: Missing and murdered indigenous women and girls. *Source:* Photo by the author. Designed by a student in the graduate class GRI 710 in spring 2024.

Figure A.8. *Rabia*, page 7: A list of names. *Source:* Photo by the author. Designed by a student in the graduate class GRI 710 in spring 2024.

Ashley Amber Shetters, Missing
Ella Mae Begay, Missing
Allison Maria Castro, Murdered
Heather Leann Cameron, Missing
Kim Lertjuntharangool, Missing
Danielle Nicole Lauramore, Missing
Carrie Marie Jones, Missing
Tina Marie Finley, Missing
Renee Printup, Murdered
Rita Janelle Papakee, Missing
Victoria Valdez, Missing
Jessie "Twilight" Crooks, Murdered
Sally Ann Hines, Murdered
Virginia Sue Pictou Noyes, Missing
Nannette Oleson, Suspicious Death
Yvonne Renee Scott, Missing
Nevaeh Kingbird, Missing
Pauline Williams, Missing
Freida Louise Franks, Missing
Shacaiah Blue Harding, Missing
Rose Marie Fields, Missing
Audrey Sky Paulsen, Missing
Ranelle Rose Bennett, Missing
Kimberly Michelle Ratushniak, Missing
Marie Walkingstick Pheasant, Murdered
Olivia Lone Bear, Suspicious Death
Hannah Marie Redkey, Missing
Ida Beard, Missing
Pauline Ann Aishanna, Missing
Gloria High Hawk, Missing
Michelle Elbow Shield, Missing
Ricarda Tillman-Locket, Missing
Maria Isabel Elizalde, Missing
Deidre Ryan Begay, Missing
Freda Knowshisgun, Missing
Aubree Staves, Missing
Dawn Day, Murdered

Nellie Angutiguluk, Murdered
Tanya Jean Brooks, Murdered
Chantel Moore, Killed by Police
Simone Sanderson, Killed
Chelsea Poorman, Suspicious Death
Chrystal Dawn Beairsto, Murdered
Adele Morin, Died in Police Custody
Misty Potts, Missing
Mary Susan Evans-Harlick, Murdered
Charlene Catholique, Missing
Loretta Ann Frank, Missing
Vanessa Tagoona, Suspicious Death
Charnelle Jenny Masakeyash,
Suspicious Death

Figure A.9. *Rabia*, page 8: We are not disposable. *Source:* Photo by the author. Designed by a student in the graduate class GRI 710 in spring 2024.

Figure A.10. *Rabia*, page 9: The vortex of gender violence. *Source:* Photo by the author. Designed by a student in the graduate class GRI 710 in spring 2024.

were someone. Stop killing nos. Patriarchy kills. Mujer sin
Stop killing us. We are not disposable. No more
someone. Ni una menos. Patriarchy kills. Mujer sin miedo. No more
Stop killing us. We are not disposable. No more
No + feminicidios. Ni una menos. Patriarchy kills. They were
sin miedo. No + feminicidios. They were
Ni una menos. They were stolen sisters.
disposable. No more stolen sisters.
We are not
Stop killing us. We are not disposable. No more stolen sisters. They were someone. Ni una menos. Ni una menos. No + feminicidios. Ni una menos. We are us. We + feminicidios. They are

Figure A.11. *Rabia*, page 10: Power. *Source:* Photo by the author. Designed by a student in the graduate class GRI 710 in spring 2024.

Figure A.12. *Rabia,* page 11: Gender violence at the intersections. *Source:* Photo by the author. Designed by a student in the graduate class GRI 710 in spring 2024.

Figure A.13. *Rabia*, page 12: Say her name. *Source:* Photo by the author. Designed by a student in the graduate class GRI 710 in spring 2024.

Figure A.14. *Rabia*, page 13: Transinclusive feminism. *Source:* Photo by the author. Designed by a student in the graduate class GRI 710 in spring 2024.

Figure A.15. *Rabia*, page 14: Women at leisure. *Source:* Photo by the author. Designed by a student in the graduate class GRI 710 in spring 2024.

Figure A.16. *Rabia*, page 15: Transnational feminism. *Source:* Photo by the author. Designed by a student in the graduate class GRI 710 in spring 2024.

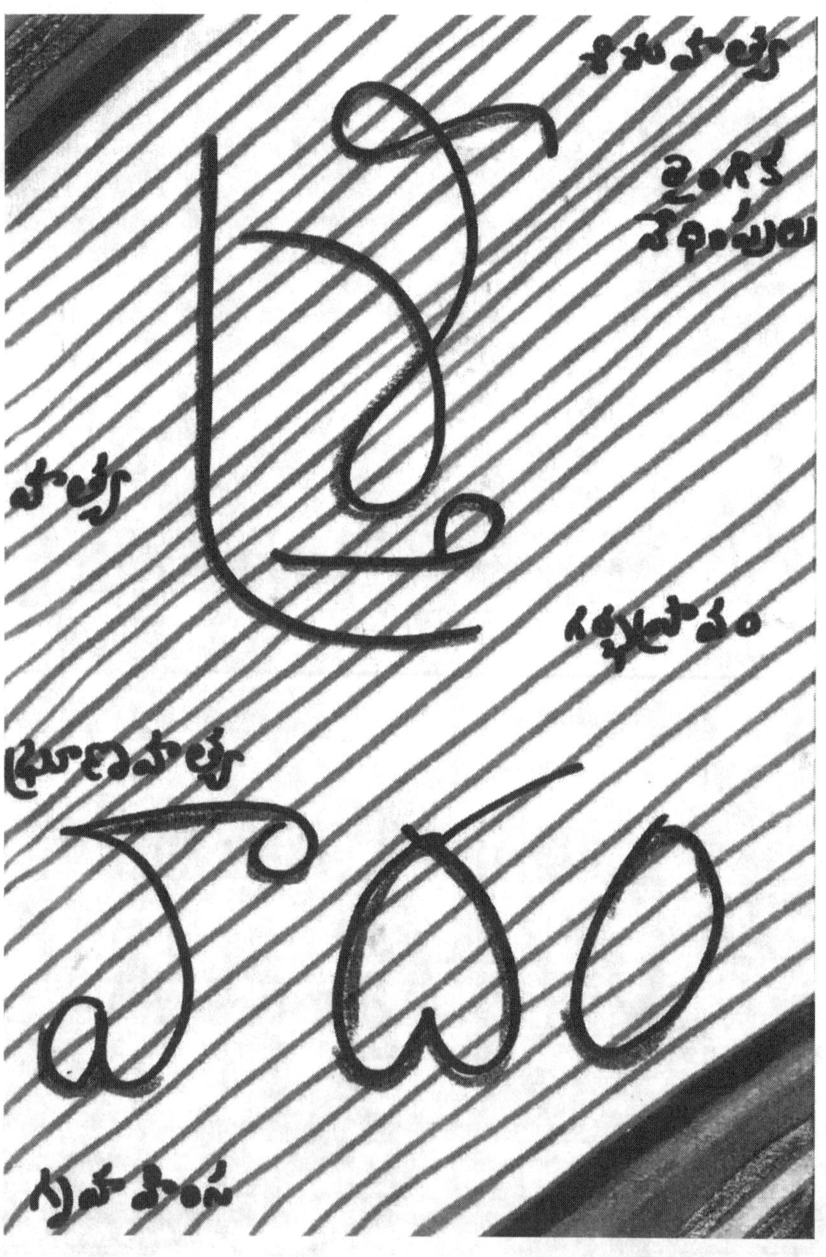

Figure A.17. *Rabia*, page 16: What is the story? *Source:* Photo by the author. Designed by a student in the graduate class GRI 710 in spring 2024.

Figure A.18. *Rabia*, page 17: There was #niunamenos before #NIUNAMAS. *Source:* Photo by the author. Designed by a student in the graduate class GRI 710 in spring 2024.

Figure A.19. *Rabia*, page 18: Our bodies, our stories. *Source:* Photo by the author. Designed by a student in the graduate class GRI 710 in spring 2024.

Figure A.20. *Rabia*, page 19: Authors of the zine. *Source:* Photo by the author. Designed by a student in the graduate class GRI 710 in spring 2024.

Bibliography

115th Congress. 2018. "S.1942—115th Congress (2017–2018): Savanna's Act." https://www.congress.gov/bill/115th-congress/senate-bill/1942.

116th Congress. 2019. "S.Res.144—116th Congress (2019–2020): A resolution designating May 5, 2019, as the "National Day of Awareness for Missing and Murdered Native Women and Girls." https://www.congress.gov/bill/116th-congress/senate-resolution/144.

"13° Mundos De Mulheres & Fazendo Gênero 11." 2017. https://www.wwc2017.eventos.dype.com.br/?lang=pt-br.

Acosta, Marina. 2018. "Ciberactivismo Feminista: La Lucha De Las Mujeres Por La Despenalización Del Aborto En Argentina." *Sphera Publica* 2, no. 18: 2–20. http://hdl.handle.net/10952/5763

"Acuerdo No. LXV/Urgen/0432/2018 II D.P." 2018. Congreso de Chihuahua. http://www.congresochihuahua2.gob.mx/biblioteca/iniciativas/archivosIniciativas/8651.pdf.

African American Policy Forum. n.d. "Say Her Name." Accessed July 5, 2025. https://www.aapf.org/sayhername.

African American Policy Forum. 2020. "About the #SayHerName Campaign." https://web.archive.org/web/20200718184018/https://aapf.org/sayhername/.

Ahmed, Sara. 2014. *Cultural Politics of Emotion*. Edinburgh University Press.

Ahmed, Sara. 2017. *Living a Feminist Life*. Duke University Press.

Ahmed, Sara. 2021. *Complaint!* Duke University Press.

Ahmed, Sara. 2023. *The Feminist Killjoy Handbook*. Random House.

Alcalá Iberri, María del Socorro. 2004. *Las Muertas De Juárez*. Mexico City: Editorial Libra.

Alsema, Adriaan. 2016. "Bogota Blames Homicide Victim for Her Own Death." *Colombia News*, May 16. https://colombiareports.com/bogota-blames-homicide-victim-death/.

Altman, Dennis. 2001. *Global Sex*. https://doi.org/10.7208/chicago/9780226016047.001.0001.

Alvarez, Sonia E. 1990. *Engendering Democracy in Brazil: Women's Movements in Transition Politics.* Princeton University Press. https://doi.org/10.2307/j.ctv1fkgddt.

AMDOC: American Documentary. 2002. "Case Studies: Señorita Extraviada." https://web.archive.org/web/20160819235532/http://www.amdoc.org/outreach_case studies_se.php.

Amuchie, Nnennaya. 2016. "'The Forgotten Victims': How Racialized Gender Stereotypes Lead to Police Violence Against Black Women and Girls: Incorporating an Analysis of Police Violence into Feminist Jurisprudence and Community Activism." *Seattle Journal for Social Justice* 14, no. 3. https://digitalcommons.law.seattleu.edu/sjsj/vol14/iss3/8.

Amnesty International. 2003. *Muertes Intolerables Diez Años De Desapariciones Y Asesinatos De Mujeres En Ciudad Juárez Y Chihuahua.* Madrid.

Amnesty International. 2008. "Stolen Sisters: A Human Rights Response to Discrimination and Violence Against Indigenous Women in Canada." *Canadian Woman Studies* 26, nos. 3–4: 105.

Anderson, Kim, Maria Campbell, and Christi Belcourt. 2018. *Keetsahnak: Our Missing and Murdered Indigenous Sisters.* University of Alberta Press.

Andreas, Peter, and Kelly M. Greenhill. 2011. *Sex, Drugs, and Body Counts: The Politics of Numbers in Global Crime and Conflict.* Cornell University Press.

Aragon, Kylee. 2022. "The Body Articulated: Gender Violence and the Performative Turn in Mexico." *UNM Digital Repository.* Museum Studies Thesis, University of New Mexico. https://digitalrepository.unm.edu/msst_etds/2.

Araluce, Olga Aikin. 2011. *Activismo social trasnacional: Un análisis en torno a los feminicidios en Ciudad Juárez.* Mexico: Iteso.

Arenas, Natalia. 2022. "Susana Chávez, La Poeta De Ciudad Juárez Que Gritó Ni Una Menos Por Primera Vez—Cosecha Roja." *Cosecha Roja,* June 3, 2022. https://www.cosecharoja.org/susana-chavez-la-poeta-de-ciudad-juarez-que-grito-ni-una-menos-por-primera-vez/.

Aristegui Noticias. 2020. "Hallan muerta en Ciudad Juárez a activista Isabel Cabanillas; FEM da detalles." https://aristeguinoticias.com/1901/mexico/revelan-causa-de-muerte-de-la-activista-mexicana-isabel-cabanillas-en-ciudad-juarez/.

Armstrong, Julie P. C. 1998. "El Depredadors: Mueder in Mexico." Paper presented at the 5th Annual International Investigative Psychology Conference, London.

Arteaga Botello, Nelson, ed. 2010. *Por Eso La Mate: Una Aproximación Sociocultural a La Violencia Contra Las Mujeres.* Mexico City: Miguel Ángel Porrúa.

Associação Nacional de Travestis e Transexuais (ANTRA). 2018. *Mapa Dos Assassinatos De Travestis E Transexuais No Brasil Em 2017.* https://antrabrasil.org/wp-content/uploads/2018/02/relatc3b3rio-mapa-dos-assassinatos-2017-antra.pdf.

Associated Press. 2024. "Canadian Serial Killer Robert Pickton Dies After Assault in Prison." *The Guardian,* May 31, 2024. https://www.theguardian.com/world/article/2024/may/31/serial-killer-robert-pickton-dies.

Athos [Luh Maza]. 2019. "35 | Liniker—Forever Young." https://www.youtube.com/watch?v=5KHta5xSdys.

Aujla, Wendy, Myrna Dawson, Crystal J. Giesbrecht, Nneka MacGregor, and Shiva Nourpanah. 2023. "Femicide in Canada." In *The Routledge International Handbook of Femicide and Feminicide*, edited by Myrna Dawson and Saide Mobayed Vega. https://doi.org/10.4324/9781003202332.

Báez, Susana. 2006. "De La Impotencia a La Creación Testimonial Y La Denuncia Social: 'El Silencio Que La Voz De Todas Quiebra.'" In *Entre Las Duras Aristas De Las Armas: Violencia Y Victimización En Ciudad Juárez*, edited by Patricia Ravelo Blancas and Héctor Domínguez Ruvalcaba, 185–219. Mexico City: Casa Chata (Centro de Investigaciones y Estudios Superiores en Antropología Social [CIESAS]).

Bailey, Jane, and Sara Shayan. 2016. "Missing and Murdered Indigenous Women Crisis: Technological Dimensions." *Canadian Journal of Women and the Law* 28, no. 2: 321–41.

Balfour, Gillian. 2008. "Falling Between the Cracks of Retributive and Restorative Justice." *Feminist Criminology* 3, no. 2: 101–20. https://doi.org/10.1177/1557085108317551.

Barad, Karen. 2003. "Posthumanist Performativity: Toward an Understanding of How Matter Comes to Matter." *Signs* 28, no. 3: 801–31. https://doi.org/10.1086/345321.

Barad, Karen. 2007. *Meeting the Universe Halfway*. Duke University Press. https://doi.org/10.1215/9780822388128.

Bard, Patrick. 2004. *La Frontera: Una Novela De Denuncia Sobre Las Muertas De Ciudad Juárez*. Mexico City: Grijalbo Intriga.

Barifouse, Rafael. 2023. "Marielle: Quem mandou matar a vereadora e outras perguntas sem resposta 5 anos após o crime." *BBC News Brasil*, March 14, 2023. https://www.bbc.com/portuguese/articles/c3g7917eqp5o.

BBC News Brasil. 2018. "#EleNão: A manifestação histórica liderada por mulheres no Brasil vista por quatro ângulos." *BBC News Brasil*, September 30, 2018. https://www.bbc.com/portuguese/brasil-45700013.

Bedrosian, A. 2022. How #NiUnaMenos Used Discourse and Digital Media to Reach the Masses in Argentina. *Latin American Research Review* 57, no. 1: 100–116. https://doi.org/10.1017/lar.2022.6.

Belotti, Francesca, Francesca Comunello, and Consuelo Corradi. 2020. "Feminicidioand #NiUna Menos: An Analysis of Twitter Conversations During the First 3 Years of the Argentinean Movement." *Violence Against Women* 27, no. 8: 1035–63. https://doi.org/10.1177/1077801220921947.

Belotti, Francesca, Vittoria Bernardini, Francesca Comunello, and Karen Boyle. 2024. "Hashtag Feminism Straddling the Americas: A Comparison Between #NiUnaMenos and #MeToo." In *The Routledge Companion to Gender, Media and Violence*, 1st ed., edited by Karen Boyle and Susan Berridge.

Bejarano, Cynthia. 2023. "Witnessing Across Borders: Truth-Telling About Feminicides in México and the MMIWG2S in Canada and the US." In *The Routledge International Handbook of Femicide and Feminicide*, edited by Myrna Dawson and Saide Mobayed Vega. https://doi.org/10.4324/9781003202332.

Bemporad, Elissa, and Joyce W. Warren. 2018. *Women and Genocide: Survivors, Victims, Perpetrators.* Indiana University Press.

Benevides, Bruna G. 2023a. "2023: Brasil invicto como campeão no consumo de pornografia trans no mundo (e de assassinatos)." *Portal Catarinas.* https://catarinas.info/colunas/brasil-invicto-como-campeao-no-consumo-de-pornografia-trans-no-mundo-e-de-assassinatos/.

Benevides, Bruna G. 2023b. "Dossiê: Assassinatos E Violências Contra Travestis E Transexuais Brasileiras Em 2022." Dossiê. Distrito Drag; ANTRA. https://antrabrasil.org/wp-content/uploads/2023/01/dossieantra2023.pdf.

Benevides, Bruna G. 2024. "Dossiê: Assassinatos E Violências Contra Travestis E Transexuais Brasileiras Em 2023." Dossiê. Distrito Drag; ANTRA. https://antrabrasil.org/wp-content/uploads/2024/01/dossieantra2024-web.pdf.

Benevides, Bruna G. 2025. "Dossiê: Assassinatos E Violências Contra Travestis E Transexuais Brasileiras Em 2024." Dossiê. Distrito Drag; ANTRA. https://antrabrasil.org/wp-content/uploads/2025/01/dossie-antra-2025.pdf.

Benítez, Rohry et al. 1999. *El silencio de la voz que todas quiebra.* Chihuahua City: Ediciones del Azar.

Bennet, Lance, and Alexandra Segerberg. 2012. "The Logic of Connective Action." *Information, Communication & Society* 15, no. 5: 739–68. http://dx.doi.org/10.1080/1369118X2012.670661.

Bento, Berenice. 2014. "Brasil: País Do Transfeminicídio." *Centro Latino-Americano Em Sexualidade E Direitos Humanos (CLAM).* https://clam.org.br/uploads/arquivo/Transfeminicidio_Berenice_Bento.pdf.

Bento, Berenice. 2016. "Transfeminicídio: Violência de gênero e o gênero da violência." In *Dissidências Sexuais E De Gênero,* edited by Leandro Colling, 43–68. Salvador, Brazil: Editora da UFBA.

Bergamo, Mônica. 2018. "Desembargadora diz que Marielle estava engajada com bandidos e é 'cadáver comum.'" *Folha De S. Paulo,* March 16, 2018. https://www1.folha.uol.com.br/colunas/monicabergamo/2018/03/desembargadora-diz-que-marielle-estava-envolvida-com-bandidos-e-e-cadaver-comum.shtml.

Berlant, Lauren. 2011. *Cruel Optimism.* Duke University Press.

Berlant, Lauren. 2012. *Desire/Love.* Dead Letter Office, BABEL Working Group.

Berman, Sabina. 2004. "Traspatio." *Gestos.*

Bertrán, Antonio. 1999. "Propone Una Versión No 'Oficial' De Los Crimenes." *Reforma,* September 8, 1999.

Betasamosake Simpson, None Leanne. 2016. "Indigenous Resurgence and Co-resistance." *Critical Ethnic Studies* 2, no. 2: 19. https://doi.org/10.5749/jcritethnstud.2.2.0019.

Biroli, Flávia, and Mariana Caminotti. 2020. "The Conservative Backlash Against Gender in Latin America." *Politics & Gender* 16, no. 1. https://doi.org/10.1017/S1743923X20000045.

Black, Abigail, Monserrat Valerio, and Raleigh Blasdell. 2023. "United States Violence Against Women Act (VAWA)." In *Springer eBooks*, 1–10. https://doi.org/10.1007/978-3-030-85493-5_1684-1.

Blanco, Marisa Revilla. 2019. "Del ¡Ni Una Más! Al #NiUnaMenos: Movimientos De Mujeres Y Feminismos En América Latina." *Política Y Sociedad* 56, no. 1: 47–67. https://doi.org/10.5209/poso.60792.

Blatter, Madison, Lia Harelson, and Christopher Courtheyn. n.d. "The Fight Against Femicide: An Analysis of Globalization Through Instagram in #NiUnaMás and #NiUnaMenos." *ScholarWorks*. https://scholarworks.boisestate.edu/under_showcase_2023/28.

Bobrow, Emily. 2008. "The Fascination of What's Difficult." *Observer*, November 20, 2008. https://observer.com/2008/11/the-fascination-of-whats-difficult/.

Bolaño, Roberto. 2004. *2666*. Barcelona: Anagrama.

Bolaño, Roberto. 2008. *2666*. New York: Farrar, Straus & Giroux.

Bolin, Erik. 2019. "550-mile walk along Red River honors missing and murdered indigenous women." Video, *InForum*. https://www.inforum.com/550-mile-walk-along-red-river-honors-missing-and-murdered-indigenous-women.

BOMB Magazine. 2004. "Santiago Sierra by Teresa Margolles." *BOMB Magazine*, January 1, 2004. https://bombmagazine.org/articles/2004/01/01/santiago-sierra/.

Bonfil, Carlos. "Señorita Extraviada." *La Jornada*, December 12, 2002.

Botello, Nelson Arteaga. 2010. *Por Eso La Maté: Una Aproximación Sociocultural a La Violencia Contra Las Mujeres*. Mexico City: Miguel Angel Porrua.

Bourgeois, Robyn Sanderson. 2014. *Warrior Women: Indigenous Women's Anti-Violence Engagement with the Canadian State*. https://tspace.library.utoronto.ca/bitstream/1807/68238/1/Bourgeois_Robyn_S_201411_PhD_thesis.pdf.

Bourgeois, Robyn Sanderson. 2015. "Colonial Exploitation: The Canadian State and the Trafficking of Indigenous Women and Girls in Canada." *UCLA Law Review* 62, no. 6: 1426–63. https://www.safetylit.org/citations/index.php?fuseaction=citations.viewdetails&citationIds[]=citjournalarticle_502129_20.

Bourgeois, Robyn Sanderson. 2017. *Violence Against Indigenous Women: Literature, Activism, Resistance*. Wilfrid Laurier University Press.

Bourgeois, Robyn Sanderson. 2023. "Colonial Femicide: Missing and Murdered Indigenous Women and Girls in Canada." In *The Routledge International Handbook of Femicide and Feminicide*, edited by Myrna Dawson and Saide Mobayed Vega. https://doi.org/10.4324/9781003202332.

Bowden, Charles. 1998. *Juárez: The Laboratory of Our Future*. New York: Aperture.

Boyd, D. 2011. "Social Network Sites as Networked Publics: Affordances, Dynamics and Implications." In *A Networked Self: Identity, Community and Culture on Social Network Sites*, edited by Z. Papacharissi, 39–58. Routledge.

Brasil de Fato. 2022. "Dois anos de Saudades de Fernanda Benvenutty." *Brasil De Fato—Paraíba*, February 2, 2022. https://www.brasildefatopb.com.br/2022/02/02/dois-anos-de-saudades-de-fernanda-benvenutty.

Breihan, Tom. 2015. "Janelle Monáe, Jidenna, St. Beauty, Deep Cotton & Roman GianArthur—"Hell You Talmbout." *Stereogum*, August 13, 2015. https://www.stereogum.com/1823862/janelle-monae-jidenna-st-beauty-deep-cotton-roman-gianarthur-hell-you-talmbout/news/.

Brock, André, Jr. 2020. *Distributed Blackness: African American Cybercultures*. NYU Press.

Brunke, Laura Isabella. 2015. "Political Homophobia in Brazil: An Evaluation of the Pentecostal Threat to the Human Rights of Sexual and Gender Minorities" (master's thesis, University of London).

Bruns, Axel. 2019. "Big social data approaches in internet studies: The case of Twitter." In *Second International Handbook of Internet Research*, edited by J. Hunsinger, L. Klastrup, and M. Allen, 1–17. Springer.

Bruns, Axel, and Stefan Stieglitz. 2014. "Metrics for understanding communication on Twitter." In *Twitter and Society*, edited by Katrin Weller, Axel Bruns, Jean Burgess, Merja Mahrt, and Cornelius Puschmann. Peter Lang.

Bubar, Roe, and Pamela Jumper Thurman. 2004. "Violence Against Native Women." *Social Justice* 31, no. 4: 70. https://www.jstor.org/stable/29768276.

Burciaga, Betzabel. 2000. "Author Discusses Murders in Juárez at New Mexico State University." *University Wire*, March 13, 2000.

Burnette, Catherine. 2008. "Historical Oppression and Intimate Partner Violence Experienced by Indigenous Women in the United States: Understanding Connectons." *Social Service Review* 89, no. 3: 531. https://doi.org/10.1086/683336.

Burnette, Catherine, and Timothy S. Hefflinger. 2017. "Identifying Community Risk Factors for Violence Against Indigenous Women: A Framework of Historical Oppression and Resilience." *Journal of Community Psychology* 45, no. 5: 587–600. https://doi.org/10.1002/jcop.21879.

Busis, Hillary. 2024. " 'True Detective' Season 4: All the References and Easter Eggs You May Have Missed in 'Night Country.' " *Vanity Fair*, February 19, 2024. https://www.vanityfair.com/hollywood/true-detective-season-4-night-country-easter-eggs?srsltid=AfmBOop2TGBUb33X7FuSSE4TsIqbjoYy6INCFci8GBWRDh8paQ_xYUis.

Butler, Judith. 2004. *Precarious Life: The Powers of Mourning and Violence*. Verso Books.

Butler, Judith. 2021. *The Force of Nonviolence: An Ethico-Political Bind*. Verso Books.

Caballero, E. S., and T. Gravante, eds. 2017. *Networks, Movements and Technopolitics in Latin America: Critical Analysis and Current Challenges*. Springer.

Caballero, Jorge. 2009. "De Cara a La Realidad." *La Jornada*, February 8, 2009.

Cajete, Gregory. 1993. *Look to the Mountain*. J. Charlton. https://files.eric.ed.gov/fulltext/ED375993.pdf.

Cajete, Gregory. 2000. *Native Science: Natural Laws of Interdependence*. Clear Light. http://ci.nii.ac.jp/ncid/BA52271117.

Cajete, Gregory. 2015. *Indigenous Community: Rekindling the Teachings of the Seventh Fire*. Living Justice.

Campos, Carmen Hein De. 2011. "Teoria Feminista Do Dereito E Lei Maria Da Penha." In *Lei Maria Da Penha Comentada Em Uma Perspectiva Jurídico-Feminista*, edited by Carmen Hein De Campos, 1–12. Libraria e Editora Lumen Juris Ltda.

Carbajal, Mariana. 2019. "Ni Una Menos: La Consigna Que Se Convirtió En Movimiento Social." Book. In *Se va a Caer: Conceptos Básicos de Los Feminismos*, edited by Susana Gamba, 1a ed., 199–205. PIXEL Editora. https://facebook.com/pixeleditora.

Carneiro, Sueli, and Regina Camargo. 2016. "Women in Movement." *Meridians* 14, no. 1: 30–49. https://doi.org/10.2979/meridians.14.1.03.

Carone, Renata Rodrigues. 2018. "A Atuação do Movimento Feminista no Legislativo Federal: Caso Da Lei Maria Da Penha." *Lua Nova Revista De Cultura E Política*, no. 105 (September): 181–216. https://doi.org/10.1590/0102-181216/105.

Carrera, Carlos, dir. 2008. *Backyard*. Argos and FOPROCINE.

Carvalho, Mario Felipe de Lima, and Sérgio Carrara. 2013. "Em direção a um futuro trans? Contribuição para a história do movimento de travestis e transexuais no Brasil." *Revista Lationoamerica: Sexualidad, Salud y Sociedad* 14, no. 2: 319–51.

Carvalho, Mario Felipe de Lima, and Sérgio Carrara. 2015. "Ciberativismo Trans: Considerações sobre uma nova geração militante. Contemporânea: Comunicação e cultura." *Póscom* 13, no. 2: 382–99.

Casa Amiga Centro de Crisis, A. C. 2009. "El Feminicidio." http://www.casa-amiga.org.mx/index.php/Contenido/el-feminicidio.html.

Castells, M. 2009. *Communication Power*. Oxford University Press.

Castells, M. 2012. *Networks of Outrage and Hope: Social Movements in the Internet Age*. Polity.

Castillo, Debra A., and María Socorro Tabuenca Córdoba. 2002. *Border Women: Writing from La Frontera*. University of Minnesota Press.

Cave, Damien. "Wave of Violence Swallows More Women in Juárez." *New York Times*, June 23, 2012. https://www.nytimes.com/2012/06/24/world/americas/wave-of-violence-swallows-more-women-in-juarez-mexico.html.

CEJIL. 2021. "Historic! Brazil is held responsible for the improper use of parliamentary immunity as an obstacle to the investigation and trial of the feminicide of Márcia Barbosa, according to the sentence of the Inter-American Court." https://cejil.org/en/press-releases/historic-brazil-is-held-responsible-for-the-improper-use-of-parliamentary-immunity-as-an-obstacle-to-the-investigation-and-trial-of-the-feminicide-of-marcia-barbosa-according-to-the-sentence-of-the/.

Cerqueira, Daniel, Samira Bueno, Renato Sérgio De Lima et al. 2025. "Atlas Da Violência 2025." *IPEA*. https://www.ipea.gov.br/atlasviolencia/publicacoes.

Chávez Castillo, Susana. 2020. *Primera Tormenta*. Canal. https://estepais.com/wp-content/uploads/2021/04/Primera-Tormenta-Susana-Chavez-Castillo-Canal-Press-digital.pdf.

Chávez, Karma R. 2013. *Queer Migration Politics: Activist Rhetoric and Coalitional Possibilities*. University of Illinois Press.

Chen, Gina Masullo, Paromita Pain, and Briana Barner. 2018. " 'Hashtag Feminism': Activism or Slacktivism?" In *Feminist Approaches to Media Theory and Research*, 197–218. Springer. https//doi:1007/978-3-319-90838-0_14.

Chenault, Venida. 2011. *Weaving Strength, Weaving Power: Violence and Abuse Against Indigenous Women*. Carolina Academic Press.

Chenou, Jean-Marie, and Carolina Cepeda-Másmela. 2019. "#NiUnaMenos: Data Activism from the Global South." *Television & New Media* 20, no. 4: 396–411. https://doi.org/10.1177/1527476419828995.

Cho, Eunice Hyunhye, Tessa Wilson, ACLU et al. 2024. *Deadly Failures: Preventable Deaths in U.S. Immigration Detention*. ACLU, American Oversight, and PHR Report. https://assets.aclu.org/live/uploads/2024/06/2024-07-01-ICE-Detainee-Deaths.pdf.

Clark, Natalie. 2016. "Shock and Awe: Trauma as the New Colonial Frontier." *Humanities* 5, no. 1: 14. https://doi.org/10.3390/h5010014.

Clemens, Elisabeth S. 1997. *The People's Lobby: Organizational Innovation and the Rise of Interest Group Politics in the United States, 1890–1925*. University of Chicago Press.

Coacci, Thiago. 2014. "Encontrando o transfeminismo brasileiro: Um mapeamento preliminar de uma corrente em ascensão." *História Agora: Revista de história do tempo presente*, vol. 1: 134–61.

Cohen, Marina, and Juliana Castro. 2014. "Protesto 'Não Mereço Ser Estuprada' Movimenta Facebook Após Resultado De Pesquisa." *O Globo*, March 29, 2014. https://oglobo.globo.com/politica/protesto-nao-mereco-ser-estuprada-movimenta-facebook-apos-resultado-de-pesquisa-12018281.

Collectif Féminicides Par Compagnons ou Ex et al. 2023. "Feminicide Data Activism." In *The Routledge International Handbook of Femicide and Feminicide*, edited by Myrna Dawson and Saide Mobayed Vega. https://doi.org/10.4324/9781003202332.

Comisión Interamericana de Derechos Humanos (CIDH). 2003. *Informe Sobre Ciudad Juárez*. https://www.cidh.oas.org/annualrep/2002sp/cap.vi.juarez.htm.

Comisión Nacional de Derechos Humanos de México (CNDHM). 1998. *Informe Sobre Los Homicidios De Mujeres En Ciudad Juárez*. Mexico City.

Conexión Migrante. 2021. "Respetttrans: El Primer Albergue LGBTI+ En Ciudad Juárez." *Conexión Migrante*, December 3, 2021. https://conexionmigrante.com/2021-/12-/02/respetttrans-el-primer-albergue-lgbti-en-ciudad-juarez/.

Conteúdo, Estadão. 2018. " 'Marielle' alcança 1o lugar nos trending topics do Twitter." *EXAME*, March 15, 2018. https://exame.com/brasil/marielle-alcanca-1o-lugar-nos-trending-topics-do-twitter/.

Coomaraswamy, Radhika. 1997. *Report on the Mission of the Special Rapporteur to Brazil on the Issue of Domestic Violence (15–26 July 1996)*. Economic and Social Council. https://digitallibrary.un.org/record/238390?ln=en&v=pdf.

Corradi, Consuelo, Chaime Marcuello-Servós, Santiago Boira, and Shalva Weil. 2016. "Theories of femicide and their significance for social research." *Current Sociology* 64, no. 7, 975–95. https://doi.org/10.1177/0011392115622256

Correa-Cabrera, Guadalupe, and Michelle Keck. 2022. "A Dangerous Journey to the U.S. and a 'New Deal' for Migrant Women and Girls." *Brown Journal of World Affairs* 28, no. 11. https://bjwa.brown.edu/28-2/a-dangerous-journey-to-the-u-s-and-a-new-deal-for-migrant-women-and-girls/.

Corry, John. 1801. *A Satirical View of London at the Commencement of the Nineteenth Century.* http://ci.nii.ac.jp/ncid/BA84428580.

Craft, Aimée. 2014. *Breathing Life into the Stone Fort Treaty: An Anishnabe Understanding of Treaty One.* UBC.

Craft, Aimée. 2020. *Treaty Words: For as Long as the Rivers Flow.* Annick.

Craig, Elaine. 2014. "Person(s) of Interest and Missing and Murdered Women: Legal Abandonment in the Downtown Eastside." *McGill Law Journal* 60, no. 1: 1–42.

Crenshaw, Kimberlé.. 1991. "Mapping the Margins: Intersectionality, Identity Politics, and Violence Against Women of Color." *Stanford Law Review* 43, no. 6: 1241–99. https://doi.org/10.2307/1229039.

Crenshaw, Kimberlé. 2016. "Race Liberalism and the Deradicalization of Racial Reform." *Harvard Law Review* 130, no. 9: 2298.

Crenshaw, Kimberlé, and the African American Policy Forum. 2023. *#SayHerName: Black Women's Stories of Police Violence and Public Silence.* Haymarket Books.

"Cronologia Dos Direitos Das Mulheres." 2016. Dossiê Feminicídio. November 2, 2016. https://dossies.agenciapatriciagalvao.org.br/feminicidio/cronologia-dos-direitos-das-mulheres/.

Culhane, Dara. 2003. "Their Spirits Live Within Us: Aboriginal Women in Downtown Eastside Vancouver Emerging into Visibility." *American Indian Quarterly* 27, nos. 3/4: 593–606.

Cunha, Magali Do Nascimento. 2017. "Construções Imaginárias Sobre a Categoria 'Gênero' no Contexto do Conservadorismo Político Religioso no Brasil Dos Anos 2010." *Perspectiva Teológica* 49, no. 2: 253. https://doi.org/10.20911/21768757v49n2p253/2017.

Da Silva, Cleusa Gomes, Juliane Mayer Grigoleto, and Rafael De Lima Kurschner. 2023. "Reflexões Sobre Bolsonarismo E Violência Policial: Assassinatos E Violações De Direitos Humanos De Travestis E Transgêneros No Brasil." *Brazilian Journal of Development* 9, no. 3: 9979–10002. https://doi.org/10.34117/bjdv9n3-075.

Darnell, Tim. 2025. "Laken Riley's Mother, Sister Attending President Trump's Congressional Speech." *Atlanta News First*, March 4, 2025. https://www.atlantanewsfirst.com/2025/03/04/georgia-democrats-bringing-guests-showing-opposition-trump-during-first-joint-congress-speech/.

Davis, Angela Yvonne. 1981. *Women, Race & Class.* Random House.

Davis, Angela Yvonne. 1989. *Women, Culture & Politics.* Vintage.

Davis, Angela Yvonne. 1999. *The Prison Industrial Complex*. AK.

Dawson, Myrna, and Saide Mobayed Vega, eds. 2023. *The Routledge International Handbook of Femicide and Feminicide*. https://doi.org/10.4324/9781003202332.

Dean, Amber. 2015. *Remembering Vancouver's Disappeared Women: Settler Colonialism and the Difficulty of Inheritance*. Toronto University Press.

De Carvalho, Raiana. 2024. "Remembering Marielle Franco: Haunting Online Presence and the Memorialization of Resistance on Social Media." *Media Culture & Society* 46, no. 5: 1010–26. https://doi.org/10.1177/01634437241228734.

De Cultura De La Ciudad De México, Secretaría. 2020. "En El Zócalo Capitalino, Piden Un Alto a La Violencia Contra La Mujer Mon Laferte, Ana Tijoux Y Sara Curruchich." Secretaría De Cultura De La Ciudad De México. https://cultura.cdmx.gob.mx/comunicacion/nota/0261-20.

De Freitas, Viviane. 2018. "Marifonia." In *Marielle, Presente*, edited by João Gomes, 19–20. Vida Secreta. https://www.miradajanela.com/2020/03/marielle-presente-antologia.html.

De Maio, Mariana. 2023. "#NiUnaMenos: The Story of a Tweet That Revolutionized Feminism and Changed How Media Covers Violence Against Women in Argentina." In *Palgrave Studies in Journalism and the Global South*, 57–84. https://doi.org/10.1007/978-3-031-30911-3_3.

De Marinis, Natalia. 2016. "Mujeres indígenas ante los escenarios del miedo en México: (In)seguridad y resistencias en la región triqui de San Juan Copala, Oaxaca." *Estudios Latinoamericanos*, no. 37: 65–86.

De Mattos Rocha, Lia. 2019. "The life and battles of Marielle Franco." *openDemocracy*, March 20, 2019. https://www.opendemocracy.net/en/democraciaabierta/life-and-battles-marielle-franco/.

De Oliveira, Helma Janielle Souza, Marcela Zamboni, Emylli Tavares Do Nascimento, and Diego Brito Da Cunha Leite. 2020. "La (re)production d'une sentence: Récits à l'unisson sur le féminicide dans les cours d'assises." *Revista Crítica de Ciências Sociais*, no. 122 (September): 31–52. https://doi.org/10.4000/rccs.10593.

De Souza Nascimento, Silvana, and Luz Gonçalves Brito. 2022. "Transfeminine Bodies: Survival and Resilience Experiences in Brazil." In *IntechOpen eBooks*. https://doi.org/10.5772/intechopen.102849.

"Decreto No 7.393, de 15 de Dezembro De 2010." n.d. Presidência Da República Casa Civil Subchefia Para Assuntos Jurídicos. https://www.planalto.gov.br/ccivil_03/_ato2007-2010/2010/decreto/d7393.htm.

Deer, Ka'nhehsí:io. 2022. "A National Shame, Say Advocates About Lack of Progress on MMIWG Action Plan." *CBC News*, June 8, 2022. https://www.cbc.ca/news/indigenous/mmiwg-action-plan-update-1.6476685.

Deer, Sarah. 2004. "Federal Indian Law and Violent Crime: Native Women and Children at the Mercy of the State." *Social Justice* 31, no. 4: 17–30.

Deer, Sarah. 2009. "Decolonizing Rape Law: A Native Feminist Synthesis of Safety and Sovereignty." *Wicazo Sa Review* 24, no. 2 (2009): 149–67. https://www.jstor.org/stable/40587785

Deer, Sarah. 2015. *The Beginning and End of Rape*. University of Minnesota Press. https://doi.org/10.5749/minnesota/9780816696314.001.0001.

Deer, Sarah, Bonnie Clairmont, and Carrie Martell, eds. 2008. *Sharing Our Stories of Survival: Native Women Surviving Violence*. AltaMira.

Delgadillo, Victoria, and Rigo Maldonado. 2003. "Journey to the Land of the Dead: A Conversation with the Curators of the *Hijas De Juárez* Exhibition." *Aztlán* 28, no. 2: 179–202. https://doi.org/10.1525/azt.2003.28.2.179.

Deloria, Vine, Jr. 1995. *Red Earth, White Lies: Native Americans and the Myth of Scientific Fact*. Fulcrum.

Deloria, Vine, Jr. 1999. *Spirit & Reason: The Vine Deloria, Jr., Reader*. Fulcrum. http://ci.nii.ac.jp/ncid/BA49438032.

Deloria, Vine, Jr., and Daniel R. Wildcat. 2001. *Power and Place: Indian Education in America*. Fulcrum.

"Detainee Death Reporting." 2025. ICE. May 23, 2025. https://www.ice.gov/detain/detainee-death-reporting.

Dickinson, Peter. "Murdered and Missing Women: Performing Indigenous Cultural Memory in British Columbia and Beyond." *Theatre Survey* 55, no. 2: 202–32.

Diniz, Débora. 2011. "Conscientious objection and abortion: Rights and duties of public sector physicians." *Revista de Saúde Pública* 45, no. 5: 981–85.

Diniz, Débora. 2012. "Harm Reduction and Abortion." *Developing World Bioethics* 12, no. 3: ii. http://10.1111/dewb.12003.

Diniz, Débora. 2015. *Cadeia: Relatos sobre mulheres*. Rio de Janeiro: Civilização Brasileira.

Diniz, Débora. 2019. "Bolsonaro threatens survival of Brazil's Indigenous population." *The Lancet*, no. 394 (10197): 444. https://www.thelancet.com/journals/lancet/article/PIIS0140-6736(19)31801-X/fulltext.

Diniz, Débora. 2020. "Maternal mortality: When a pandemic overlaps with the anti-gender crusade." *Developing World Bioethics* 20, no. 3: 116–17. https://doi.org/10.1111/dewb.12288

Domínguez Ruvalcaba, Héctor. 2011. Email.

Domínguez Ruvalcaba, Héctor, and Ignacio Corona. 2010. *Gender Violence at the U.S.–Mexico Border: Media Representation and Public Response*. University of Arizona Press.

Domínguez Ruvalcaba, Héctor, and Patricia Ravelo Blancas. 2003. "La Batalla De Las Cruces: Los Crímenes Contra Mujeres En La Frontera Y Sus Intérpretes." *Desacatos*, no. 13: 122–33. https://www.scielo.org.mx/pdf/desacatos/n13/a9.pdf.

Domínguez Ruvalcaba, Héctor, and Patricia Ravelo Blancas. 2010. "Obedience Without Compliance: The Role of the Government, Organized Crime, and NGOs in the System of Impunity That Murders the Women of Ciudad Juárez." In *Terrorizing Women: Feminicides in the Américas*, edited by Cynthia Bejerano and Rosa-Linda Fregoso, 182–96. Duke University Press.

Domínguez Ruvalcaba, Héctor, and Patricia Ravelo Blancas. 2011. *Desmantelamiento De La Ciudadanía: políticas de terror en la frontera norte*. Mexico City: Ediciones Eón.

Domínguez Ruvalcaba, Héctor, and Patricia Ravelo Blancas, Ileana Rodríguez, and Mónica Szurmuk. 2015. "Literature About Feminicide in Ciudad Juárez." In *The Cambridge History of Latin American Women's Literature*, edited by Ileana Rodríguez and Mónica Szurmuk, 543–58. https://doi.org/10.1017/cho9781316050859.037.

Driskill, Qwo-Li, Chris Finley, Brian Joseph Gilley, and Scott Lauria Morgansen, eds. 2011. *Queer Indigenous Studies: Critical Interventions in Theory, Politics, and Literature*. University of Arizona Press.

Driver, Alice Laurel. 2011. "Cultural Production and Ephemeral Art: Feminicide and the Geography of Memory in Ciudad Juárez, 1998–2008." PhD dissertation, University of Kentucky. https://uknowledge.uky.edu/cgi/viewcontent.cgi?article=1001&context=hisp_etds.

Driver, Alice Laurel. 2015. *More or Less Dead: Feminicide, Haunting, and the Ethics of Representation in Mexico*. University of Arizona Press. https://muse.jhu.edu/book/38137.

Duluth News Tribune. 2019. " 'Something's wrong': Disappearance of pregnant Fargo woman still a mystery." *Duluth News Tribune*, June 10, 2019. https://www.duluthnewstribune.com/news/somethings-wrong-disappearance-of-pregnant-fargo-woman-still-a-mystery.

Dunbar-Ortiz, Roxanne. 2015a. "Native Land and African Bodies, the Source of US Capitalism." *Monthly Review* 66, no. 9: 47–55.

Dunbar-Ortiz, Roxanne. 2015b. "Roxanne Dunbar-Ortiz: Settler-Colonialism and Genocide Policies in North America." https://www.youtube.com/watch?v=gZxZv5LCHtQ.

Dunbar-Ortiz, Roxanne. 2015c. *An Indigenous Peoples' History of the United States*. Beacon .

El Paso Times. "Special Report: 'Juárez Deserves the Title of Most Dangerous City in the World.' " *El Paso Times*, June 7, 2010.

Esther Chávez Cano Collection. n.d. "Esther Chávez Cano Collection." Ms-0471. New Mexico State University Library, Archives and Special Collections Department.

Excélsior. 2010. "Ejecución De La Activista Marisela Escobedo Fue Por Venganza Del Presunto Criminal, Dice Gobernador De Chihuahua." *Excélsior*, December 17, 2010. https://www.excelsiorcalifornia.com/2010/12/17/ejecucin-de-la-activista-marisela-escobedo-fue-por-venganza-del-presunto-criminal-dice-gobernador-de-chihuahua/.

Excélsior. 2011. "Asesinan a activista en Juárez tras resistirse a violación." *Excélsior*, January 11, 2011. https://www.excelsior.com.mx/node/703310.

Federici, Silvia. 2004. *Caliban and the Witch: Women, the Body and Primitive Accumulation*. Autonomedia. https://openlibrary.org/books/OL8696448M/ Caliban_and_the_Witch.

Federici, Silvia, Liz Mason-Deese, Susana Draper, and Betty Ruth Lozano Lerma. 2021. *Feminicide and Global Accumulation: Frontline Struggles to Resist the Violence of Patriarchy and Capitalism*. Common Notions.

Fernandez, Marcos, and Jean-Christophe Rampal. 2007. *La Ciudad De Las Muertas: Indiferencia Política, Ineptitud Oficial, Indignación Mundial Y Los Asesinatos Siguen*. Mexico City: Grijalbo.

Figueroa Romero, Dolores. 2019. "Políticas de feminicidio en México: Perspectivas interseccionales de mujeres indígenas para reconsiderar su definición teórica-legal y las metodología de recolección de datos." *Journal of International Women's Studies* 20, no. 8: 64–86.

Finnegan, Nuala. 2021. *Cultural Representations of Feminicidio at the US–Mexico Border*. Routledge.

"Fiscalía Solicita Condena De Acusados Por Asesinar a Marielle Franco." 2025. *Agência Brasil,*May 14, 2025. https://agenciabrasil.ebc.com.br/es/justica/ noticia/2025-05/fiscalia-solicita-condena-de-acusados-por-asesinar-marielle-franco.

Florini, Sarah. 2019. *Beyond Hashtags: Racial Politics and Black Digital Networks*. NYU Press.

Fonseca, Maria Fernanda Soares, Maria da Luz Alves Ferreira, Rizza Maria de Figueiredo, and Ágatha Silva Pinheiro. 2018. "O feminicídio como uma manifestação das relações de poder entre os gêneros." *JURIS-Revista da Faculdade de Direito* 28, no. 1: 49–66.

Fórum Brasileiro de Segurança Pública. 2023. *Anuário Brasileiro De Segurança Pública*. FBSP. https://forumseguranca.org.br/wp-content/uploads/2023/07/ anuario-2023.pdf.

Fórum Brasileiro de Segurança Pública. 2024. *Anuário Brasileiro De Segurança Pública*. FBSP. https://forumseguranca.org.br/wp-content/uploads/2024/07/ anuario-2024.pdf

Fórum Brasileiro de Segurança Pública. 2025. *Visível E Invisível: A Vitimização De Mulheres No Brasil*. FBSP. https://forumseguranca.org.br/wp-content/ uploads/2025/03/relatorio-visivel-e-invisivel-5ed-2025.pdf?v=13-03.

Fotopoulou, Aristea. 2016. "Digital and networked by default? Women's organizations and the social imaginary of networked feminism." *New Media & Society* 18, no. 6: 989–1005. https://doi.org/10.1177/1461444814552264.

Fregoso, Rosa-Linda. 2023. *The Force of Witness: Contra Feminicide*. Duke University Press.

Fregoso, Rosa-Linda, and Cynthia L. Bejarano. 2010. "Introduction." In *Terrorizing Women: Feminicide in the Americas*, edited by Rosa Linda Fregoso and Cynthia L. Bejarano, 1–44. Duke University Press.

Frías, Sonia M. 2021. "Femicide and feminicide in Mexico: Patterns and trends in Indigenous and non-Indigenous regions." *Feminist Criminology* 18, no. 1: 3–23. https://doi.org/10.1177/15570851211029377.

Frosch, Dan. 2009. "Bodies Found but Mystery Lingers for Kin of Missing Women." *New York Times*, March 24, 2009. https://www.nytimes.com/2009/03/24/us/24prostitute.html?searchResultPosition=2&login=email&auth=login-email.

G1. 2018a. "Manifestações de sábado, 29 de setembro, contra e a favor de Bolsonaro; FOTOS." *Política*, September 30, 2018. https://g1.globo.com/politica/noticia/2018/09/30/manifestacoes-de-sabado-29-de-setembro-contra-e-a-favor-de-bolsonaro-fotos.ghtml.

G1. 2018b. "Solução Do Caso Marielle Franco Pode Levar Até 60 Dias, Preveem Fontes Da Polícia Civil." *Política*, March 16, 2018. https://g1.globo.com/politica/blog/matheus-leitao/post/2018/03/16/solucao-do-caso-marielle-franco-pode-levar-ate-60-dias-preveem-fontes-da-policia-civil.ghtml.

G1. 2023. "Mulher trans é morta a facadas e amordaçada no RJ." *Rio de Janeiro*, July 27, 2023. https://g1.globo.com/rj/rio-de-janeiro/noticia/2023/07/27/mulher-trans-e-morta-a-facadas-e-amordacada-no-rj.ghtml.

G1. 2024. "Irmãos Brazão mandaram matar Marielle por frustrar interesses da dupla e para intimidar PSOL no Rio, aponta PGR." *Rio de Janeiro*, May 9, 2024. https://g1.globo.com/rj/rio-de-janeiro/noticia/2024/05/09/pgr-denuncia-irmaos-brazao-rivaldo-barbosa-morte-marielle-psol.ghtml.

Gabbatt, Adam. 2024. "Father of Laken Riley Decries Politicization of Daughter's Murder." *The Guardian*, March 19, 2024. https://www.theguardian.com/us-news/2024/mar/18/laken-riley-father-statement.

Gago, Verónica. 2017. *Neoliberalism from Below: Popular Pragmatics and Baroque Economies*. Duke University Press.

Gago, Verónica. 2020. *Feminist International: How to Change Everything*. Verso Books.

García, José Manuel. "Las Muertas De Victor Ronquillo, 'Se Apropió De Investigaciones Ajenas.'" *Proceso*, October 17, 1999.

García, José Manuel. "Las Muertas De Juárez De Víctor Ronquillo: El Morbo De La Razón Cínica." *Al Margen*, March 23, 2005.

García, Ma. Aidé Hernández, and Patricia Fabiola Coutiño Osorio. 2016. *Cultura De La Violencia Y Feminicidio En México*. Mexico City: Fontamara.

García, Martha Estela Pérez. 2011. *Luchas De Arena: Las Mujeres En Ciudad Juárez*. Mexico: Universidad Autonoma de Ciudad Juárez.

García-Del Moral, Paulina. 2011. "Representation as Technology of Violence: On the Representation of the Murders and Disappearances of Aboriginal Women in Canada and Women in Ciudad Juárez." *Canadian Journal of Latin American and Caribbean Studies* 36, no. 72: 33–63.

García-Del Moral, Paulina. 2020. "Practicing Accountability, Challenging Gendered State Resistance: Feminist Legislators and Feminicidio in Mexico." *Gender & Society* 34, no. 5: 844–68. https://doi.org/10.1177/0891243220948217.

García-Del Moral, Paulina, Dolores Figueroa Romero, Patricia Torres Sandoval, and Laura Hernández Pérez. 2023. "Feminicide/Femicide and Colonialism." In *The Routledge International Handbook of Femicide and Feminicide*, edited by Myrna Dawson and Saide Mobayed Vega. https://doi.org/10.4324/9781003202332.

Garza, Cristina Rivera. 2023. *Liliana's Invincible Summer (Pulitzer Prize winner): A Sister's Search for Justice*. Hogarth.

Gaspar de Alba, Alicia. 2005. *Desert Blood: The Juárez Murders*. Houston: Arte Publico.

Gayles, Prisca. 2025. *Pain into Purpose: Mobilizing Emotions in Argentina's Black Resistance Movement*. Cambridge University Press.

Gayles, Prisca, and Muñoz-Muñoz, Marilena. 2022. "Unveiling Latin American White multiculturalism: Black women's politics in Argentina and Costa Rica." *Latin American and Caribbean Ethnic Studies* 18, no. 2: 200–216. https://doi.org/10.1080/17442222.2022.2058443.

Gayón, Mariana Berlanga. 2018. *Una Mirada Al Feminicidio*. Mexico City: Universidad Autonoma de la Ciudad De Mexico.

Gerbaudo, Paolo, and Emiliano Treré. 2015. "In search of the 'we' of social media activism: Introduction to the special issue on social media and protest identities." *Information Communication & Society* 18, no. 8: 865–71. https://doi.org/10.1080/1369118X.2015.1043319.

Gill-Peterson, Jules. 2024. *A Short History of Trans Misogyny*. Verso Books.

Giraldo-Luque, Santiago, Núria Fernández-García, and José-Cristian Pérez-Arce. 2018. "La Centralidad Temática De La Movilización #NiUnaMenos En Twitter." *El Profesional De La Informacion* 27, no. 1: 96. https://doi.org/10.3145/epi.2018.ene.09.

Glenn, Evelyn Nakano. 2015. "Settler Colonialism as Structure: A Framework for Comparative Studies of U.S. Race and Gender Formation." *Sociology of Race and Ethnicity* 1 no. 1: 52–72. https://doi.org/10.1177/2332649214560440.

Gobby, Jen, and Lucy Everett. 2022. "Policing Indigenous Land Defense and Climate Activism: Learnings from the Frontlines of Pipeline Resistance In Canada." In *Enforcing Ecocide: Power, Policing & Planetary Militarization*, edited by Alexander Dunlop and Andrea Brock, pp. 89–121. Cham: Springer International.

Gonzales, Lélia. 1984. "Racismo e Sexismo na Cultura Brasileira." *Revista Ciências Sociais Hoje*, 223–44.

González Rodríguez, Sergio. 2002. *Huesos En El Desierto*. Crónicas/Anagrama. Barcelona: Editorial Anagrama.

Goodman, Leslee. 2018. "Women are the first environment: An interview with Mohawk elder Katsi Cook." *Medium*, April 13, 2018. https://moonmagazineeditor.medium.com/women-are-the-first-environment-an-interview-with-mohawk-elder-katsi-cook-40ae4151c3c0.

Gould, Deborah B. 2009. *Moving Politics*. https://doi.org/10.7208/chicago/9780226305 318.001.0001.

Government of Canada. 2024. "Truth and Reconciliation Commission of Canada." May 28, 2024. https://www.rcaanc-cirnac.gc.ca/eng/1450124405592/152910 6060525.

Gravante, T. 2016. *Cuando la gente toma la palabra: Medios digitales y cambio social en la Insurgencia de Oaxaca*. Ediciones Ciespal.

Grazer, Brian, and Charles Fishman. 2015. *A Curious Mind: The Secret to a Bigger Life*. Simon & Schuster.

Guerrera, Frida. 2018. *#Ni Una Más / #Not One More*. National Geographic Books.

Gumprecht, Blake. 2017. "What exactly happened to Savanna LaFontaine-Greywind? Here's what we know and don't know." *Twin Cities*, September 18, 2017. https://www.twincities.com/2017/09/18/what-exactly-happened-to-savanna-lafontaine-greywind-heres-what-we-know-and-dont-know/.

Gurr, Barbara. 2014. *Reproductive Justice: The Politics of Health Care for Native American Women*. Rutgers University Press.

Hargreaves, Allison. 2017. *Violence Against Indigenous Women: Literature, Activism, Resistance*. Wilfrid Laurier University Press.

Harjo, Sterlin, Taika Waititi, and Sydney Freeland, writers. 2021. "Come Get Your Love." *Reservation Dogs*. Season 1, episode 5. Directed by Blackhorse Lowe. Aired August 30, 2021. FX on Hulu.

Harjo, Sterlin, Chad Charlie, and Taika Waititi, writers. 2022a. "Roofing." *Reservation Dogs*. Season 2, episode 3. Directed by Erica Tremblay. Aired August 10, 2022. FX on Hulu.

Harjo, Sterlin, Taika Waititi, and Blackhorse Lowe, writers. 2022b. "This Is Where the Plot Thickens." *Reservation Dogs*. Season 2, episode 8. Directed by Blackhorse Lowe. Aired September 14, 2022. FX on Hulu.

Harjo, Sterlin, Taika Waititi, and Chad Charlie, writers. 2023. "Deer Lady." *Reservation Dogs*. Season 3, episode 3. Directed by Danis Goulet. Aired August 9, 2023. FX on Hulu.

Harry, Debra. 2005. "Acts of Self-Determination and Self-Defense: Indigenous People's Responses to Biocolonialism." In *Rights and Liberties in the Biotech Age*, edited by Sheldon Krimsky and Peter Shorett, 87–97. Rowman & Littlefield.

Harry, Debra. 2006. "Asserting Tribal Sovereignty over Cultural Property: Moving Towards Protection of Genetic Material and Indigenous Knowledge." *Seattle Journal for Social Justice* 5, no. 1.

Harry, Debra. 2011. "Biocolonialism and Indigenous Knowledge in United Nations Discourse." *Griffith Law Review* 20, no. 3: 702–28. https://doi.org/10.1080/10383441.2011.10854717.

Harry, Debra. 2017. "Decolonizing Colonial Constructions of Indigenous Identity: A Conversation Between Debra Harry and Leonie Pihama" In *Great Vanishing*

Act: Blood Quantum and the Future of Native Nations, edited by Norbert S. Hill and Kathleen Ratteree, 98–110. Fulcrum.

Harry, Debra, and Le'a Malia Kanehe. 2007. "Asserting Tribal Sovereignty over Cultural Property: Moving Towards Protection of Genetic Material and Indigenous Knowledge." *Seattle Journal for Social Justice* 5, no. 1: 13. https://digitalcommons.law.seattleu.edu/cgi/viewcontent.cgi?article=1592&context=sjsj.

Hartman, Saidiya. 2008. "Venus in Two Acts." *Small Axe* 12, no. 2: 1–14. https://muse.jhu.edu/article/241115.

Hayes, Lenny. 2020. "Including and Caring for Two Spirit Relatives in the MMIWG2 Movement." In *MMIWG2 &MMIP Organizing Toolkit: A Publication by Sovereign Bodies Institute, in Partnership with MMIWG2 Families, Indigenous Survivors of Violence, and Their Allies*, 34–50. https://www.sovereign-bodies.org/_files/ugd/6b33f7_2585fecaf9294450a595509cb701e7af.pdf.

Hayes, Lenny, Anne LaFrinier-Ritchie, Nicole Matthews et al. 2023. "Two-Spirit Identity and Adolescent Survey Measures: Considerations of Appropriation, Transparency, and Inclusion." *American Journal of Public Health* 113, no. 11: 1153–56. https://doi.org/10.2105/AJPH.2023.307387.

Heart, Maria Yellow Horse Brave. 1999. "Gender Differences in the Historical Trauma Response Among the Lakota." *Journal of Health & Social Policy* 10, no. 4: 1–21. https://doi.org/10.1300/j045v10n04_01.

Heiser, Jörg, and Pablo Larios. 2016. "Manifesta 11." *Frieze*, August 19, 2016. https://www.frieze.com/article/manifesta-11-0.

Herrera, Sonia, Laila Ferrera, Marta Muixi, Dolors Sierra, and Xavier Giró. 2010. "Documentaries on Feminicide in Ciudad Juárez." In *Materials of Peace and Human Rights*, 18. Barcelona: Government of Catalonia.

Hesford, Wendy S. 2021. *Violent Exceptions: Children's Human Rights and Humanitarian Rhetorics*. Ohio State University Press.

Hibberd, James. 2023. "Taylor Sheridan Does Whatever He Wants: I Will Tell My Stories My Way." *The Hollywood Reporter*, December 26, 2023. https://www.hollywoodreporter.com/tv/tv-features/taylor-sheridan-yellowstone-interview-1235519261/.

Hill Collins, Patricia. 2004. *Black Sexual Politics: African Americans, Gender, and the New Racism*. Routledge.

Hill, Annie. 2024. *Trafficking Rhetoric: Race, Migration, and the Making of Modern-Day Slavery*. Ohio State University Press.

"História." 2018. Associação Nacional De Travestis E Transexuais, February 17, 2018. https://antrabrasil.org/historia/.

Hochschild, Arlie Russell. 2016. *Strangers in Their Own Land: Anger and Mourning on the American Right*. New Press.

H.R.1585—116th Congress (2019–2020): Violence Against Women Reauthorization Act of 2019 (April 10). https://www.congress.gov/bill/116th-congress/house-bill/1585/text.

Holmes, Cindy, Sarah Hunt, and National Collaborating Centre for Aboriginal Health. 2017. "Indigenous Communities and Family Violence: Changing the Conversation." National Collaborating Centre for Aboriginal Health. https://www.nccih.ca/docs/emerging/RPT-FamilyViolence-Holmes-Hunt-EN.pdf.

Huerta Moreno, Lydia. 2015. "Hablar Sobre La Violencia De Género En Las Redes Sociales: El Caso De Diana, La Cazadora." In *Tácticas Y Estrategias Contra La Violencia De Género*, edited by Patricia Ravelo Blancas, 137–58. Mexico City: Ediciones Eón.

Hutta, Jan Simon. 2022. "Necropolitics Beyond the Exception: Parapolicing, Milícia Urbanism, and the Assassination of Marielle Franco in Rio de Janeiro." *Antipode* 54, no. 6: 1829–58. https://doi.org/10.1111/anti.12866.

Illesinghe, Vathsala, Ahora Que Sí Nos Ven, Femi(ni)cide Watch Poland et al. "Femicide/Feminicide Observatories and Watches: Perspectives from Argentina, Colombia, Israel, Spain, Panama, and Poland." 2023. In *The Routledge International Handbook of Femicide and Feminicide*, edited by Myrna Dawson and Saide Mobayed Vega, 114–25. https://doi.org/10.4324/9781003202332.

Illuminative. 2024. "Home page—*Illuminative*." June 5, 2024. https://illuminative.org/.

Indian Law Resource Center. 2020. "Savanna's Act and the Not Invisible Act Signed into Law." *Indian Law Resource Center*, October 13, 2020. https://indianlaw.org/swsn/savanna_not_invisible_laws#_ftn1.

Indspire. 2020. "Tekatsi:tsia'kwa Katsi Cook." September 23, 2020. https://indspire.ca/laureate/sherrill-katsi-cook-barreiro/.

Ingram, Suzanne. 2016. "Silent Drivers | Driving Silence—Aboriginal Women's Voices on Domestic Violence." *Social Alternatives* 1, no. 35: 6–12. https://socialalternatives.com/wp-content/uploads/2021/02/Ingram-SOC_ALT_Vol-35_1.pdf.

Instituto Chihuahuense de la Mujer (ICHMujer). 2015. *Su historia, logros y retos.* Chihuahua: ICHMujer.

Instituto Nacional de Ciencias Penales (INCP). 2004. *Homicidios Y Desapariciones De Mujeres En Ciudad Juárez.* Mexico City: Instituto Nacional de Ciencias Penales.

Inter-American Court of Human Rights. 2009. "Inter-American Court of Human Rights Case of González et al. ('Cotton Field') v. Mexico." *Corteidh*, 1161. https://www.corteidh.or.cr/docs/casos/articulos/seriec_205_ing.pdf.

Inter-American Court of Human Rights. 2021. "Inter-American Court of Human Rights Case of *Barbosa de Souza et al. v. Brazil.*" *Corteidh*, 51–53. https://www.corteidh.or.cr/docs/casos/articulos/seriec_435_ing.pdf.

IPEA. 2014. "Tolerância Social À Violência Contra as Mulheres." https://portalantigo.ipea.gov.br/agencia/images/stories/PDFs/SIPS/140327_sips_violencia_mulheres_novo.pdf.

Iturralde, Christina. 2010. "Searching for Accountability on the Border: Justice for the Women of Ciudad Juárez." In *Terrorizing Women: Feminicide in the Américas*, edited by Rosa-Linda Fregoso and Cynthia Bejarano, . Duke University Press.

Jackson, Sarah J., Moya Bailey, and Brooke Foucault Welles. 2020. *#HashtagActivism: Networks of Race and Gender Justice*. MIT Press.

Jacobs, Beverly. 2005. "Gender Discrimination Under the Indian Act: Bill C31 and First Nations Women." In *Feminism, Law, Inclusion: Intersectionality in Action*, edited by Gayle MacDonald, Rachel Osborne, and Charles Smith, 175–99. Toronto: Sumach.

Jacobs, Beverly. 2018. "Decolonizing the Violence Against Indigenous Women." In *Whose Land Is It Anyway? A Manual for Decolonization*, edited by Peter McFarlane and Nicole Schabus, 47–51. Federation of Post-Secondary Educators of BC.

Jacobs, Beverly, and Andrea Williams. 2008. "Legacy of Residential Schools: Missing and Murdered Aboriginal Women." In *From Truth to Reconciliation: Transforming the Legacy of Residential Schools*, edited by Marlene Brant Castellano, Linda Archibald, and Mike DeGangné, 119–42. Ottawa: Aboriginal Healing Foundation.

Jalalzai, Farida, and Pedro G. Dos Santos. 2015. "The Dilma Effect? Women's Representation Under Dilma Rousseff's Presidency." *Politics & Gender* 11, no. 1: 117–45. https://doi.org/10.1017/s1743923x14000579.

Jankowski, Christian. 2020. "Manifesta 11—Teresa Margolles." https://vimeo.com/462685822.

Johnson, Daniel. 2023. "Kimberlé Crenshaw Honors the Stories of Black Women in New Book." *Black Enterprise*, July 26, 2023. https://www.blackenterprise.com/kimberle-crenshaw-honors-black-women-new-book/.

Johnson, Jazzlyn. 2019. "Struggle for Justice: The Women Behind Hanna's Act." *Native News Project*, University of Montana, May 19, 2019. https://nativenews.jour.umt.edu/2019/northern-cheyenne/.

Johnston, Lyla June. 2018. "Lyla June—Mamwlad Official Video." https://www.youtube.com/watch?v=TeGLDwfrvb8.

Johnston, Lyla June. 2022. "Architects of Abundance: Indigenous Regenerative Food and Land Management Systems and the Excavation of Hidden History." PhD diss., University of Alaska Fairbanks.

Jones, Loring. 2007. "The Distinctive Characteristics and Needs of Domestic Violence Victims in a Native American Community." *Journal of Family Violence* 23, no. 2: 113–18. https://doi.org/10.1007/s10896-007-9132-9.

Kulick, Don. 1998. *Travesti: Sex, Gender, and Culture Among Brazilian Transgendered Prostitutes*. University of Chicago Press.

Kuokkanen, Rauna. 2014. "Gendered Violence and Politics in Indigenous Communities." *International Feminist Journal of Politics* 17, no. 2: 271–88. https://doi.org/10.1080/14616742.2014.901816.

Kurian, P.A., D. Munshi, and A. Mundkar. 2015. "The dialectics of power and powerlessness in transnational feminist networks: Online struggles around gender-based violence." In *The Oxford Handbook of Transnational Feminist Movements*, edited by R. Baksh and W. Harcourt, 871–94. Oxford University Press.

La Cadera de Eva. 2022. "El Origen Del Movimiento 'Ni Una Más.'" n.d. *La Cadera De Eva*. https://lacaderadeeva.com/actualidad/el-origen-del-movimiento-ni-una-mas/4872.

La Casa del Encuentro. 2020. *Por Ellas: 10 Años De Informes De Feminicios En Argentina*. Buenos Aires: Asociación Civil La Casa del Encuentro. https://www.lacasadelencuentro.org/descargas/femicidios-10-anios.pdf

La Jornada. 2010a. "La Jornada: Absuelven En Juicio Oral Al Asesino Confeso De Rubí Frayre En Juárez." *La Jornada*, May 2, 2010. https://www.jornada.com.mx/2010/05/02/estados/030n1est.

La Jornada. 2010b. "La Jornada: Asesinato De Marisela Escobedo Desata Indignación En Diversos Sectores Del País." *La Jornada*, December 18, 2010. https://www.jornada.com.mx/2010/12/18/politica/012n1pol.

La Jornada. 2011. "La Jornada: Marchan En Reforma Para Protestar Por Feminicidios." *La Jornada*, January 16, 2011. https://www.jornada.com.mx/2011/01/16/politica/007n1pol.

Lagarde y de los Ríos, Marcela. 1993. *Los Cautiverios De Las Mujeres: Madresposas, Monjas, Putas, Presas Y Locas*. Mexico City: Universidad Nacional Autónoma de México.

Lagarde y de los Ríos, Marcela. 2006. "Introduction." In *Feminicidio: Una perspectiva global*, edited by Diana E. Russell and Roberta A. Harmes, 15–42. Mexico City: Universidad Autónoma de Mexico.

Lagarde y de los Ríos, Marcela. 2010. "Preface." In *Terrorizing Women: Feminicides in the Américas*, edited by Cynthia Bejerano and Rosa-Linda Fregoso. Durham, North Carolina: Duke University Press.

Lamb, Christina. 2020. *Our Bodies, Their Battlefield: What War Does to Women*. HarperCollins UK.

Laudano, Claudia. 2016. "Feministas en la red: Reflexiones en torno a las potencialidades y restricciones de la participación en el ciberspacio." In *Sin Feminismos no hay democracia: Género y ciencias sociales*, edited by F. Rovetto and L. Fabbri, 31–54. Rosario, Argentina: Universidad Nacional de Rosario Ediciones.

Lee, Lloyd Lance, and Gregory Cajete. 2014. *Diné Perspectives: Revitalizing and Reclaiming Navajo Thought*. University of Arizona Press eBooks. http://ci.nii.ac.jp/ncid/BB17502139.

Lei n.12.015/2009 Artigo 213. 2009. *Lei nº 12.015, de 7 de agosto de 2009. Altera o Título VI da Parte Especial do Decreto-Lei nº 2.848, de 7 de dezembro de 1940 – Código Penal, e o art. 1º da Lei nº 8.072, de 25 de julho de 1990, que trata dos crimes hediondos*. Diário Oficial da União, August 10, 2009. https://www.jusbrasil.com.br/legislacao/818585/lei-12015-09.

Levischi, Beatriz. 2019. "Contra o machismo: Relembre 8 hashtags que mudaram um pouco o mundo." *UOL Universa*, March 18, 2019. https://www.uol.com.br/universa/noticias/redacao/2019/03/18/oito-hashtags-transformadoras-de-mulheres-e-para-mulheres.htm.

Lewis, Patricia C., Nadine J. Kaslow, Yuk Fai Cheong, Dabney P. Evans, and Kathryn M. Yount. 2024. "Femicide in the United States: A Call for Legal Codification and National Surveillance." *Frontiers in Public Health* 12 (February). https://doi.org/10.3389/fpubh.2024.1338548.

Lheidli T'enneh First Nation, Carrier Sekani Tribal Council, Prince George Native Friendship Centre, and Prince George Nechako Aboriginal Employment & Training Association. 2006. *Highway of Tears Symposium Recommendations Report.* https://highwayoftears.org/wp-content/uploads/2022/04/Highway-of-Tears-Symposium-Recommendations-Report-January-2013.pdf.

López, Issa, dir. 2024. *True Detective: Night Country.* Season 4. HBO.

López, María Pia. 2020. *Not One Less: Mourning, Disobedience and Desire.* Polity.

Loureiro, Gabriela Silva. 2020. "To Be Black, Queer and Radical: Centring the Epistemology of Marielle Franco." *Open Cultural Studies* 4, no. 1: 50–58. https://doi.org/10.1515/culture-2020-0005.

Lozano, Nina Maria. 2019. *Not One More! Feminicidio on the Border.* Ohio State University Press.

Lucchesi, Annita. 2018. "'Mapping for Social Change: Cartography and Community Activism in Mobilizing Against Colonial Gender Violence.'" *Mapping Meaning* 2, no. 1: 14–21.

Lucchesi, Annita. 2019. "Mapping Geographies of Canadian Colonial Occupation: Pathway Analysis of Murdered Indigenous Women and Girls." *Gender, Place and Culture* 26, no. 6: 868–87. https://doi.org/10.1080/0966369x.2018.1553864.

Lucchesi, Annita. 2022. "Mapping Violence Against Indigenous Women and Girls: Beyond Colonizing Data and Mapping Practices." *University of Arizona*, 2022. https://repository.arizona.edu/handle/10150/666446.

Lugones, María. 2003. *Peregrinajes.* Rowman & Littlefield.

Lugones, María. 2008. "The Coloniality of Gender." *Worlds & Knowledges Otherwise*, no. 2: 1–17.

Lugones, María. 2010. "Toward a Decolonial Feminism." *Hypatia* 25, no. 4 (2010): 742–59. http://www.jstor.org/stable/40928654.

"Lula cria pacto nacional de prevenção a feminicídios." 2023. *Agência Brasil*, August 16, 2023. https://agenciabrasil.ebc.com.br/politica/noticia/2023-08/lula-cria-pacto-nacional-de-prevencao-feminicidios.

Luna-Firebaugh, Eileen. 2006. "Violence Against American Indian Women and the Services-Training-Officers-Prosecutors Violence Against Indian Women (STOP VAIW) Program." *Violence Against Women* 12, no. 2: 125–36.

Macaulay, Fiona. 2005. "Private Conflicts, Public Powers: Domestic Violence Inside and Outside the Courts in Latin America." In *The Judicialization of Politics in Latin America*, edited by Alan Angell, Line Schjolden, and Rachel Sieder. Palgrave Macmillan.

Macaulay, Fiona. 2021. *Transforming State Responses to Feminicide: Women's Movements, Law and Criminal Justice Institutions in Brazil.* Emerald.

Maciel, Débora Alves. 2011. "Ação Coletiva, Mobilização Do Direito E Institu-ições Políticas: O Caso Da Campanha Da Lei Maria Da Penha." *Revista Brasileira De Ciências Sociais* 26, no. 77: 97–112. https://doi.org/10.1590/s0102-69092011000300010.

Machado, Isadora Vier, and Maria Lígia Ganacim Granado Rodrigues Elias. 2018. "Feminicídio Em Cena: Da Dimensão Simbólica À Política." *Tempo Social* 30, no. 1: 283–304. https://doi.org/10.11606/0103-2070.ts.2018.115626.

Machado, Maria Das Dores Campos. 2018. "O Discurso Cristão Sobre a 'Ideologia De Gênero.'" *Revista Estudos Feministas* 26, no. 2. https://doi.org/10.1590/1806-9584-2018v26n247463.

Maracle, Lee. 1988. *I Am Woman: A Native Perspective on Sociology and Feminism.* Press Gang.

Maracle, Lee, Columpa Bobb, and Tania Carter. 2019. *Hope Matters.* Bookhug.

Marcus, George E. 2010. *Sentimental Citizen: Emotion in Democratic Politics.* Penn State University Press.

Margolles, Teresa. 2016a. *Pistas de baile.* Photographs. https://jamescohan.viewin-grooms.com/artworks/21787-teresa-margolles-pistas-de-baile-2016/.

Margolles, Teresa. 2016b. *Póker de damas.* Performance. https://www.manifesta.org/editions/manifesta-11-zurich/participants/1571.

Marques, Elionay Rodrigues, and Janine Gomes da Silva. 2024. "Ideologia de Gênero e Fake News no Site Escola Sem Partido." In *A Internet Como Campo de Disputas de Genero,* edited by Cristina Scheibe Wolff and Elaine Schmitt, 77–88. Cultura e Barbárie Editora. https://doi.org/10.29327/5366407.1-8.

Marques, Moama Lorena Lacerda. 2022. "O luto público como luta política: Marielle Franco e as primeiras respostas da poesia." *Revista de Estudos de Literatura, Cultura e Alteridade-Igarapé* 15, no. 4: 31–46.

Martin, Carol Muree, Harsha Walia, Catherine Moses et al. 2019. *Red Women Rising.* Downtown Eastside Women's Centre. https://dewc.ca/content/wp-content/uploads/2019/04/MMIW-Report-Final-March-10-WEB.pdf.

Martín, María. 2014. "O Ipea Corrige Os Resultados Da Pesquisa Sobre O Estupro Uma Semana Depois." *El País Brasil,* April 4, 2014. https://brasil.elpais.com/brasil/2014/04/04/sociedad/1396641232_381697.html.

Martins, Raphael. 2017. "Pedófilos assediam participante do MasterChef pelo Twitter." *EXAME,* August 2, 2017. https://exame.com/brasil/pedofilos-assediam-participante-do-masterchef-pelo-twitter/.

Matamonasa-Bennett, Arieahn. 2014. "'A Disease of the Outside People.'" *Psychology of Women Quarterly* 39, no. 1: 20–36. https://doi.org/10.1177/0361684314543783.

Mauthner, Natasha S. 2016. "Un/Re-Making Method: Knowing/Enacting Posthumanist Performative Social Research Methods Through 'Diffractive Genealogies' and 'Metaphysical Practices.'" In *Mattering: Feminism, Science, and Materialism,* edited by Victoria Pitts-Taylor, 258–83. NYU Press.

Mbembe, Achille. 2003. "Necropolitics." *Public Culture* 15, no. 1: 11–40. https://doi.org/10.1215/08992363-15-1-11.

Mbembe, Achille. 2019. *Necropolitics*. Duke University Press eBooks. https://doi.org/10.1215/9781478007227.

Martínez Prado, Hérika. 2023. "Cruces Rosas Y Negras, Un Ícono Mundial." *El Diario*, March 12, 2023. https://diario.mx/juarez/cruces-rosas-y-negras-un-icono-mundial-20230312-2033907.html.

McCoy, Terrence, Marina Lopes, and Teo Armus. 2019. "'This Will Not Stick': Brazilian President Lashes Out over Alleged Links to Left-Wing Politician's Killing." *Washington Post*, October 30, 2019. https://www.washingtonpost.com/nation/2019/10/30/jair-bolsonaro-marielle-franco-murder-link/.

McDiarmid, Jessica. 2020. *Highway of Tears: A True Story of Racism, Indifference, and the Pursuit of Justice for Missing and Murdered Indigenous Women and Girls*. National Geographic Books.

McGillivray, Anne, and Brenda Comaskey. 1999. *Black Eyes All of the Time: Intimate Violence, Aboriginal Women, and the Justice System*. Toronto: University of Toronto Press.

Meadows, Ruthie. 2023. *Efficacy of Sound: Power, Potency, and Promise in the Translocal Ritual Music of Cuban Ifá-Òrìsà*. University of Chicago Press.

Medeiros, Priscila, and Natália Flores. 2021. "Simbologia De Marielle Franco Nas Guerras Culturais Do Brasil Polarizado: Uma Análise Discursiva." *Revista ECO-Pós* 24, no. 2: 64–89. https://doi.org/10.29146/ecopos.v24i2.27694.

Medeiros, Priscila, and Natália Flores. 2022. "Social Media in a Post-Truth Age: Discursive Roles of Fake News About Marielle Franco." In *The Politics of Technology in Latin America. Vol. 2, Digital Media, Daily Life and Public Engagement*, edited by David Ramirez Plascencia, Barbara Carvalho Gurgel, and Avery Plaw, 179–93. Routledge.

Medeiros, Silvia. 2017. "Mulheres do mundo todo ocupam as ruas de Florianópolis." CUT—Central Única Dos Trabalhadores, August 3, 2017. https://www.cut.org.br/noticias/mulheres-do-mundo-todo-ocupam-as-ruas-de-florianopolis-395c.

Medellín, María Luisa. "Agrega Piezas Al Misterio De Las Mujeres De Juárez." *El Norte*, October 17, 1999.

Mendizabal Bermúdez, Gabriela, and Agustina Bonino. 2019. "Ni una más, ni una menos, manifestaciones de mujeres como fuente del derecho." *Inventio* 13, no. 29: 5–12. https://inventio.uaem.mx/index.php/inventio/article/view/189/191

Mesquita, Lígia. 2018. "Os Últimos Momentos De Marielle Franco Antes De Ser Morta Com Quatro Tiros Na Cabeça." *g1*, March 15, 2018. https://g1.globo.com/rj/rio-de-janeiro/noticia/os-ultimos-momentos-de-marielle-franco-antes-de-ser-morta-com-quatro-tiros-na-cabeca.ghtml.

Messing, Jill Theresa, Millan A. AbiNader, Jesenia M. Pizarro, April M. Zeoli, Em Loerzel, Tricia Bent-Goodley, and Jacquely Campbell. 2023. "Femicide in the United States." In *The Routledge International Handbook of Femicide and*

Feminicide, edited by Myrna Dawson and Saide Mobayed Vega. https://doi. org/10.4324/9781003202332.

Messinger, Adam M., and Xavier L. Guadalupe-Diaz. 2020. *Transgender Intimate Partner Violence: A Comprehensive Introduction*. NYU Press.

Ministério das Mulheres. 2024. "Pacto Nacional de Prevenção aos Feminicídios lança plano de ação com 73 medidas para enfrentar a violência contra mulheres." *Ministério das Mulheres*, March 19, 2024. https://www.gov.br/mulheres/ pt-br/central-de-conteudos/noticias/2024/marco/pacto-nacional-de-prevencao-aos-feminicidios-lanca-plano-de-acao-com-73-medidas-para-enfrentar-a-violencia-contra-mulheres.

Miranda, Deborah A. 2010. "Extermination of the *Joyas*: Gendercide in Spanish California." *GLQ* 16, no. 1–2: 253–84. https://doi.org/10.1215/10642684-2009-022.

Miranda, Justino. "Mujeres Provocativas Son Causa De Agresiones: Fiscal." *El Universal*, November 17, 2009.

Moïsi, Dominique. 2008. *The Geopolitics of Emotion: How Cultures of Fear, Humiliation, and Hope Are Reshaping the World*. Anchor Books.

Molloy, Molly. 2002. "Pirating the Story." *Texas Observer*, August 30, 2002, 24–25.

Monárrez Fragoso, Julia Estela. 2000. "La cultura del feminicidio en Ciudad Juárez, 1993–1999." *Frontera norte* 12, no. 23: 87–117. https://doi.org/10.17428/ rfn.v12i23.1396.

Monárrez Fragoso, Julia Estela. 2003. *Aztlán* 28, no. 2: 153–78. https://doi.org/10. 1525/azt.2003.28.2.153.

Monárrez Fragoso, Julia Estela. 2009. *Trama de una injusticia: Feminicidio sexual sistemico en Ciudad Juárez*. Ciudad Juárez: Colegio de la Frontera Norte.

Monárrez Fragoso, Julia Estela. 2023. "Systemic Sexual Feminicide: Colonial Scars in Bodies and Territories." In *The Routledge International Handbook of Femicide and Feminicide*, edited by Myrna Dawson and Saide Mobayed Vega. https:// doi.org/10.4324/9781003202332.

Monárrez Fragoso, Julia Estela, Luis E. Cervera Gomez, and Rodolfo Rubio Salas. 2010. *Violencia contra las mujeres e inseguriad ciudadana en Ciudad Juárez*. Mexico City: Miguel Angel Porrua.

Monárrez Fragoso, Julia Estela, and Maria Socorro Tabuenca. 2007. *Bordeando la violencia contra las mujeres en la frontera norte de Mexico*. Ciudad Juárez: Colegio de la Frontera Norte.

Mojad, Shahrzad, Patricia Godinho Gomes, Aura Estela Cumes et al. 2021. "Causes of Violence Against Women and the Relationship Between the Murder of Women and Global Accumulation." In *Feminicide and Global Accumulation: Frontline Struggles to Resist the Violence of Patriarchy and Capitalism*, edited by Silvia Federici, Liz Mason-Deese, Susana Draper, and Betty Ruth Lozano Lerma, 37–47. Common Notions.

Moreira, Vitória. 2023. "Gendering Populism: The Rise of Right-Wing Populism and Anti-Gender Politics in Brazil." In *Edward Elgar eBooks*, 148–65. https:// doi.org/10.4337/9781802209549.00012.

Moreno, Maria. 2016. "Elogio De La Furia." *Página 12 Contratapa*, June 10, 2016. https://www.pagina12.com.ar/diario/contratapa/13-301412-2016-06-10.html.

Moreno, Norberto. 2006. *444 Ciudad Juárez 93-06: Expedientes Del Feminicidio.* Mexico City: Norberto Moreno.

MUAC. 2020. "Trans-Migrantes-Trans." https://www.facebook.com/MUAC.UNAM/videos/trans-migrantes-transuna-conversaci%C3%B3n-que-acompa%C3%B1a-la-pieza-p%C3%B3ker-de-damas-de-te/316321599549539/.

Museo Universitario Arte Contemporáneo. 2020. " 'Trans-Migrantes-Trans.' " https://www.youtube.com/watch?v=FtIAC2B9Up8.

Nagle, Mary Katheryn. 2023. "Illuminative." *X (formerly Twitter).* https://x.com/IllumiNative/status/1672345036640460800?ref_src=twsrc%5Etfw%7Ctwcamp%5Etweetembed%7Ctwterm%5E1672345036640460800%7Ctwgr%5E8c47e31b64a5064a400c5a421a9edb56f2ca92d7%7Ctwcon%5Es1_&ref_url=https%3A%2F%2Fwww.yahoo.com%2Flifestyle%2Fnative-activists-hit-back-at-yellowstone-creators-claim-that-his-film-changed-a-law-affecting-indigenous-people-201419562.html.

National Inquiry into Missing and Murdered Indigenous Women and Girls. 2019. *Reclaiming Power and Place: Final Report of the National Inquiry into Missing and Murdered Indigenous Women and Girls.* https://www.mmiwg-ffada.ca/wp-content/uploads/2019/06/Final_Report_Vol_1a-1.pdf.

Návar, Jose Xavier. "Desaparecen Las Muertas De Juárez." *El Mañana,* March 15, 2009.

Nava, Gregory, dir. 2007. *Bordertown.*

Nelson, Jennifer. 2003. *Women of Color and the Reproductive Rights Movement.* NYU Press.

Ni Una Menos. 2018. *Amistad Política + Inteligencia Colectiva Documentos Y Manifiestos 2015/2018.* https://niunamenos.org.ar/wp-content/uploads/2018/12/amistad-poli%CC%81tica-inteligencia-colectiva-libro-num.pdf.

Nicas, Jack, and Flávia Milhorance. 2024. "Brazil Police Arrest 3 for Murder of Marielle Franco." *New York Times,* March 24, 2024. https://www.nytimes.com/2024/03/24/world/americas/brazil-marielle-franco-assassination-arrest.html.

"Nuestras Hijas de Regreso a Casa" 2008. https://nuestrashijasderegresoacasa.blogspot.com/.

Nussbaum, Martha C. 2001. *The Fragility of Goodness: Luck and Ethics in Greek Tragedy and Philosophy.* Cambridge University Press.

Nussbaum, Martha C. 2013. *Creating Capabilities: The Human Development Approach.* Harvard University Press.

Nussbaum, Martha C. 2019. *The Monarchy of Fear: A Philosopher Looks at Our Political Crisis.* Simon & Schuster.

Office on Violence Against Women. 2024. "History." Office on Violence Against Women, U.S. Department of Justice, March 21, 2024. https://www.justice.gov/ovw/history.

Oficina en México del Alto Comisionado de las Naciones Unidas para los Derechos Humanos (OACNUDH). 2009. *Feminicidio.* Mexico City: OACNUDH.

ONU Mujeres. 661st Legislatura, Cámara De Diputados, Comisión Especial Para Conocer Y Dar Seguimiento Puntual Y Exhaustivo a Las Acciones Que Han Emprendido Las Autoridades Competentes En Relación a Los Feminicidios Registrados En México, ONU Mujeres, Entidad de las Naciones Unidas para la igualdad de Género y el Empoderamiento de las Mujeres, and Instituto Nacional de las Mujeres. 2012. *Violencia Feminicida En México: Características, Tendencias Y Nuevas Expresiones En Las Entidades Federativas, 1985–2010.* Impreso y hecho en México. https://www.unwomen.org/sites/default/files/ Headquarters/Attachments/Sections/Library/Publications/2013/2/Feminicidio_ Mexico-1985-2010%20pdf.pdf.

Oppal, Wally T. 2012. *Forsaken: The Final Report of the Missing Women Commission of Inquiry.* https://missingwomen.library.uvic.ca/index.html%3Fp=30.html

Oros Peters, Tia. 2020. "To Be a Good Ancestor: Resisting Colonial Violence & Uplifting Native Women & Girls." In *MMIWG2 &MMIP Organizing Toolkit: A Publication by Sovereign Bodies Institute, in Partnership With MMIWG2 Families, Indigenous Survivors of Violence, and Their Allies*, 7–10. https://www. sovereign-bodies.org/_files/ugd/6b33f7_2585fecaf9294450a595509cb701e7af. pdf.

Ortega, Gregorio. 1999. *Las Muertas De Ciudad Juárez: El Caso De Elizabeth Castro Garcìa Y Abdel Latif Sharif Sharif.* Mexico: Fontamara.

Pacheco, Nick. 2003. "Resolution Urging the Investigations of the Murders in Ciudad Juárez." *Aztlán* 28, no. 2: 203–4. https://doi.org/10.1525/azt.2003.28.2.203.

Padilla, Martha E., and Héctor Pérez. 2002. "Interpretaciones Locales Sobre La Violencia En Contra De Las Mujeres En Ciudad Juárez." *La Ventana*, no. 15: 195–230.

Padilla, Sergio Contreras. 2002. "Señorita Extraviada." *Cimacnoticias*, July 26, 2002. http://www.cimacnoticias.com.mx/noticias/02jul/02072601.html.

Palmater, Pamela. 2014. "Genocide, Indian Policy, and Legislated Elimination of Indians in Canada." *Aboriginal Policy Studies* 3, no. 3. https://doi.org/10.5663/ aps.v3i3.22225.

Palmater, Pamela. 2016. "Shining Light on the Dark Places: Addressing Police Racism and Sexualized Violence Against Indigenous Women and Girls in the National Inquiry." *Canadian Journal of Women and the Law* 28, no. 2: 253–84. https://doi.org/10.3138/cjwl.28.2.253.

Palomino, Sally. 2016. " 'No More Femicides, We're All Rosa Elvira.' " *EL PAÍS English*, May 18, 2016. https://english.elpais.com/elpais/2016/05/17/inenglish/ 1463494726_319553.html.

Paredez, Deborah. 2009. *Selenidad.* Duke University Press eBooks. https://doi. org/10.1215/9780822390893.

Park, Sehee. 2018. "Scholar Sarah Deer Speaks on Victims' Rights." *The Amherst Student*, April 17, 2018. https://amherststudent.amherst.edu/article/2018/04/17/ scholar-sarah-deer-speaks-victims%E2%80%99-rights.html.

PBS. "POV: Señorita Extraviada." *PBS*, August 20, 2002. http://www.pbs.org/pov/senoritaextraviada/.

Pedro, Joana Maria, Cristina Scheibe Wolff, and Janine Gomes Da Silva. 2022. "Desafios Dos Feminismos Na História Do Brasil Contemporâneo." *História (São Paulo)* 41 (January). https://doi.org/10.1590/1980-4369e2022016.

Pedwell, Carolyn. 2014. *Affective Relations: The Transnational Politics of Empathy.* Springer.

Pérez Osorio, Carlos, dir. 2020. *Las Tres Muertes De Marisela Escobedo / The Three Deaths of Marisela Escobedo.* Scorpio and Netflix Studios.

Pérez-Espino, A. "Falta De Ética E Impunidad." *Proceso*, October 17, 1999.

Perrone, Joana. 2023. "Feminicide in Brazil." In *The Routledge International Handbook of Femicide and Feminicide*, edited by Myrna Dawson and Saide Mobayed Vega. https://doi.org/10.4324/9781003202332.

Phillips, Dom. 2018. "Protests held across Brazil after Rio councillor shot dead." *The Guardian*, March 26, 2018. https://www.theguardian.com/world/2018/mar/15/marielle-franco-shot-dead-targeted-killing-rio.

Phillips, Dom. 2021. "Men tweeted creepy things about a Brazilian girl on 'MasterChef Junior.' Here's how Brazilian women fought back." *Washington Post*, December 1, 2021. https://www.washingtonpost.com/news/worldviews/wp/2015/11/06/men-tweeted-creepy-things-about-a-brazilian-girl-on-masterchef-junior-heres-how-brazilian-women-fought-back/.

Phillips, Tom. 2024. "Who killed Marielle Franco? Arrests lay bare nexus of politicians, police and paramilitaries." *The Guardian*, March 26, 2024. https://www.theguardian.com/world/2024/mar/26/marielle-franco-assassination-brazil-rio-police-arrests.

Piatti-Crocker, Adriana. 2021. "Diffusion of #NiUnaMenos in Latin America: Social Protests amid a Pandemic." *Journal of International Women's Studies* 22, no. 12: 7–24.

Piscitelli, Adriana. 2014. "Transnational Sisterhood? Brazilian Feminisms Facing Prostitution." *Latin American Policy* 5, no. 2: 221–35. https://doi.org/10.1111/lamp.12046.

Piscitelli, Adriana. 2017. "'#Queroviajarsozinhasemmedo': Novos Registros Das Articulações Entre Gênero, Sexualidade E Violência No Brasil." *Cadernos Pagu*, no. 50. https://doi.org/10.1590/18094449201700500008.

Piscitelli, Adriana. 2022. "Love and Anger: Putafeminismos / Whore Feminisms in Brazil." *Global Public Health* 17, no. 10: 2401–14. https://doi.org/10.1080/17441692.2022.2110916.

"Póker de damas." 2020. Facebook, uploaded by Mor Charpentier. https://www.facebook.com/mor.charpentier/videos/in-the-midst-of-teresa-margolles-work-photographing-trans-sex-workers-in-ciudad-/285882145965138/.

Poniatowska, Elena. 1971. *La Noche De Tlatelolco: Testimonios De Historia Oral.* Mexico City: Ediciones Era.

Poniatowska, Elena. 2002. "Las Ciudades Fronterizas Son Hoteles De Paso." *La Jornada*, April 1, 2002.

Portillo, Lourdes, dir. 2001. *Señorita Extraviada*. Xochitl Productions.

Portillo, Lourdes. 2003. "Filming *Señorita Extraviada*." *Aztlán* 28, no. 2: 229–34. https://doi.org/10.1525/azt.2003.28.2.229.

Primera Tormenta (blog). 2001 (May). https://primeratormenta.blogspot.com/.

Procuraduría General De la República (PGR). 2012. "Informe De Las Acciones de la GR en los Homicidios De Mujeres En Cd. Juárez, Chihuahua." https://web.archive.org/web/20120607234140/http://www.pgr.gob.mx/Temas%20Relevantes/Casos%20de%20Interes/Muertas%20de%20Juarez/Presentacion.asp.

Puntos Suspensivos Comunicación. 2020. "Canción Sin Miedo #MonLaferte #VivirQuintana Y #ElPalomar..." https://www.youtube.com/watch?v=_J_V4WFPTzo.

Quijano, Aníbal. 2007. "Coloniality and Modernity/Rationality." *Cultural Studies* 21, no. 2–3): 168–78. doi:10.1080/09502380601164353.

Quintana, Victor. 2009. "Mujeres En Éxodo Por La Vida." *La Jornada*, November 13, 2009. https://www.jornada.com.mx/2009/11/13/opinion/021a2pol.

Radford, Jill, and Diana H. Russell, 1992. *Femicide: The Politics of Woman Killing*. Twayne.

Raheja, Michelle H. 2011. *Reservation Reelism: Redfacing, Visual Sovereignty, and Representations of Native Americans in Film*. University of Nebraska Press.

Ramirez, Reyna. 2004. "Healing, Violence, and Native American Women." *Social Justice* 31, no. 4: 103–16.

Ramos, Dulce. 2012. "Los 18 Activistas Asesinados En 2011: Primera Parte." *Animal Politico*, January 16, 2012. https://www.animalpolitico.com/2012/01/los-18-activistas-asesinados-en-2011-primera-parte.

Rangel Oliveros, Alejandra, and Valentina García Marín. 2021. "The Uncertainty of Feminicides in Transwomen: Approaches to Trans Genocides Among Racialized Women." In *Feminicide and Global Accumulation: Frontline Struggles to Resist the Violence of Patriarchy and Capitalism*, edited by Silvia Federici, Liz Mason-Deese, Susana Draper, and Betty Ruth Lozano Lerma, 66–71. Common Notions.

Rausch, Natasha. 2019. "550-mile walk along Red River honors missing and murdered Indigenous women." *InForum*, August 1, 2019. https://www.inforum.com/newsmd/550-mile-walk-along-red-river-honors-missing-and-murdered-indigenous-women.

Rausch, Natasha. 2024. "Crisis of missing Indigenous people sparks activists, self-taught searchers to help families awaiting answers." *InForum*, March 6, 2024. https://www.inforum.com/news/crisis-of-missing-indigenous-people-sparks-activists-self-taught-searchers-to-help-families-awaiting-answers.

Ravelo, Ricardo. "Las Muertas De Juárez, El Libro De La Indignación." *Proceso*, October 31, 1999.

Ravelo Blancas, Patricia. 2011. *Miradas etnológicas: Violencia sexual y de género en Ciudad Juárez, Chihuahua: Estructura, política, cultura y subjetividad.* Mexico City: Eón.

Ravelo Blancas, Patricia, and Rafael Bonilla. 2006. *La Batalla De Las Cruces.* Mexico City: Campo Imaginario and CIESAS.

Ravelo Blancas, Patricia, Lourdes Carrillo Domínguez, and Sergio Sánchez Díaz. 2000. "Movimiento feminista en Chihuahua: Convergencias y divergencias." Document prepared for Encuentro de la Asociación de Estudios Latinoamericanos. Miami, March 16–18, 2000.

Ravelo Blancas, Patricia, and Héctor Domínguez Ruvalcaba. 2006. *Entre Las Duras Aristas De Las Armas.* Mexico City: CIESAS.

Rcalc, Nicolette. 2023. "Femicide in Brazil: Inter-American Condemnation." *Harvard International Review*, July 3, 2023. https://hir.harvard.edu/femicide-in-brazil-inter-american-condemnation/.

Redação Marie Claire. 2019. "Liniker Canta Forever Young Em Campanha Sobre a Expectativa De Vida De Pessoas Trans." *Revista Marie Claire*, June 11, 2019. https://revistamarieclaire.globo.com/Mulheres-do-Mundo/noticia/2019/06/liniker-canta-forever-young-em-campanha-sobre-expectativa-de-vida-de-pessoas-trans.html.

RedCorn, Princella. 2018. "Wind River Feature Film Tackles the Subject of Missing and Murdered Native Women." In *Restoration of Native Sovereignty and Safety for Native Women*, 15:32–35. https://www.niwrc.org/sites/default/files/files/magazine/restoration.15.1.pdf.

Reid, Jennifer. 2010. "The Doctrine of Discovery and Canadian Law." *Canadian Journal of Native Studies*, no. 30. https://caid.ca/CanDocDis2010.pdf.

"Remembering Our Dead." n.d. *Remembering Our Dead.*https://tdor.translivesmatter.info/reports?action=recent.

Resende, Thiago. 2022. "Bolsonaro cortou 90% da verba de combate à violência contra a mulher." *Folha De S.Paulo*, October 2, 2022. https://www1.folha.uol.com.br/cotidiano/2022/09/bolsonaro-cortou-90-da-verba-de-combate-a-violencia-contra-a-mulher.shtml.

Reuters. 2018. "Thousands protest murder of Brazilian activist politician." Reuters, March 19, 2018. https://www.reuters.com/news/picture/thousands-protest-murder-of-brazilian-ac-idUSRTS1NZP6/.

Revilla Blanco, Marisa. 2019. "Del ¡Ni una más! al #NiUnaMenos: Movimientos de mujeres y feminismos en América Latina." *Política y Sociedad* 59, no. 1: 47–67. https://doi.org/10.5209/poso.60792.

Revista Fernanda. "Backyard: El Traspatio." *Revista Fernanda*, February 4, 2009.

Ritchie, Andrea. 2017. *Invisible No More: Police Violence Against Black Women and Women of Color.* 1st ed. Beacon.

Rivera Cusicanqui, Silvia. 2020. *Ch'ixinakax Utxiwa: On Decolonising Practices and Discourses.* Polity.

Roberts, Dorothy E. 1997. *Killing the Black Body: Race, Reproduction, and the Meaning of Liberty*. Pantheon.

Robertson, Kimberly, and Jenell Navarro. 2020. "Mass Incarceration Since 1492." In *Otherwise Worlds: Against Settler Colonialism and Anti-Blackness*, edited by Tiffany Lethabo King, Jenell Navarro, and Andrea Smith, 297–319. Duke University Press.

Rodríguez, Ileana. 2009. *Liberalism at Its Limits*. University of Pittsburgh Press. https://doi.org/10.2307/j.ctt9qh6vz.

Rodríguez, Teresa. 2007. *Las Hijas De Juárez: Un Auténtico Relato De Asesinatos En Serie Al Sur De La Frontera*. ATRIA Books.

Rolnik, Suely. 2023. *Spheres of Insurrection: Notes on Decolonizing the Unconscious*. Polity.

Ronquillo, Victor. 1999a. "Defiende Su Libro Victor Ronquillo." *Reforma*, October 31, 1999.

Ronquillo, Victor. 1999b. *Las Muertas De Juárez*. Mexico City: Booket.

Ross, Loretta, and Rickie Solinger. 2017. *Reproductive Justice: An Introduction*. University of California Press.

Rovira-Sancho, Guiomar, and Jordi Morales-i-Gras. 2022. "Femitags for Feminist Connected Crowds in Latin America and Spain." *Acta Psychologica*, no. 230 (October): 103756. https://doi.org/10.1016/j.actpsy.2022.103756.

Russell, Diana E. H., and Nicole Van de Ven, eds. 1976. *Crimes Against Women: Proceedings of the International Tribunal*. https://www.dianarussell.com/f/Crimes_Against_Women_Tribunal.pdf.

Russell, Diana E. H., and Roberta A. Harmes. 2001. *Femicide in Global Perspective*. Athene Series. Teachers College Press.

Sabri, Bushra, Veronica P. S. Njie-Carr, Jill T. Messinget al. 2018. "The weWomen and ourCircle Randomized Controlled Trial Protocol: A Web-Based Intervention for Immigrant, Refugee and Indigenous Women With Intimate Partner Violence Experiences." *Contemporary Clinical Trials*, no. 76 (December): 79–84. https://doi.org/10.1016/j.cct.2018.11.013.

Sáenz, Consuelo. 2022. "'Ni Una Menos,' Escribió Susana." *Revista Replicante*, January 21, 2022. https://revistareplicante.com/ni-una-menos-escribio-susana/.

"Sala10: Teresa Margolles." 2020. *Museo Universitario Arte Contemporáneo*, July 13, 2020. https://muac.unam.mx/exposicion/sala10-teresa-margolles.

Salvatori, Lidia. 2022. "The Deep River of Feminism." *Critical Times* 5, no. 1: 241–48. https://doi.org/10.1215/26410478-9536591.

Salzinger, Leslie. 2003. *Genders in Production: Making Workers in Mexico's Global Factories*. University of California Press.

Sánchez Avella, César, and Paula Lucía Arévalo Mutiz. 2020. "Approach to the Legal Treatment of Lethal Violence Against Trans Women in Colombia: From Femicide to Transfemicide." *Revista Vía Iuris*, no. 29 (July): 85–109. https://doi.org/10.37511/viaiuris.n29a3.

Sancho, Guiomar Rovira, and Jordi Morales-i-Gras. 2022. "*Femitags* for Feminist Connected Crowds in Latin America and Spain." *Acta Psychologica*, no. 230 (October): 103756. https://doi.org/10.1016/j.actpsy.2022.103756.

"Savanna LaFontaine-Greywind Official." 2017. Facebook. https://www.facebook.com/SavannaLaFontaineGreywind/.

Scaptura, Maria N., and Brittany E. Hayes. 2023. "Systems of Power and Femicide: The Intersection of Race, Gender, and Extremist Violence." In *The Routledge International Handbook of Femicide and Feminicide*, edited by Myrna Dawson and Saide Mobayed Vega. https://doi.org/10.4324/9781003202332.

Scheper-Hughes, Nancy. 1992. *Death Without Weeping: The Violence of Everyday Life in Brazil*. University of California Press.

Scheper Hughes, Nancy. 2008. *The Last Commodity: Post-Human Ethics, Global (in)justice, and the Traffic in Organs*. Multiversity.

Secretaria de Relaciones Exteriores. 2007. *General Law on Women's Access to a Life Free of Violence*. https://www.summit-americas.org/brief/docs/Law_on_access_to_a_life_free_violence.pdf.

Segato, Rita Laura. 2003. "Las Esturcturas Elementales De La Violencia: Contrato Y Status En La Etiologia De La Violencia." *Serie Antropologica*, no. 334.

Segato, Rita Laura. 2013. *La Escritura En El Cuerpo De Las Mujeres Asesinadas En Ciudad Juárez Territorio, Soberanía Y Crímenes De Segundo Estado*. Buenos Aires: Tinta Limon.

Segato, Rita Laura. 2016. "Patriarchy from Margin to Center: Discipline, Territoriality, and Cruelty in the Apocalyptic Phase of Capital." *South Atlantic Quarterly* 115, no. 3: 615–24. https://doi.org/10.1215/00382876-3608675.

Segato, Rita Laura, and Lívia Vitenti. 2023. "Femigenocide." In *The Routledge International Handbook of Femicide and Feminicide*, edited by Myrna Dawson and Saide Mobayed Vega. https://doi.org/10.4324/9781003202332.

Shepard, Quinn, creator. 2024. *Under the Bridge*. Hulu.

Sheridan, Taylor. 2018. "Written Testimony on S. 1942, SAVANNA'S ACT by Taylor Sheridan." *NIWRC*, 2018. https://www.niwrc.org/restoration-magazine/february-2018/written-testimony-s-1942-savannas-act-taylor-sheridan.

Sheridan, Taylor, writer. 2020. "All for Nothing." *Yellowstone*. Season 3, episode 6. Directed by Taylor Sheridan. Aired July 26, 2020. Paramount Network.

Simpson, Audra. 2014. *Mohawk Interruptus: Political Life Across the Borders of Settler States*. Duke University Press.

Smith, Andrea. 2005. *Conquest: Sexual Violence and American Indian Genocide*. South End.

Smith, Linda Tuhiwai. 1999. *Decolonizing Methodologies: Research and Indigenous Peoples*. Bloomsbury.

Smith, Morgan. 2023. "Strong Women on the Border." *Las Cruces Bulletin*, December 15, 2023. https://www.lascrucesbulletin.com/stories/strong-women-on-the-border,66963.

Sosa, Lorena. "Femicide and Intersectionality." 2023. In *The Routledge International Handbook of Femicide and Feminicide*, edited by Myrna Dawson and Saide Mobayed Vega. https://doi.org/10.4324/9781003202332.

Soto, Sandra Gayou. 2021. "Belle Delouisse adapta la Canción sin Miedo para mujeres en Yucatán." *Quadratin Yucatán*, January 5, 2021. https://yucatan.quadratin.com.mx/mujer/belle-delouisse-adapta-la-cancion-sin-miedo-para-mujeres-en-yucatan/.

Sovereign Bodies Institute. 2020. "MMIWG2 & MMIP Organizing Toolkit: A Publication by Sovereign Bodies Institute, in Partnership with MMIWG2 Families, Indigenous Survivors of Violence, and Their Allies." *Sovereign Bodies Institute*. https://www.sovereign-bodies.org/_files/ugd/6b33f7_2585fecaf929 4450a595509cb701e7af.pdf.

Spade, Dean. 2015. *Normal Life: Administrative Violence, Critical Trans Politics, and the Limits of Law*. Duke University Press.

Stanley, Eric A. 2021. *Atmospheres of Violence: Structuring Antagonism and the Trans/ Queer Ungovernable*. Duke University Press.

Staudt, Kathleen A. 2008. *Violence and Activism at the Border: Gender, Fear, and Everyday Life in Ciudad Juárez*. Inter-America Series. University of Texas Press.

Staudt, Kathleen A., Tony Payan, and Z. Anthony Kruszewski. 2009. *Human Rights Along the U.S.–Mexico Border: Gendered Violence and Insecurity*. University of Arizona Press.

Stephen, Lynn. 2016. "Gendered Transborder Violence in the Expanded United States–Mexico Borderlands." *Human Organization* 75, no. 2: 159–67. https://doi.org/10.17730/0018-7259-75.2.159.

Sudré, Lu. 2018. "Transexuais São Assassinadas Sob Gritos De 'Bolsonaro Presidente.'" *Brasil De Fato*, October 24, 2018. https://www.brasildefato.com.br/2018/10/24/transexuais-sao-assassinadas-sob-gritos-de-bolsonaro-presidente/.

Sullivan, Zoe. 2018. "LGBTQ Brazilians on Edge After Self-Described 'Homophobic' Lawmaker Elected President." *NBC News*, October 29, 2018. https://www.nbcnews.com/feature/nbc-out/lgbtq-brazilians-edge-after-self-described-homophobic-lawmaker-elected-president-n925726.

Swenson, Kyle. 2021. "Fargo woman lured pregnant neighbor to her apartment, killed her and took her unborn baby." *Washington Post*, October 25, 2021. https://www.washingtonpost.com/news/morning-mix/wp/2017/12/12/fargo-woman-lured-pregnant-neighbor-to-her-apartment-killed-her-and-took-her-unborn-baby/.

Tabuenca, Socorro, and Ricardo Aguilar. 2000. *Lo Que El Viento a Juárez*. Torreón, Mexico: Nimbus.

Tenaglia, Kabyr Barakat Faretta, and Daniel Canavese de Oliveira. 2025. "Barreiras de Acesso ao Sistema Único de Saúde." *Saberes Plurais Educação Na Saúde* 9, no. 1: e144857. https://doi.org/10.54909/sp.v9i1.144857.

"Teresa Margolles." 2006. Station Museum of Contemporary Art. https://www.stationmuseum.com/past-exhibitions/frontera-450/teresa-margolles/.

Tgeu. 2024. "Will the Cycle of Violence Ever End? TGEU's Trans Murder Monitoring Project Crosses 5,000 Cases." *TGEU—Transgender Europe* (blog). November 13, 2024. https://tgeu.org/will-the-cycle-of-violence-ever-end-tgeus-trans-murder-monitoring-project-crosses-5000-cases/.

Thomas Jefferson to James Monroe. 1801. Manuscript and other material. https://www.loc.gov/item/mtjbib010767/.

Thomas, Joy. 2020. "#SayHerName: A Digital Memorial." *Electric Marronage*, July 24, 2020. https://www.electricmarronage.com/electricblog/2020/7/2/sayhername.

Thoreau, Henry David. 2016. "Walking." In *The Making of the American Essay*, edited by John D'Agata, 167–95. Graywolf.

Threadcraft, Shatema. 2023. "North American Necropolitics and Gender: On Black Lives Matter and Black Femicide." In *The Routledge International Handbook of Femicide and Feminicide*, edited by Myrna Dawson and Saide Mobayed Vega. https://doi.org/10.4324/9781003202332.

Toledo Vázquez, Patsilí. 2009. *Feminicidio*. Consultancy for the Mexico Office of the United Nations High Commissioner for Human Rights, Mexico.

Toledo Vázquez, Patsilí. 2023. "Femicide/Feminicide and Legislation." In *The Routledge International Handbook of Femicide and Feminicide*, edited by Myrna Dawson and Saide Mobayed Vega. https://doi.org/10.4324/978100320 2332.

Transgender Law Center. 2024. "Roxsana Hernandez—Transgender Law Center." June 24, 2024. https://transgenderlawcenter.org/case/roxsana-hernandez/.

"Trans-Migrantes-Trans." 2020. https://www.facebook.com/MUAC.UNAM/videos/trans-migrantes-transuna-conversaci%C3%B3n-que-acompa%C3%B1a-la-pieza-p%C3%B3ker-de-damas-de-te/316321599549539/.

TV UNAM. 2020. "¿Cuál Es El Papel Del Artista En Situaciones De Violencia? Teresa Margolles." https://www.youtube.com/watch?v=Y12_KY7SLo0.

Tyree, Tia C. M., and Marnel Niles Goins. 2021. "Speak Up, Sis: Black Women, Race, and News Coverage of the Me Too Movement." In *The Routledge Handbook of Gender and Communication*, 1st ed., 1:475–94. https://doi.org/10.4324/9780429448317-33.

UN Committee on the Elimination of Discrimination Against Women (28th session 2003 New York) [CEDAW]. 2003. "Report of the Committee on the Elimination of Discrimination Against Women, 28th Session (13–31 January 2003) [and] 29th Session (30 June-18 July 2003)." New York: UN. https://digitallibrary.un.org/record/503158?ln=en&v=pdf.

Urban Indian Health Institute. 2017. *Our Bodies, Our Stories: Sexual Violence Among Native Women in Seattle*.

Urban Indian Health Institute. 2018. *Missing and Murdered Indigenous Women and Girls: A Snapshot of Data from 71 Urban Cities in the United States*.

Urzúa Martínez, Sergio. 2019. "Aportes a Una Etnografía De Los Movimientos Feministas: Recursos Expresivos En Las Marchas #Ni Una Menos Y #8M En

Santiago De Chile." *Antípoda Revista De Antropología Y Arqueología*, no. 35 (April): 115–24. https://doi.org/10.7440/antipoda35.2019.06.

U.S. Department of State. 2005. *Country Reports on Human Rights Practices*. Washington, DC.

Valencia, Sayak. 2010. *Capitalismo Gore*. Barcelona: Melusina.

Valencia, Sayak. 2018. *Gore Capitalism*. MIT Press.

Valencia, Sayak, and Olga Arnaiz Zhuravleva. 2019. "Necropolitics, Postmortem/Transmortem Politics, and Transfeminisms in the Sexual Economies of Death." *Transgender Studies Quarterly* 6, no. 2: 180–93. https://doi.org/10.1215/23289252-7348468.

Valencia, Sayak, and Liliana Falcón. 2023. "Continuities and Discontinuities Between the Concepts of Feminicide and Transfeminicide in Mexico." In *The Routledge International Handbook of Femicide and Feminicide*, edited by Myrna Dawson and Saide Mobayed Vega. https://doi.org/10.4324/9781003202332.

Vega, Saide Mobayed, Sonia M. Frías, Fabiola de Lachica Huerta, and Aleida Luján-Pinelo. 2023. "Feminicide in Mexico." In *The Routledge International Handbook of Femicide and Feminicide*, edited by Myrna Dawson and Saide Mobayed Vega. https://doi.org/10.4324/9781003202332.

Velázquez, Susana. 2003. *Violencias Cotidianad, Violencia De Genero: Escuchar, Comprender, Ayudar*. Buenos Aires: Editorial Paidos.

Violence on the Land, Violence on Our Bodies: Building an Indigenous Response to Environmental Violence. 2017. Women's Earth Alliance. http://landbodydefense.org/uploads/files/VLVBReportToolkit_2017.pdf.

Violence Policy Center. 2023. *When Men Murder Women: A Review of 25 Years of Female Homicide Victimization in the United States*. https://www.vpc.org/studies/wmmw2023.pdf.

Vizenor, Gerald Robert. 1999. *Manifest Manners: Narratives on Postindian Survivance*. University of Nebraska Press.

Vizenor, Gerald Robert. 2008. *Survivance: Narratives of Native Presence*. University of Nebraska Press.

Voces sin Eco. 1998. *Cruz de los Feminicidios*.

Washington Valdez, Diana. 2005. *Cosecha De Mujeres: Safari En El Desierto Mexicano*. Mexico City: Oceano.

Washington Post. "Names of the women found dead in Ciudad Juárez." *Washington Post*, June 24, 2000. https://www.washingtonpost.com/archive/politics/2000/06/25/names-of-the-women-found-dead-in-ciudad-juarez/8a19ec10-339f-4664-8a17-5ef2833b6685/.

Webb, Kathryn. 2023. "Almost 30 Years Later: Anti-Femicide Activism in Mexico from 1993–2022." *Butler Journal of Undergraduate Research*, no. 9. https://digitalcommons.butler.edu/bjur/vol9/iss1/8.

The White House. 2023. "FACT SHEET: Biden-Harris Administration Celebrates the Twenty-Ninth Anniversary of the Violence Against Women Act." September 13, 2023. https://bidenwhitehouse.archives.gov/briefing-room/statements-releases/2023/09/13/fact-sheet-biden-harris-administration-celebrates-the-twenty-ninth-anniversary-of-the-violence-against-women-act/.

Williams, Robert A., Jr. 1990. *The American Indian in Western Legal Thought: The Discourses of Conquest.* Oxford University Press.

Wilson, Shawn. 2008. *Research Is Ceremony: Indigenous Research Methods.* Brunswick Books.

Winfrey-Harris, Tamara. 2020. "The Reckoning Will Be Incomplete Without Black Women and Girls." *The Atlantic,* November 5, 2020. https://www.theatlantic.com/ideas/archive/2020/06/revolution-will-be-incomplete-without-black-women-and-girls/613045/.

Winton, Jenna. 2014. "Rebranding Valentine's Day: A Day for Honoring Murdered and Missing Indigenous Women." *Cultural Survival,* February 18, 2014. https://www.culturalsurvival.org/news/rebranding-valentines-day-day-honoring-murdered-and-missing-indigenous-women.

Woolman, Joanna, and Sarah Deer. 2014. "Protecting Native Mothers and Their Children: A Feminist Lawyering Approach." Mitchell Hamline Open Access. http://open.mitchellhamline.edu/wmlr/vol40/iss3/4.

World Bank Group. 2021. "Intentional homicides, female (per 100,000 female)." https://data.worldbank.org/indicator/VC.IHR.PSRC.FE.P5?end=2021&most_recent_year_desc=true&start=1990.

Wright, Melissa. 2006. *Disposable Women and Other Myths of Global Capitalism.* Routledge.

Wynn, James, and G. Mitchell Reyes. 2021. *Arguing with Numbers: The Intersections of Rhetoric and Mathematics.* Penn State University Press.

X, Malcolm. "The Ballot or the Bullet." In *On Violence: A Reader,* edited by Bruce B. Lawrence and Aisha Karim, 143–57. Duke University Press.

Zecha, Angelika, Naeemah Abrahams, Karine Duhamel, Cristina Fabré, María Alejandra Otamendi, Alejandra Ríos-Cázares, Heidi Stöckl, Myrna Dawson, and Saide Mobayed Vega. 2023. "Data Sources and Challenges in Addressing Femicide and Feminicide." In *The Routledge International Handbook of Femicide and Feminicide,* edited by Myrna Dawson and Saide Mobayed Vega. Routledge. https://doi.org/10.4324/9781003202332.

Index